Street by Street

CW00621790

LEEDS

GUISELEY, MORLEY, PUDSEY, ROTHWELL, YEADON

Alwoodley, Beeston, Bramley, Chapeltown, Cookridge, Cross Gates, Harehills, Headingley, Horsforth, Meanwood, Middleton, Rawdon, Roundhay

3rd edition December 2005
© Automobile Association Developments Limited 2005

Original edition printed July 2001

Ordnance Survey® This product includes map data licensed from Ordnance Survey® with the permission of the Controller of Her Majesty's Stationery Office. © Crown copyright 2005. All rights reserved. Licence number 399221.

Published by AA Publishing (a trading name of Automobile Association Developments Limited, whose registered office is Fanum House, Basing View, Basingstoke, Hampshire RG21 4EA. Registered number 1878835).

Mapping produced by the Cartography Department of The Automobile Association. (A02548)

A CIP Catalogue record for this book is available from the British Library.

Printed by Oriental Press, Dubai

Key to map pages	ii-iii
Key to map symbols	iv-1
Enlarged map pages	2-3
Main map pages	4-51
Index – towns & villages	52
Index – streets	52-68
Index – featured places	68-70
Acknowledgements	70

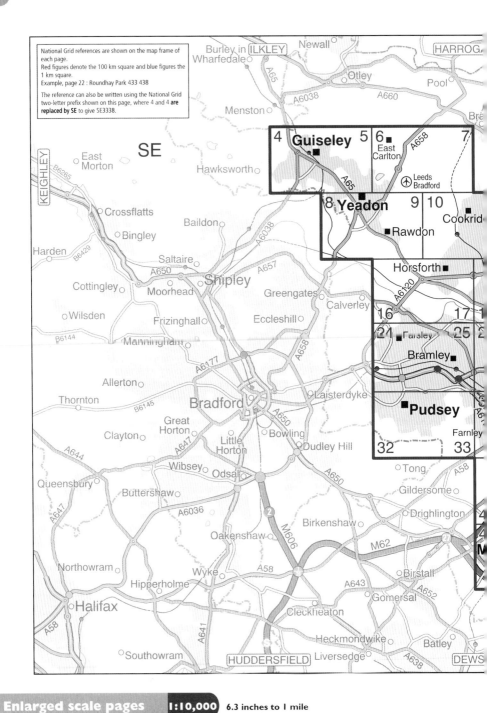

ii

National Grid references are shown on the map frame of each page.
Red figures denote the 100 km square and blue figures the 1 km square.
Example, page 22 : Roundhay Park 433 438

The reference can also be written using the National Grid two-letter prefix shown on this page, where 4 and 4 **are replaced by SE** to give SE3338.

SE

KEIGHLEY

Burley in Wharfedale ○   ILKLEY   Newall ○   HARROG

A65   Otley ○   Pool ○

A6038   A660   Pool ○

Menston ○   Br

East Morton ○   B6265

Hawksworth ○

4   Guiseley   5   6 ■
East Carlton   A658   **7**

⊕ Leeds Bradford

A65

8 Yeadon   **9**   **10**

■ Rawdon   Cookrid ■

Crossflatts ○

Baildon ○

A6038

Bingley ○

Harden ○   B6429

Saltaire ○   A650   A657

Cottingley ○   Moorhead ○

Shipley

Horsforth ■

A6120

Wilsden ○

Frizinghall ○   Eccleshill ○

Greengates ○   Calverley ○

16   **17 1**

A658

21 ■ Farsley   **25** 2

Manningham ○

B6144

A6177

Bramley ■

Allerton ○

Thornton ○   B6145

Bradford   ○ Laisterdyke

A650   A6

■ Pudsey

Great Horton   A647   Little Horton   ○ Bowling   Dudley Hill   Farnley

Clayton ○

A644   **32**   **33**

Wibsey ○   Odsal ○   A650

Queensbury ○

Buttershaw ○

○ Tong   A58

A6036   ○ Gildersome

A647   Birkenshaw ○   ○ Drighlington

2

Oakenshaw ○   M606   M62

Northowram ○   Wyke ○   A58   ○ Birstall   M

Hipperholme ○   A643   Gomersal

A652

Halifax ○   Cleckheaton   A638

A58   A641   Heckmondwike ○   Batley ○

○ Southowram   HUDDERSFIELD   Liversedge ○   DEWS

Enlarged scale pages   **1:10,000**   6.3 inches to 1 mile

0 — 1/4 — miles — 1/2

0 — 1/4 — 1/2 — kilometres — 3/4 — 1

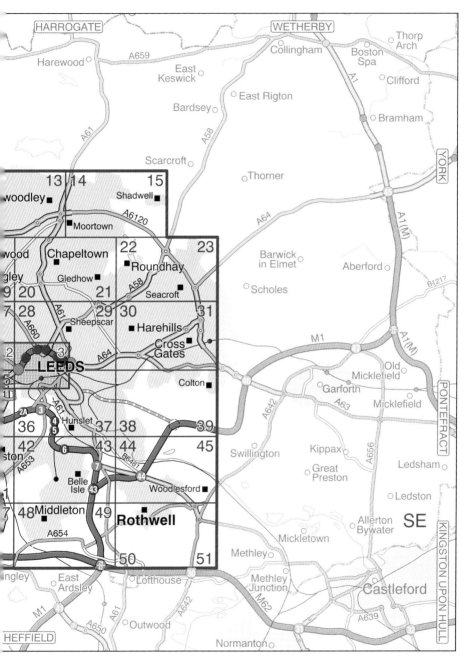

HARROGATE

WETHERBY

Thorp Arch

Harewood

A659

Collingham

Boston Spa

East Keswick

A1

Clifford

East Rigton

Bardsey

Bramham

A58

A61

Scarcroft

YORK

Thorner

A64

13 | 14 | 15

woodley

Shadwell

A6120

Moortown

A58

Barwick in Elmet

A1(M)

wood | Chapeltown | 22 | 23

Aberford

 B1217

gley | Gledhow | Roundhay

Scholes

9 | 20 | 21

A58

Seacroft

M1

7 | 28 | 29 | 30 | 31

A61

Sheepscar

Harehills

A1(M)

2 | 3

A64

Cross Gates

Old Mickfield

LEEDS

PONTEFRACT

Colton

Garforth

A63

Mickfield

2A | 3

A642

A61

4 | Hunslet | 37 | 38 | 39

A656

5

Swillington

Kippax

Ledsham

36

42 | 43 | 44 | 45

6

B6481

ston | A653 | 7

Great Preston

Ledston

Belle Isle | 43 | 44

Woodlesford

48 | Middleton | 49 | Rothwell

Allerton Bywater

SE

A654

Mickletown

KINGSTON UPON HULL

7

50 | 51

Methley

M1

Lofthouse

Methley Junction

Castleford

East Ardsley

A642

A639

HEFFIELD

A61

A650

Outwood

Normanton

M62

4.2 inches to 1 mile **Scale of main map pages** **1:15,000**

| 0 | 1/4 | miles 1/2 | 3/4 | 1 |

| 0 | 1/4 | 1/2 | kilometres 3/4 | 1 | 1 1/4 | 1 1/2 |

iv

Motorway & junction	Level crossing
Motorway service area	Tramway
Primary road single/dual carriageway	Ferry route
Primary road service area	Airport runway
A road single/dual carriageway	County, administrative boundary
B road single/dual carriageway	Mounds
Other road single/dual carriageway	Page continuation 1:15,000
Minor/private road, access may be restricted	Page continuation to enlarged scale 1:10,000
One-way street	River/canal, lake, pier
Pedestrian area	Aqueduct, lock, weir
Track or footpath	Peak (with height in metres)
Road under construction	Beach
Road tunnel	Woodland
Parking	Park
Park & Ride	Cemetery
Bus/coach station	Built-up area
Railway & main railway station	Industrial building
Railway & minor railway station	Leisure building
Underground station	Retail building
Light railway & station	Other building
Preserved private railway	

Junction 9 — Motorway & junction

Services — Motorway service area

Services — Primary road service area

LC — Level crossing

465 Winter Hill — Peak (with height in metres)

17 — Page continuation 1:15,000

3 — Page continuation to enlarged scale 1:10,000

P — Parking

P+ — Park & Ride

⊓⊔⊓⊔⊓⊔	City wall	♖	Castle
A&E	Hospital with 24-hour A&E department	⌂	Historic house or building
PO	Post Office	Wakehurst Place NT	National Trust property
📖	Public library	M	Museum or art gallery
i	Tourist Information Centre	♞	Roman antiquity
i	Seasonal Tourist Information Centre	⚱	Ancient site, battlefield or monument
⛽⛽	Petrol station, 24 hour Major suppliers only	▄▄	Industrial interest
†	Church/chapel	❈	Garden
🚻	Public toilets	◉	Garden Centre Garden Centre Association Member
♿	Toilet with disabled facilities	⚘	Garden Centre Wyevale Garden Centre
PH	Public house AA recommended	♣	Arboretum
🍴	Restaurant AA inspected	🛒	Farm or animal centre
Madeira Hotel	Hotel AA inspected	⚕	Zoological or wildlife collection
🎭	Theatre or performing arts centre	➤	Bird collection
🎥	Cinema	🐟	Nature reserve
⚑	Golf course	⬥	Aquarium
▲	Camping AA inspected	V	Visitor or heritage centre
🚐	Caravan site AA inspected	♈	Country park
▲🚐	Camping & caravan site AA inspected	◠	Cave
🏖	Theme park	🗼	Windmill
⛪	Abbey, cathedral or priory	🛢	Distillery, brewery or vineyard

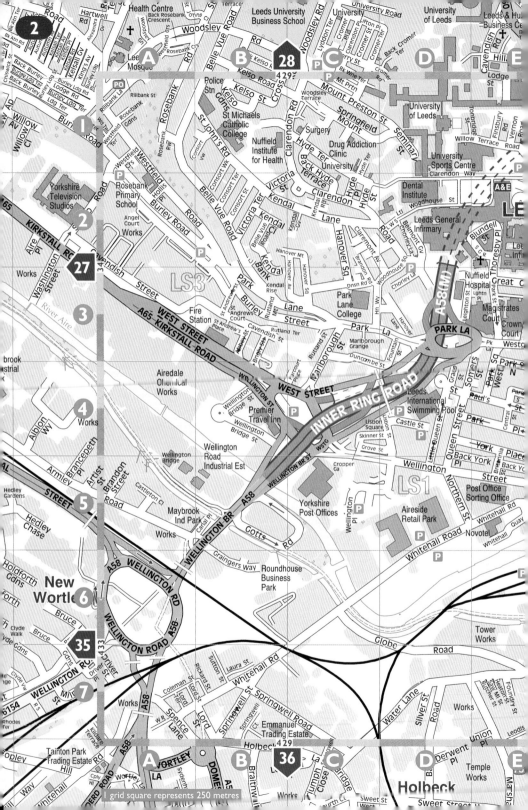

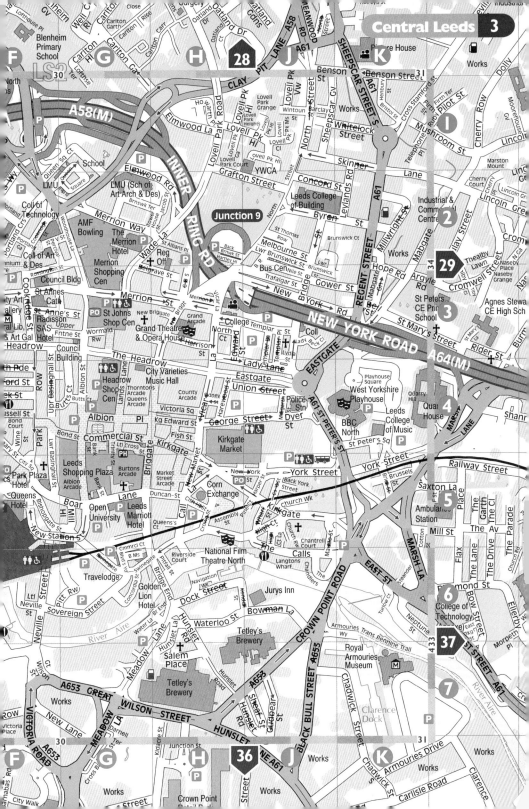

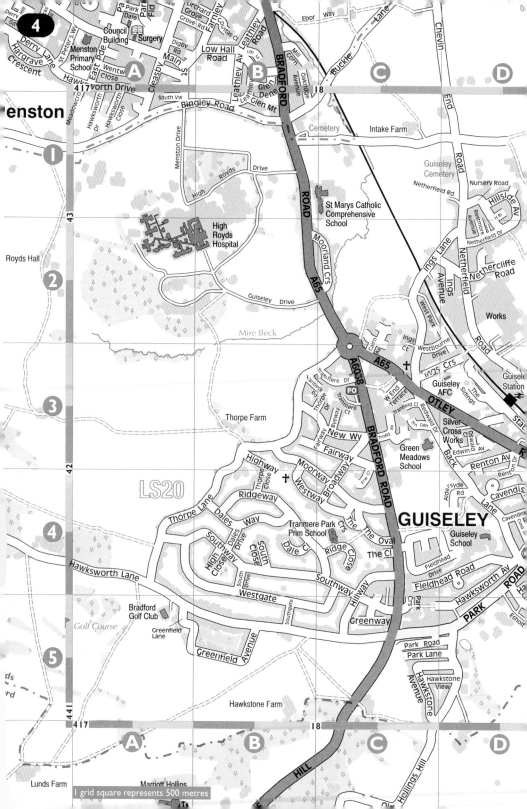

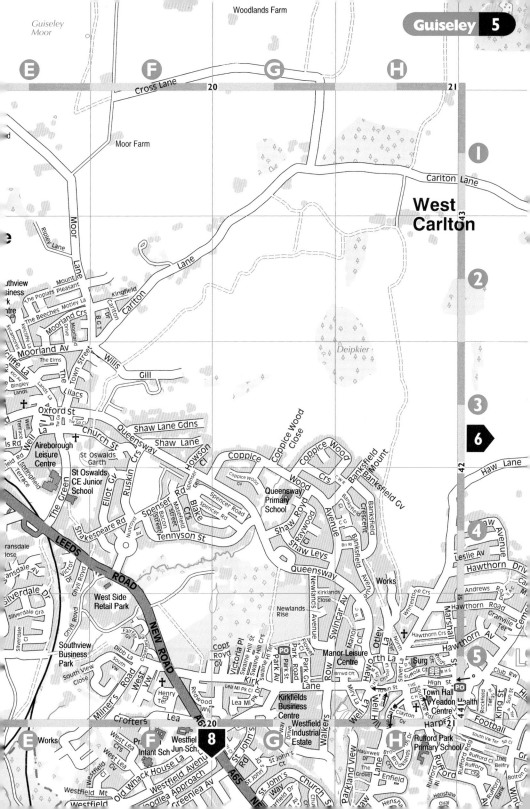

6

A 421 **B** 22 **C** **D**

1

Carlton Lane

West
Carlton

East
Carlton

Carlton Lane

†

Carlton
Manor

2

Carlton
Works

Road

Novia
Plantation

HARROGATE

Cemetery

Warren

3
5

Yeadon
Airport
Industrial
Estate

A658

Leeds Bradford
Airport Industrial Estate

Coney Lodge
Farm

Haw Lane

Novia
Farm

House

Lane

Yeadon
Cemetery

†

4

Haw

Avenue

Road

Leslie Av

P

Yeadon Moor

P

Travelodge

Whitehous

Hawthorn Drive

Carlton

Mt

P

Andrews Road

Granville Ter

Hawthorn Road

Yeadon Tarn

P

Leeds Bradford
International Airport

Whitestone Crs

Cavendish
Street

LS19

Glenmere Mt

VICTORIA AVENUE

South Side Aviation
Centre

Hawthorn Crs

Hawthorn Av

Cemetery

5

Surg

PO

Club RW

Yeadon
Cricket Club

Works

High St

Town Hall

Yeadon
Health
Centre

King St

High

Dam Lane

Moorfield

Plane Tree Grove

A 421 **B** 22 **9** **C** **D**

Rufford Park
Primary School

East VW

Grange

Avenue

Street

Moorfield
Business
Park

Premier
Travel Inn

South Vw Ter

I grid square represents 500 metres

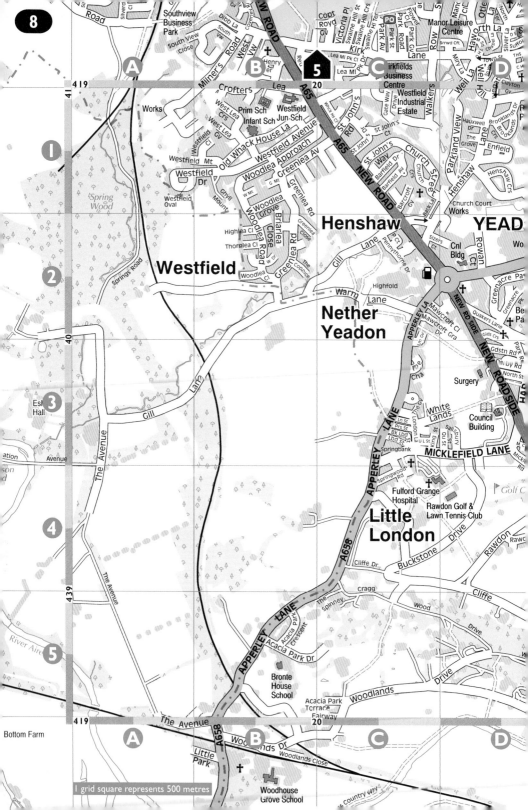

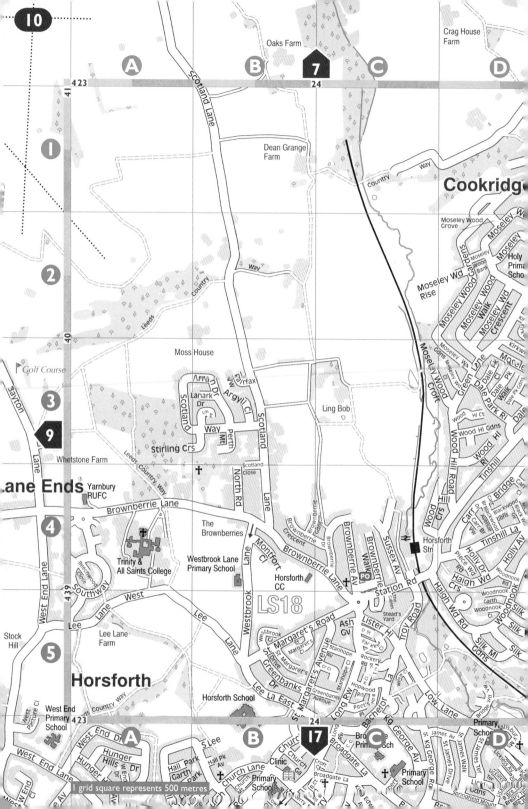

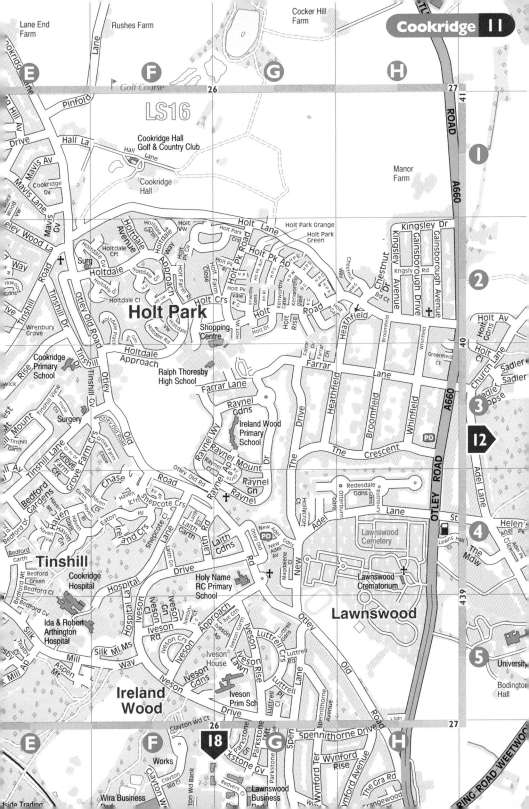

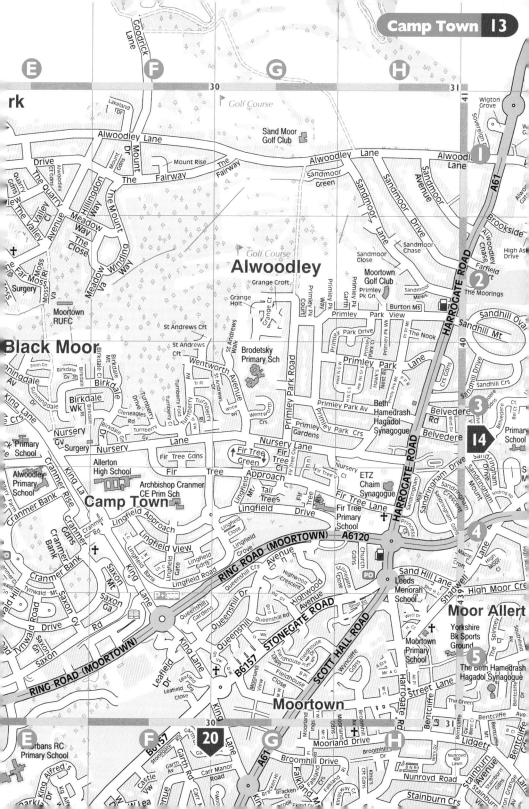

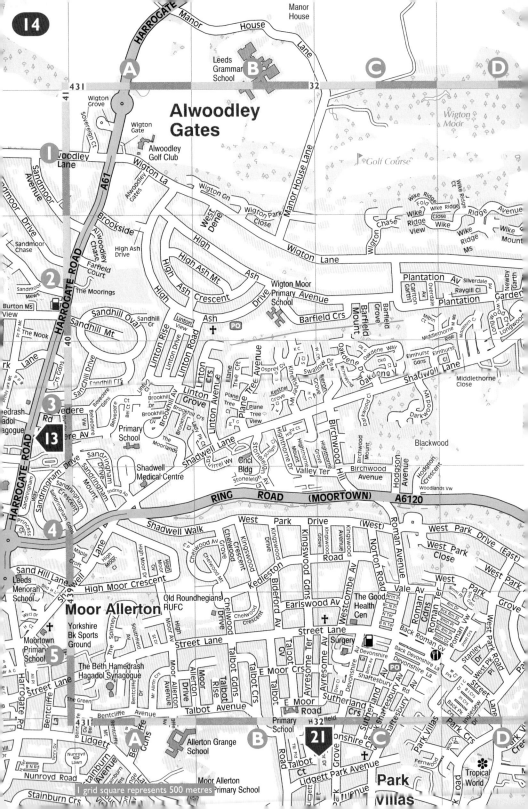

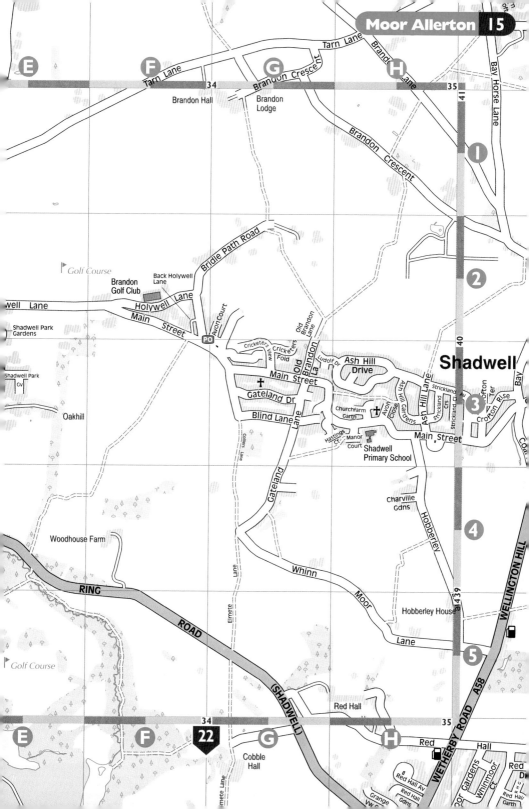

E F G H

Tarn Lane

Brandon Lane

Bay Horse Lane

34 Brandon Crescent 35 41

Brandon Hall

Brandon Lodge

Brandon Crescent

1

2

Golf Course

Bridle Path Road

Brandon Golf Club

Back Holywell Lane

Holywell Lane

well Lane

Main Street

Shadwell Park Gardens

PO

Avon Court

Old Brandon Lane

Ash Hill Drive

Shadwell

40

Shadwell Park Gv

Cricketers View

Cricketers Fold

Old Brandon La

Ludolf Dr

Ash Hill Gardens

Ash Hill Lane

Strickland Av

Strickland Crs

Strickland Cl

Crofton Ter

Crofton Rise

Bay

Oakhill

Main Street

Gateland Dr

Blind Lane

Churchfarm Garth

Avon Cross

3

Crofton

Co

Hastings Ct

Manor Court

Shadwell Primary School

Main Street

Colliers Lane

Gateland Lane

Charville Gdns

4

Woodhouse Farm

Whinn

Moor

Hobberley

A 639

Elmere Lane

Golf Course

RING

ROAD

(SHADWELL)

Lane

Hobberley House

WELLINGTON HILL

5

34 22 35

E F G H

Cobble Hall

Red Hall

Red

Hall

WETHERBY ROAD A 58

or Gardens

Whinmoor Ct

Red Hall Av

Red Hall Gdns

Grange

Red Hall

Red Dr

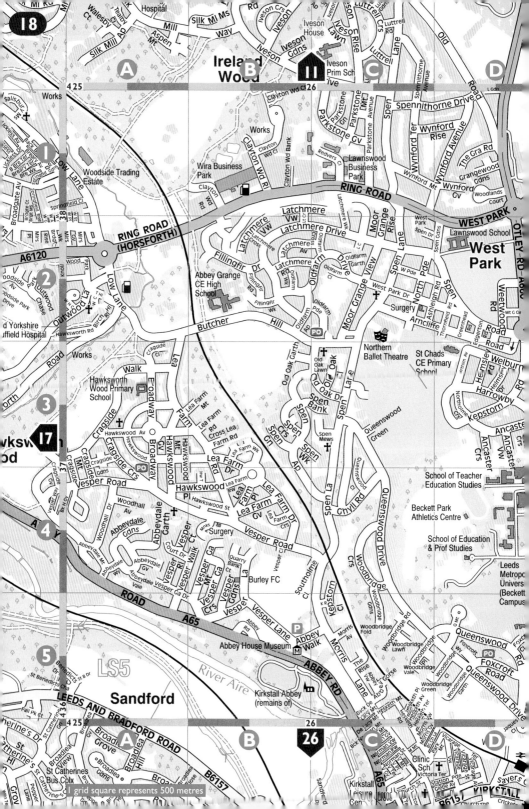

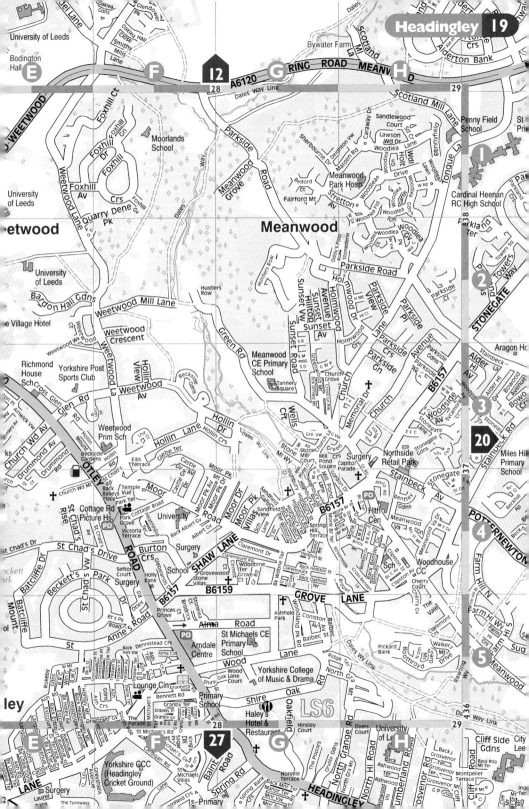

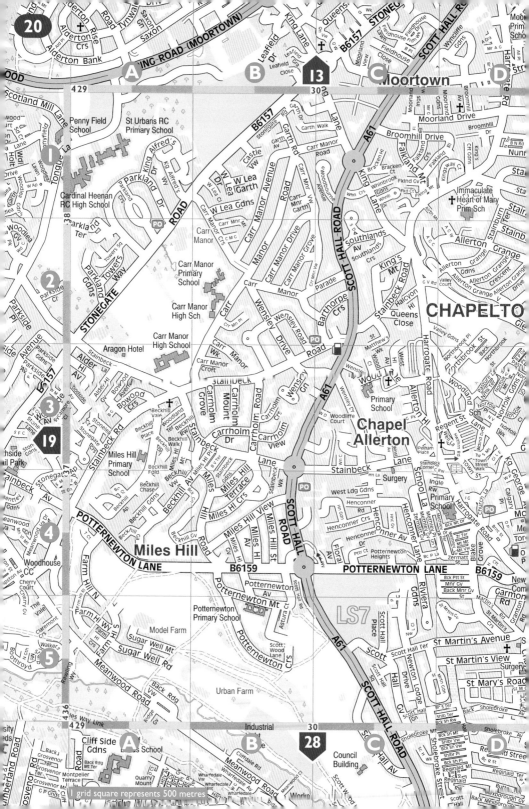

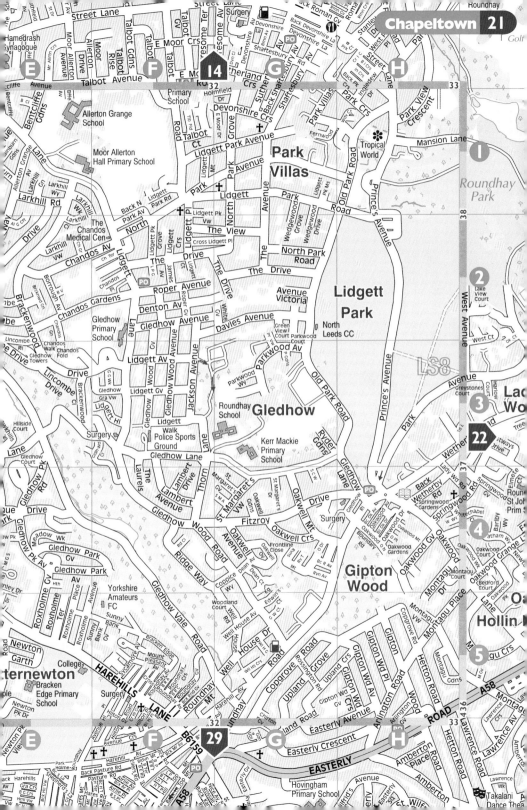

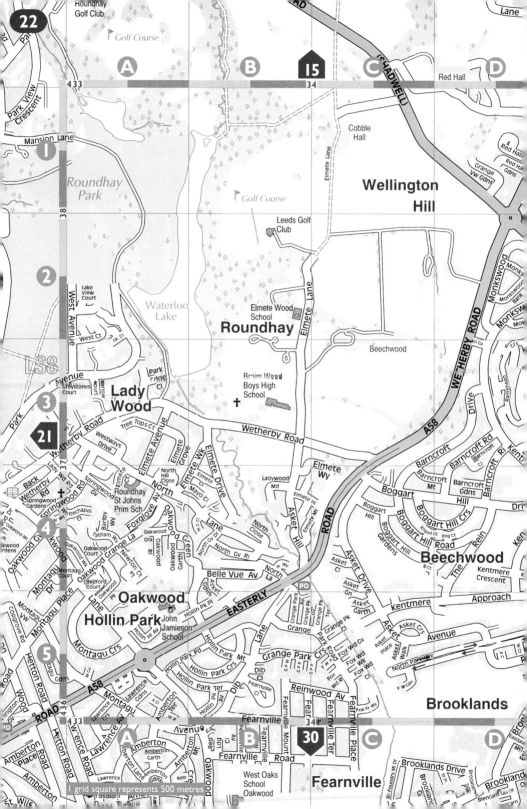

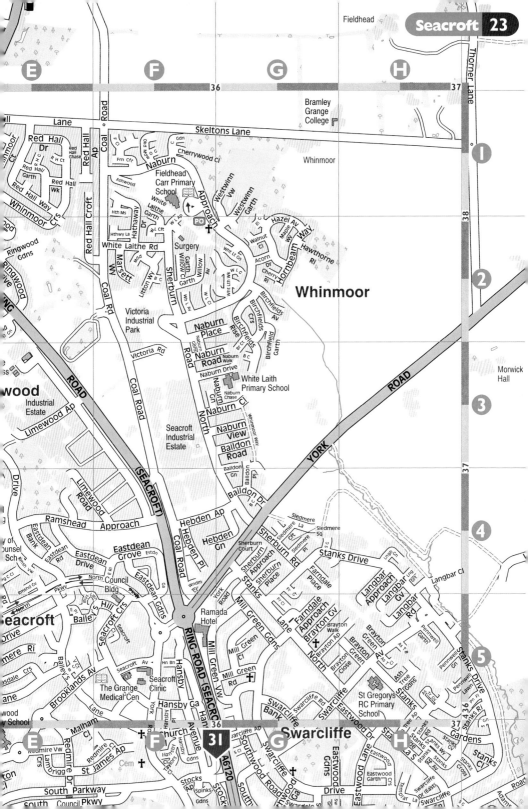

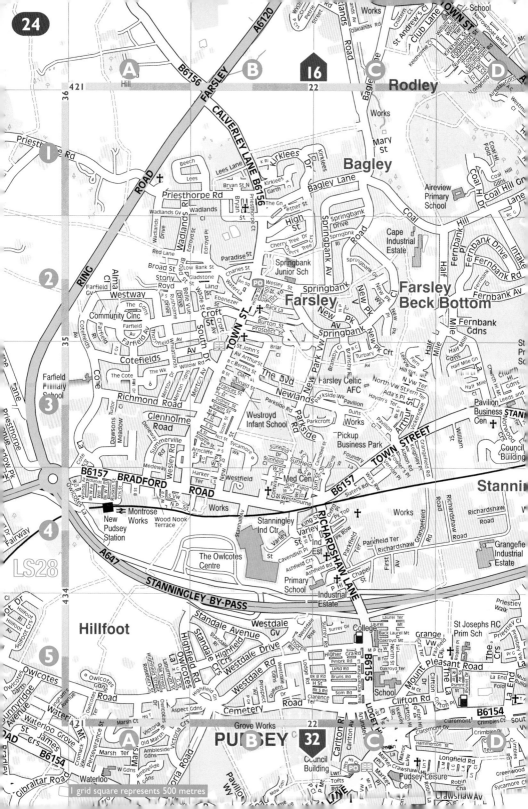

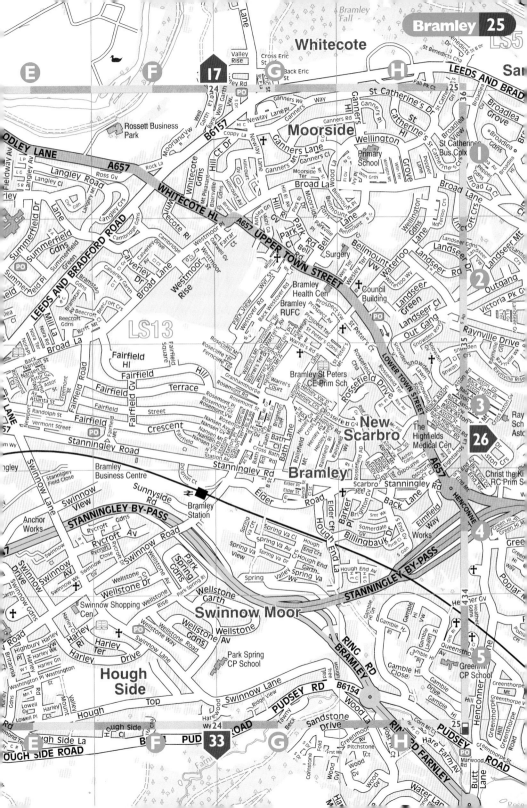

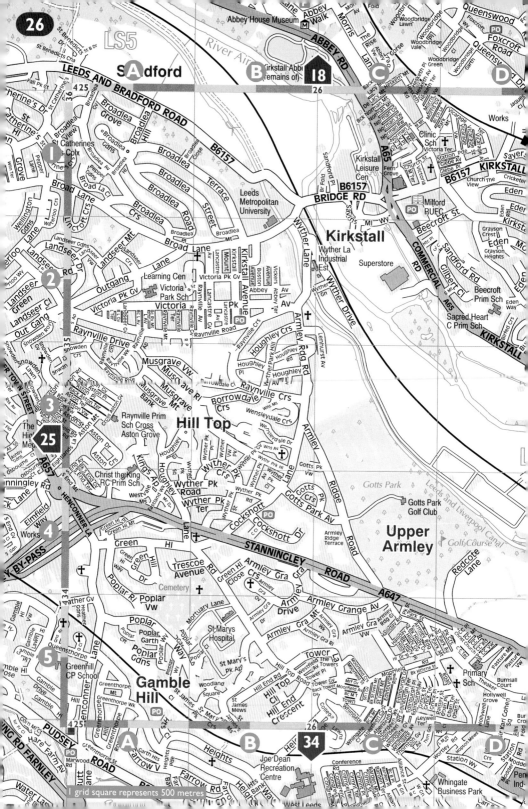

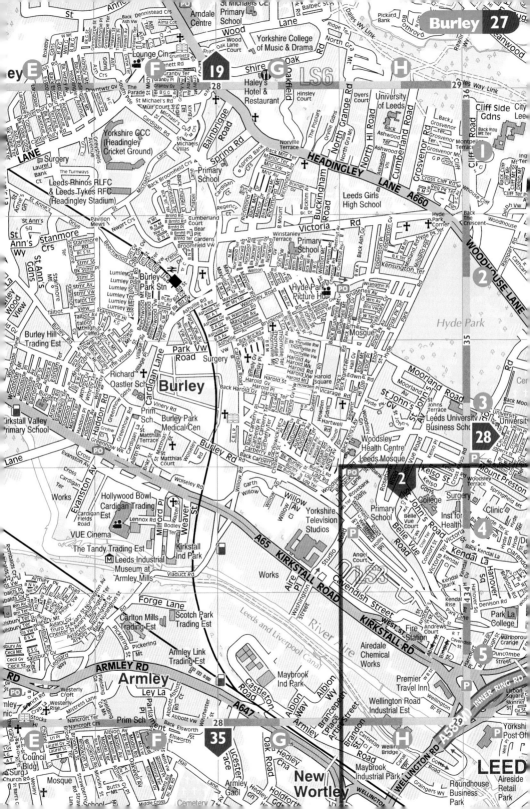

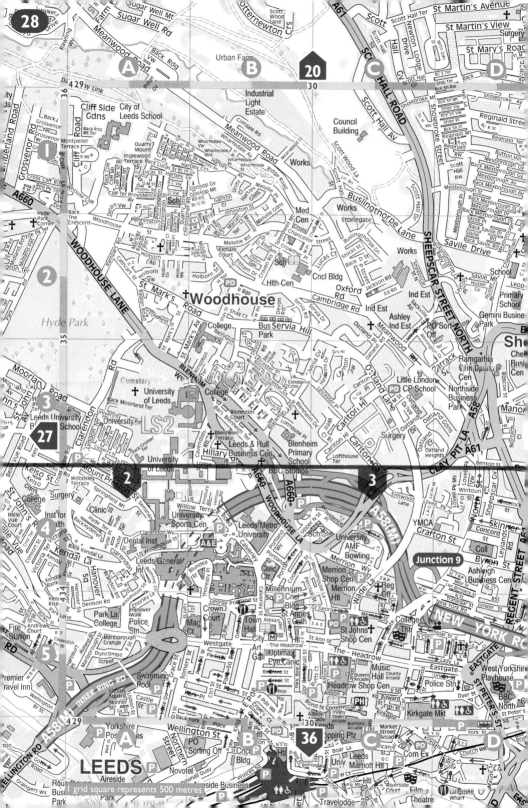

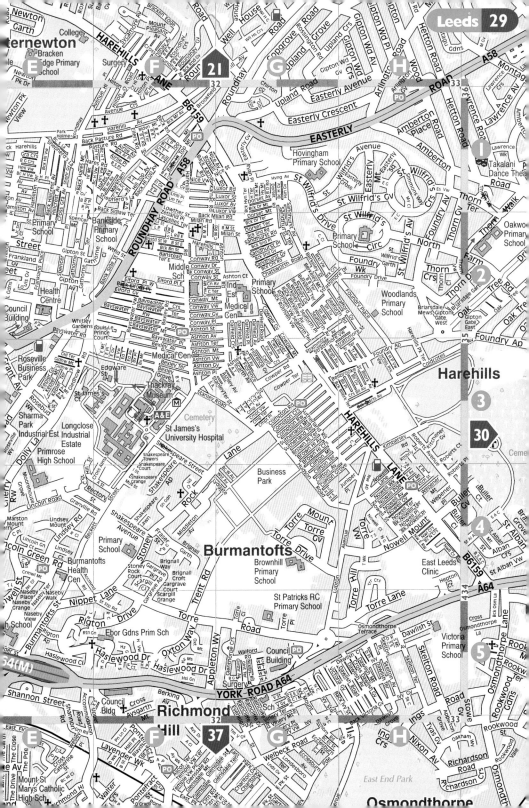

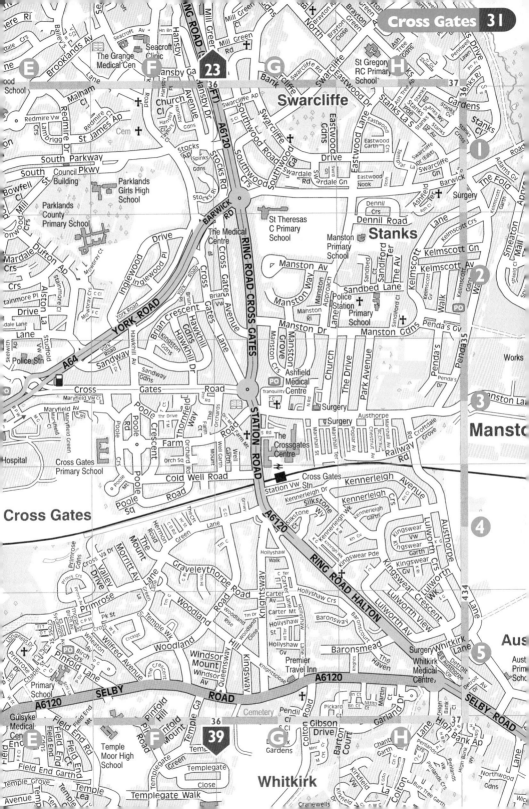

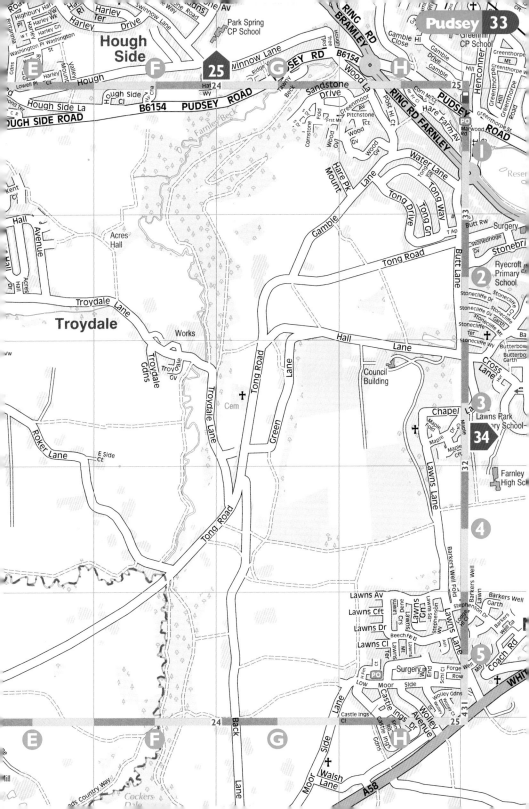

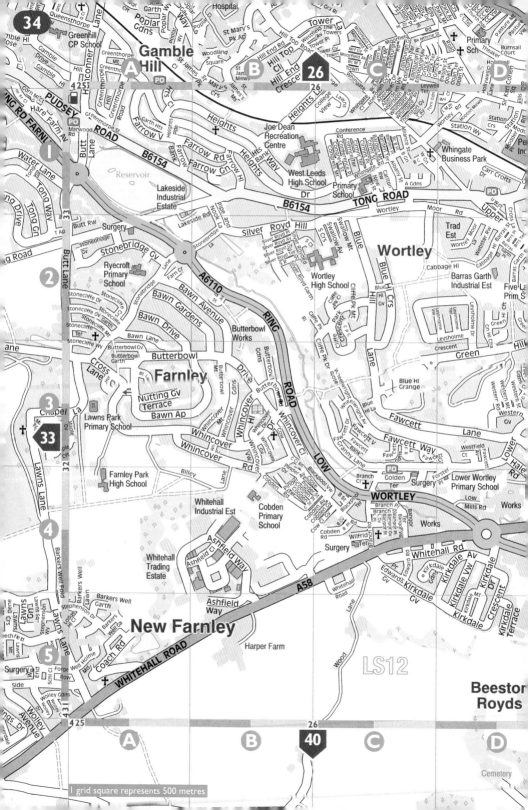

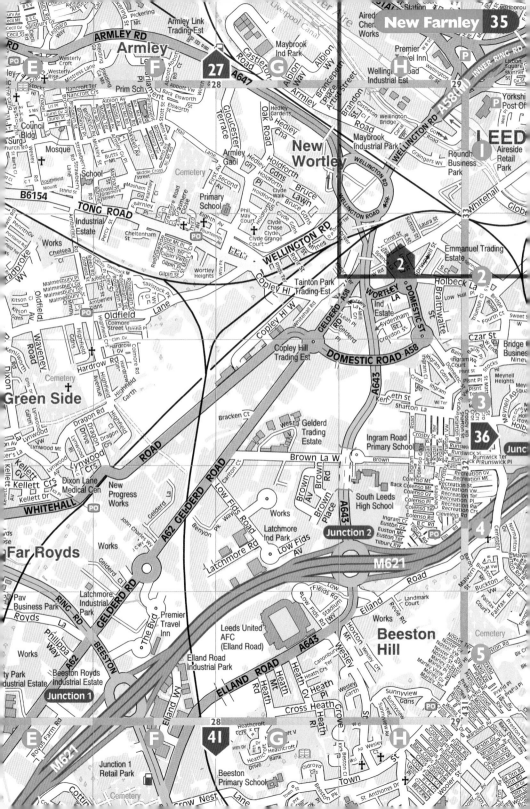

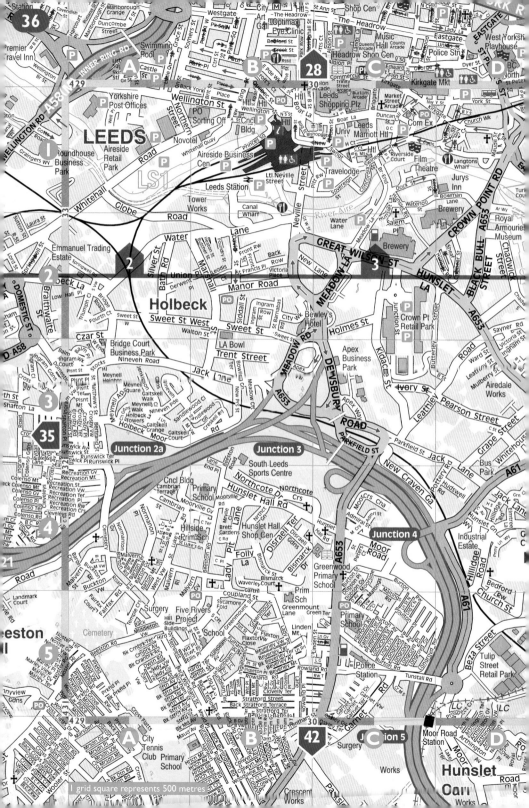

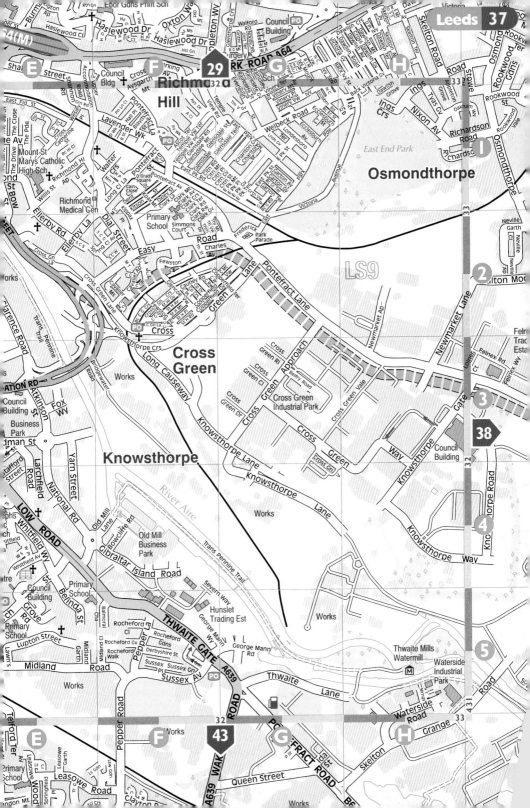

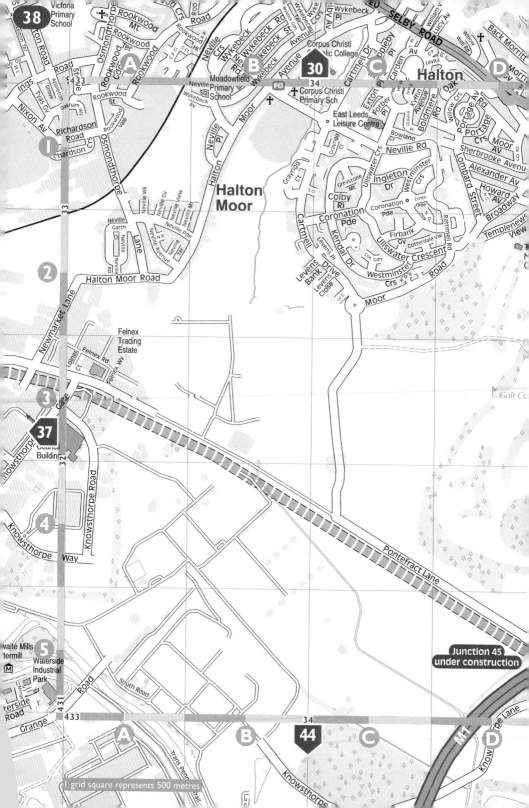

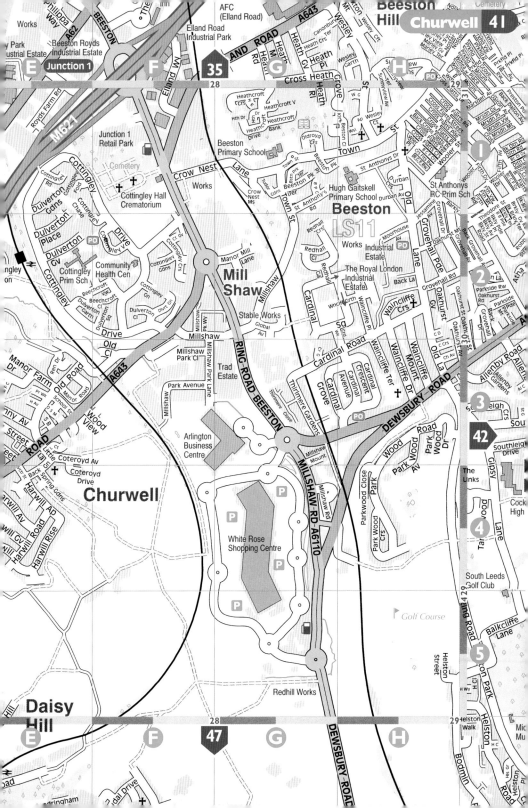

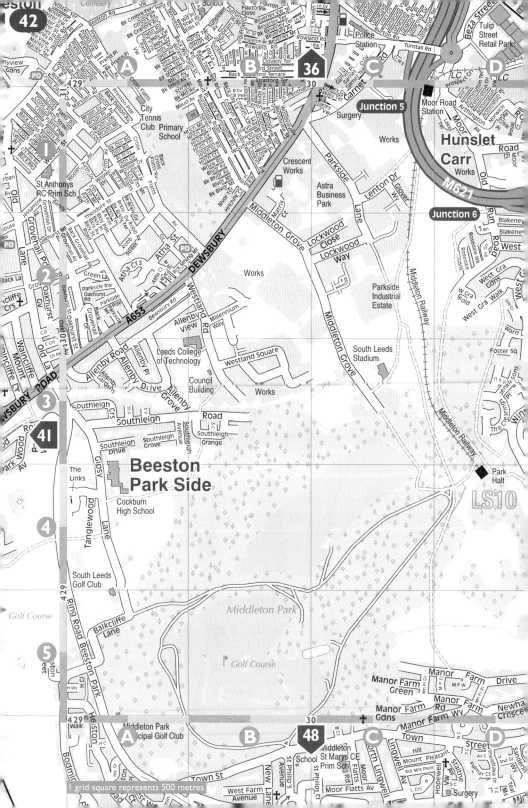

Lupton Street
Garth
Rocheford Gv
Rochford
Gdns
Rocheford
Walk
Midland Cl
Midland Rd
Derbyshire St.
George Mann Rd
Thw
Waterman
Waterside Industrial Park

Midland Road
Pepper Rd
Sussex Sussex Gn
Sussex Av

E
F
G
H

Works

PO

37
32

A639 WAKEFIELD ROAD

Thwaite Lane

Waterside Road

Grange
Road

Works

Queen Street

PONTEFRACT ROAD

Skelton

Works

Works

A639

Cemetery

Middleton Road

Parnaby Rd
Parnaby Av
Bk Parnaby Rd
Bk Parnaby Av
Westbury Pl
Westbury Mt
Westbury Ter
Clayton Rd
Clayton

Woodhouse Hill Road
Leasowe Road
Leasowe Garth
Springfield

A61

Works

Works

N Wy Dr

Stourton

I

33
31

2

Works

PONTEFRACT ROAD

Junction 7

A61

Enterprise Way

East Grange Drive
East Gra Sq
E Gra Garth
East Gra Rd
East Gra Rise
Low Gra Crs

Winrose Grove

Belle-Isle Medical Centre

Ring Road Middleton

A61

A639

Leodis Way

3

30

44 M1

Grange View
Low Grange

Windmill Road

South Leeds Art College

Windmill Primary School

Belle Isle Road

Orion View

Middleton Road

Highlands Wk
Highlands Dr
Middlecroft Rd
Middlecroft Cl

Orion Walk

Kensington

Orion Crs
Orion Gdns

Lea Park Drive

Lea Park Vale
Lea Park Cl

Bewick
Grove

Mandarin

WAKEFIELD ROAD

Works

Jawb
Industrial
Estate

4

St George's
Crs

Belle Isle

Petersfield Av

Broom Crs
Broom Rd
South Hill
South Hill Crs

Broom Terrace

Broom Nook

Hopes Farm Rd

M621

Junction 43

St George's

Low Shops Lane

Approach

Aberfield Ga

Broom
Gdns

Broom
Garth

Broom Place

Broom Mt
Broom Gv

Middleton Grange
Raylands Way

Grange Fields Way

5

Haig

A639

Nesfield VW
Nesfield Rd
Nesfield Gdns
Nesfield Crs
Nesfield View

Belle Isle Road

Ring Road Middleton

Raylands Rd
Raylands Pl
Raylands Close
Raylands Lane

Works

Street
Lanshaw Rd

Dolphin Rd

Throstle Road

Cranmore Rise
Cranmr Rd
Cranmore Crs

Cranmore Drive

Clapgate Primary School

E
F
G
H

32
49

33

Middleton Lane

WAKEFIELD ROAD

Middleton Avenue

Kingsfield

Sharp Lane

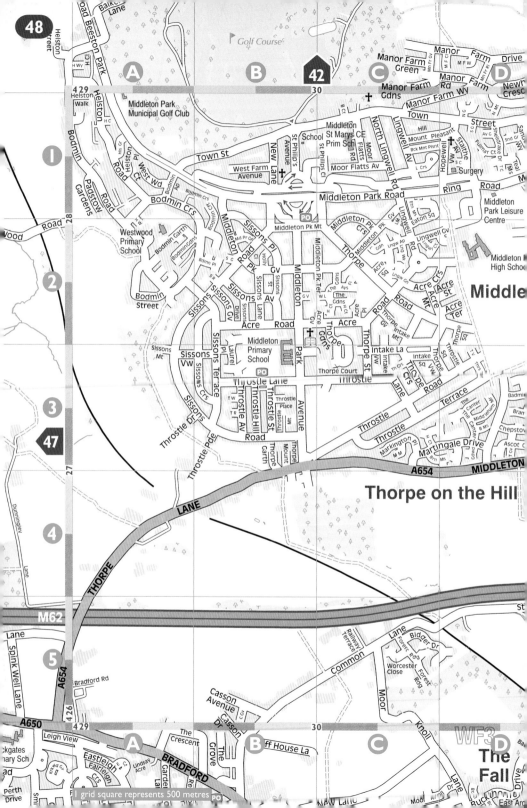

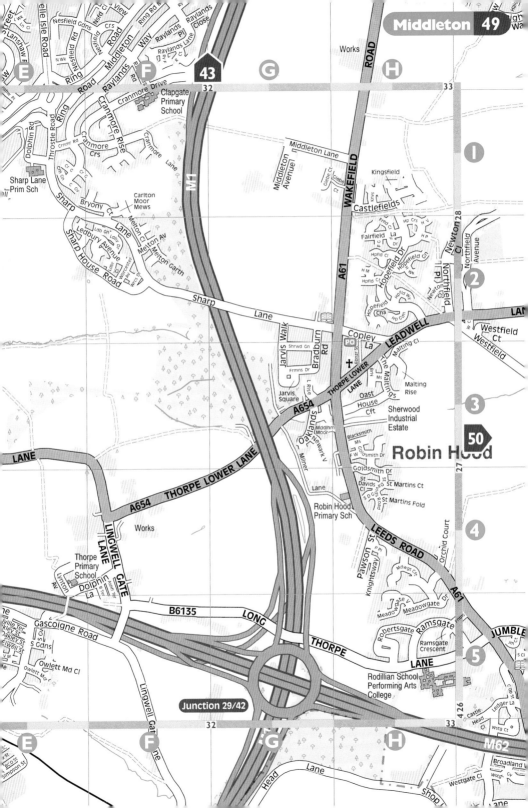

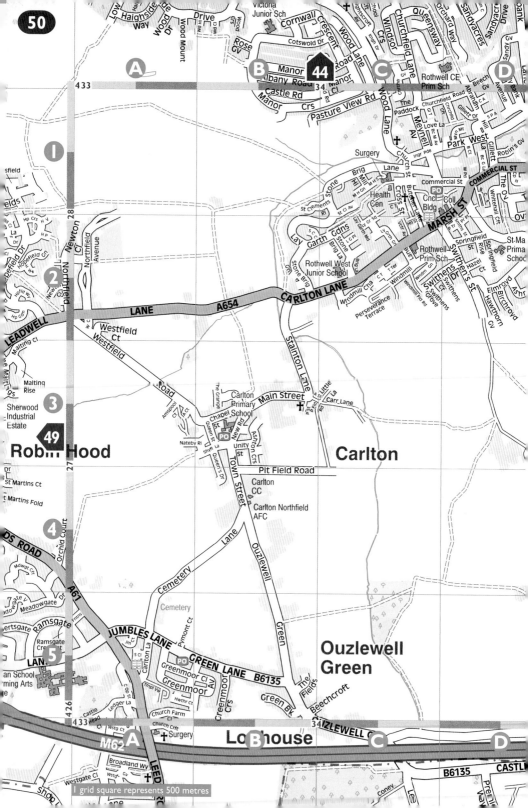

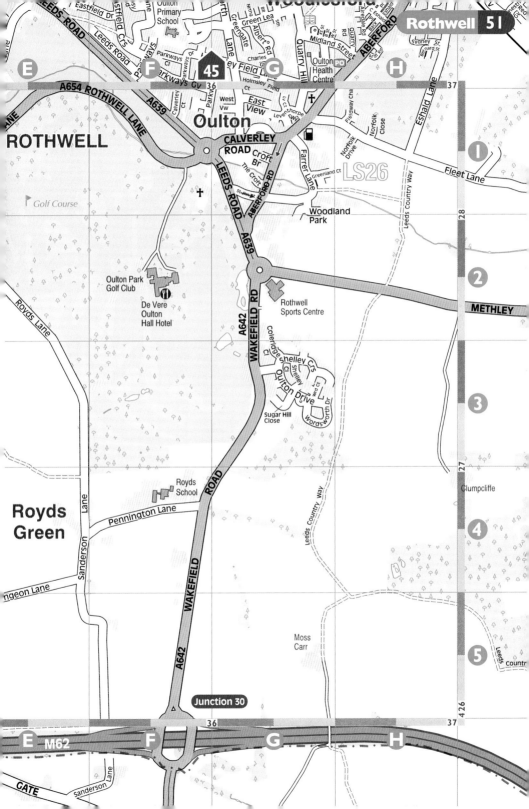

Adel	12 A3	Cookridge	10 D1	Holt Park	11 F2	Seacroft
Alwoodley	13 G2	Cragg Hill	17 G2	Horsforth	9 H5	Shadwell
Alwoodley Gates	14 A1	Cross Gates	31 E4	Horsforth Woodside	17 G2	Sheepscar
Alwoodley Park	12 D1	Cross Green	37 F5	Hough Side	25 F5	Stanks
Armley	27 F5	Daisy Hill	41 E5	Hunslet	36 D4	Stanningley
Bagley	24 C1	East Carlton	6 C1	Hunslet Carr	42 D1	Stourton
Bantam Grove	47 F2	Farnley	34 A3	intake	24 D2	Swarcliffe
Beechwood	22 C4	Far Royds	35 E4	Ireland Wood	11 F5	Swinnow Moor
Beeston	41 G2	Farsley	24 B2	John O'Gaunts	45 F4	Thorpe on The Hill
Beeston Hill	35 H5	Farsley Beck Bottom	24 C2	Kelcliffe	4 D2	Tingley
Beeston Park Side	42 A4	Fearnville	30 C1	Killingbeck	30 C3	Tinshill
Beeston Royds	34 D5	Fulneck	32 B3	Kirkstall	26 C2	Troydale
Belle Isle	43 E4	Gamble Hill	26 A5	Knowsthorpe	37 F3	Upper Armley
Birks	46 C4	Gipton	30 B2	Lady Wood	22 A3	Weetwood
Black Moor	13 E3	Gipton Wood	21 H4	Lane Ends	9 H4	Wellington Hill
Bramhope	7 G1	Gledhow	21 G5	Larkfield	9 F3	Wellroyd
Bramley	25 G4	Green Side	35 E3	Lawnswood	11 G5	West Carlton
Brooklands	22 C5	Guiseley	4 C4	Leeds	3 E2	West End
Bruntcliffe	46 A3	Halton	30 C5	Lidget Park	21 G2	Westfield
Burley	27 F3	Halton Moor	38 B1	Little London	8 C4	West Park
Burmantofts	29 F4	Harehills	29 H5	Low Fold	16 D2	Whinmoor
Calverley	16 A4	Hawksworth Wood	17 H5	Low Green	9 E4	Whitecote
Camp Town	13 F4	Headingley	18 D5	Meanwood	19 G2	Whitkirk
Carlton	50 C3	Henshaw	5 E4	Middleton	48 D2	Woodhouse
Chapel Allerton	20 C5	Hillfoot	24 A5	Miles Hill	20 A4	Woodlesford
Chapeltown	20 C2	Hill Top	26 A3	Mill Shaw	41 G2	Wortley
Churwell	41 G4	Holbeck	36 A2	Monkswood	22 D3	Yeadon
Colton	39 G2	Hollin Park	22 A5	Moor Allerton	13 H5	

Moorside	25 G1	Seacroft		
Moortown	13 G5	Shadwell		
Morley	46 B2	Sheepscar		
Nether Yeadon	8 C2	Stanks		
New Brighton	46 B2	Stanningley		
New Farnley	34 A5	Stourton		
Newsam Green	45 G2	Swarcliffe		
New Scarbro	25 H3	Swinnow Moor		
New Wortley	35 G1	Thorpe on The Hill		
Oakwood	22 A5	Tingley		
Old Bramhope	7 F1	Tinshill		
Osmondthorpe	37 H1	Troydale		
Oulton	51 F1	Upper Armley		
Ouzlewell Green	50 C5	Weetwood		
Parklands	30 C1	Wellington Hill		
Park Villas	21 G1	Wellroyd		
Potternewton	21 E5	West Carlton		
Pudsey	32 B1	West End		
Rawdon	9 E2	Westfield		
Rawdon Carrs	9 F5	West Park		
Richmond Hill	37 F1	Whinmoor		
Robin Hood	49 H5	Whitecote		
Rodley	16 C5	Whitkirk		
Rothwell	51 E1	Woodhouse		
Rothwell Haigh	51 G2	Woodlesford		
Roundhay	22 B2	Wortley		
Royds Green	51 E4	Yeadon		
Sandford	18 A5			

USING THE STREET INDEX

Street names are listed alphabetically. Each street name is followed by its postal town or area locality, the Postcode District, the page number, and the reference to the square in which the name is found.

Standard index entries are shown as follows:

Abbey Av *KSTL* LS5 ....**26** B2

Street names and selected addresses not shown on the map due to scale restrictions are shown in the index with an asterisk:

Airedale Gv *RTHW* LS26 * **45** H5

GENERAL ABBREVIATIONS

ACC	ACCESS	CTYD	COURTYARD	HLS	HILLS	MWY	MOTORWAY	SE	SOU
ALY	ALLEY	CUTT	CUTTINGS	HO	HOUSE	N	NORTH	SER	SERVI
AP	APPROACH	CV	COVE	HOL	HOLLOW	NE	NORTH EAST	SH	
AR	ARCADE	CYN	CANYON	HOSP	HOSPITAL	NW	NORTH WEST	SHOP	SH
ASS	ASSOCIATION	DEPT	DEPARTMENT	HRB	HARBOUR	O/P	OVERPASS	SKWY	
AV	AVENUE	DL	DALE	HTH	HEATH	OFF	OFFICE	SMT	
BCH	BEACH	DM	DAM	HTS	HEIGHTS	ORCH	ORCHARD	SP	
BLDS	BUILDINGS	DR	DRIVE	HVN	HAVEN	OVAL		SPR	
BND	BEND	DRO	DROVE	HWY	HIGHWAY	PAL	PALACE	SQ	
BNK	BANK	DRY	DRIVEWAY	IMP	IMPERIAL	PAS	PASSAGE	ST	
BR	BRIDGE	DWGS	DWELLINGS	IN	INLET	PAV	PAVILION	STN	
BRK	BROOK	E	EAST	IND EST	INDUSTRIAL ESTATE	PDE	PARADE	STR	
BTM	BOTTOM	EMB	EMBANKMENT	INF	INFIRMARY	PH	PUBLIC HOUSE	STRD	
BUS	BUSINESS	EMBY	EMBASSY	INFO	INFORMATION	PK	PARK	SW	SOU
BVD	BOULEVARD	ESP	ESPLANADE	INT	INTERCHANGE	PKWY	PARKWAY	TDG	
BY	BYPASS	EST	ESTATE	IS	ISLAND	PL	PLACE	TER	T
CATH	CATHEDRAL	EX	EXCHANGE	JCT	JUNCTION	PLN	PLAIN	THROL	
CEM	CEMETERY	EXPY	EXPRESSWAY	JTY	JETTY	PLNS	PLAINS	TNL	
CEN	CENTRE	EXT	EXTENSION	KG	KING	PLZ	PLAZA	TOLL	T
CFT	CROFT	F/O	FLYOVER	KNL	KNOLL	PR	PRINCE	TPK	TU
CH	CHURCH	FC	FOOTBALL CLUB	L	LAKE	PREC	PRECINCT	TR	
CHA	CHASE	FK	FORK	LA	LANE	PREP	PREPARATORY	TRL	
CHYD	CHURCHYARD	FLD	FIELD	LDG	LODGE	PRIM	PRIMARY	TWR	
CIR	CIRCLE	FLDS	FIELDS	LGT	LIGHT	PROM	PROMENADE	U/P	UND
CIRC	CIRCUS	FLS	FALLS	LK	LOCK	PRS	PRINCESS	UNI	UNI
CL	CLOSE	FLTS	FLATS	LKS	LAKES	PRT	PORT	UPR	
CLFS	CLIFFS	FM	FARM	LNDG	LANDING	PT	POINT	V	
CMP	CAMP	FT	FORT	LTL	LITTLE	PTH	PATH	VA	
CNR	CORNER	FWY	FREEWAY	LWR	LOWER	PZ	PIAZZA	VIAD	V
CO	COUNTY	FY	FERRY	MAG	MAGISTRATE	QD	QUADRANT	VIL	
COLL	COLLEGE	GA	GATE	MAN	MANSIONS	QU	QUEEN	VIS	
COM	COMMON	GAL	GALLERY	MD	MEAD	QY	QUAY	VLG	
COMM	COMMISSION	GDN	GARDEN	MDW	MEADOWS	R	RIVER	VLS	
CON	CONVENT	GDNS	GARDENS	MEM	MEMORIAL	RBT	ROUNDABOUT	VW	
COT	COTTAGE	GLD	GLADE	MKT	MARKET	RD	ROAD	W	
COTS	COTTAGES	GLN	GLEN	MKTS	MARKETS	RDG	RIDGE	WD	
CP	CAPE	GN	GREEN	ML	MALL	REP	REPUBLIC	WHF	
CPS	COPSE	GND	GROUND	ML	MILL	RES	RESERVOIR	WKS	
CR	CREEK	GRA	GRANGE	MNR	MANOR	RFC	RUGBY FOOTBALL CLUB	WLS	
CREM	CREMATORIUM	GRG	GARAGE	MS	MEWS	RI	RISE	WY	
CRS	CRESCENT	GT	GREAT	MSN	MISSION	RP	RAMP	YD	
CSWY	CAUSEWAY	GTWY	GATEWAY	MT	MOUNT	RW	ROW	YHA	YOUTH
CT	COURT	GV	GROVE	MTN	MOUNTAIN	S	SOUTH		
CTRL	CENTRAL	HGR	HIGHER	MTS	MOUNTAINS	SCH	SCHOOL		
CTS	COURTS	HL	HILL	MUS	MUSEUM				

POSTCODE TOWNS AND AREA ABBREVIATIONS

AL/HA/HU	Alwoodley/Harewood/Huby	BRAM	Bramley	HDGY	Headingley	LDSU	Leeds University	PDSY/CALV	Pudsey/C
BAIL	Baildon	BULY	Burley	HORS	Horsforth	MID	Middleton (W.Yorks)	RHAY	Ro
BEE/HOL	Beeston/Holbeck	BVRD	Belle Vue Road	IDLE	Idle	MOR	Morley	RTHW	R
BHP/TINH	Bramhope/Tinshill	CHAL	Chapel Allerton	ILK	Ilkley	MSTN/BAR	Manston/Barwick in Elmet	SCFT	S
BOW	Bowling	EARD/LOFT	East Ardsley/Lofthouse	KSTL	Kirkstall	OSM	Osmandthorpe	WOR/AKM	Wortley
		GSLY	Guiseley	LDS	Leeds City Centre			YEA	

A

Abbey Av KSTL LS5	26 B2	Abbey Rd KSTL LS5	17 H4	Aberfield Crest MID LS10	43 E5	Ackworth Av YEA LS19	9 E1	Acre Ter MID LS10
Abbey Ct HORS LS18	17 H4	Abbey St BVRD LS3	2 B5	Aberfield Dr MID LS10	43 E5	Ackworth Crs YEA LS19	9 E1	Ada's Pl PDSY/CALV LS28
Abbeydale Gdns KSTL LS5	18 A4	Abbey Ter KSTL LS5	26 B2	Aberfield Ga MID LS10	43 E4	Ackworth Dr YEA LS19	9 E1	Addingham Gdns
Abbeydale Garth KSTL LS5	18 A4	Abbey Vw KSTL LS5	18 C5	Aberfield Mt MID LS10	43 E5	Acorn Dr SCFT LS14	23 G2	WOR/ARM LS12
Abbeydale Gv KSTL LS5	18 A4	Abbey Wk KSTL LS5	18 B5	Aberfield Ri MID LS10	43 E5	Acre Crs MID LS10	48 C2	Addison Rd MSTN/BAR LS15
Abbeydale Mt KSTL LS5	18 A4	Abbott Ct WOR/ARM LS12	27 F5	Aberfield Rd MID LS10	43 E5	Acre Gv MID LS10	48 C2	Adel Garth BHP/TINH LS16
Abbeydale V KSTL LS5	18 A4	Abbott Vw WOR/ARM LS12	27 F5	Aberfield Vw MID LS10	42 D5	Acre Mt MID LS10	48 C2	Adel Grange Cft
Abbeydale Wy KSTL LS5	18 A4	Aberdeen Dr WOR/ARM LS12	34 C1	Aberford Rd RTHW LS26	51 E3	Acre Pl MID LS10	48 C2	BHP/TINH LS16 *
Abbey Gorse KSTL LS5	18 C5	Aberdeen Gv WOR/ARM LS12	34 C1	Abraham HI RTHW LS26	44 D5	Acre Rd MID LS10	48 C2	Adel Grange Ms
		Aberdeen Rd WOR/ARM LS12	34 C1	Acacia Park Crs IDLE BD10	8 B5	Acres Hall Av PDSY/CALV LS28	33 G2	BHP/TINH LS16
		Aberdeen Wk WOR/ARM LS12	34 C1	Acacia Park Dr IDLE BD10	8 B5	Acres Hall Crs PDSY/CALV LS28	33 G2	Adel Gn BHP/TINH LS16
		Aberfield Bank MID LS10	43 E5	Acacia Park Ter IDLE BD10	8 B5	Acres Hall Dr PDSY/CALV LS28	33 G2	Adel La BHP/TINH LS16
		Aberfield Cl MID LS10	43 E4	Accommodation Rd OSM LS9	29 E4	Acre Sq MID LS10	48 C2	Adel Md BHP/TINH LS16
				Ackroyd St MOR LS27	46 D2	Acre St MID LS10	48 C2	

HP/TINH LS16 ....12 B1
Cl BHP/TINH LS16 ....12 A4
Ct BHP/TINH LS16 ....12 A4
Cft BHP/TINH LS16 ...12 A4
Dr BHP/TINH LS16 ....12 A4
Gdns BHP/TINH LS16..12 A4
urs BHP/TINH LS16....12 A4
ers Ct BHP/TINH LS16.12 B4
P/TINH LS16..............12 B3
d Dr BHP/TINH LS16 ..12 B4
d Gv BHP/TINH LS16 ..12 B4
d Pl BHP/TINH LS16 ...12 B4
d Rd BHP/TINH LS16 ..12 B4
st BEE/HOL LS11........36 C4
t BULY LS4................27 E3
ft SCFT LS14.............16 D5
ft BRAM LS13.............16 D2
t HORS LS18.............16 D2
Gdns BRAM LS13........24 D1
Gv HORS LS18...........16 D2
S26 *......................45 H5
Quay BRAM LS13........25 H1
Rd RTHW LS26 *.........45 H5
ar MOR LS27.............46 D2
.............................45 H5
Vw RTHW LS26 *........45 H5
Nhf BRAM LS13..........16 D5
EA LS19...................9 E1
t 27 G4
EA LS19...................9 E1
HAY LS8...................29 F1
MSTN/BAR LS15.........39 E1
CHAL LS7.................21 E4
t RTHW LS26.............44 B5
e WOR/ARM LS12 *.....34 C1
v CHAL LS7...............21 E4
Mt AL/HA/HU LS17......14 A2
HDGY LS6.................19 F4
HORS LS18...............17 C1
MOR LS27................46 D1
S26........................45 G5
PDSY/CALV LS28.........32 B2
LDS LS1...................3 G5
LDS LS1...................3 G4
t PDSY/CALV LS28......24 A1
EARD/LOFT WF5.........50 B3
27.........................3 G4
CALV LS23...............32 D1
v WOR/ARM LS12......27 G5
Rd RHAY LS8 *..........29 F1
Rd RHAY LS8............29 F1
t RHAY LS8..............29 F1
MOR LS27................46 C4
MOR LS27................46 C4
v MOR LS27.............46 C4
t AL/HA/HU LS17........20 A3
Gv CHAL LS7............20 A3
e Rd GSLY LS20.........24 D4
Bank AL/HA/HU LS17...12 D5
Crs AL/HA/HU LS17.....12 D5
Mt AL/HA/HU LS17......12 D5
Pl AL/HA/HU LS17.......12 D5
ar MSTN/BAR LS15.....30 D1
st LDS LS13..............3 F3
a Gv HDGY LS6 *........32 A1
CALV LS28...............32 A1
a Rd HDGY LS6 *.......17 C1
LS18......................17 C1
CALV LS28...............32 A1
a Ter YEA LS19..........32 A1
MOR LS27 *.............41 E3
rs BEE/HOL LS11........42 A5
r BEE/HOL LS11..........42 A5
dns BEE/HOL LS11......42 A5
v BEE/HOL LS11.........42 A5
n BEE/HOL LS11.........42 A5
Vw BEE/HOL LS11.......42 A2
Grange Av
/HU LS17..................21 E1
Grange Cl
/HU LS17..................20 C2
Grange Crs
/HU LS17..................20 D2
Grange Cft RHAY LS8...21 E2
Grange Dr
/HU LS17..................20 D2
Grange Gdns
/HU LS17..................20 D2
Grange Ri
/HU LS17..................20 D2
Grange V
/HU LS17..................20 D2
Grange Wk
/HU LS17..................20 D2
Grange Wy RHAY LS8...20 D2
Hl CHAL LS7..............20 C3
Ms AL/HA/HU LS17......20 D3
PK CHAL LS7.............20 C3
st BULY LS4..............13 H5
st BULY LS4..............27 E5
s WOR/ARM LS12.......34 C1
t MOR LS27..............35 G2
s Cir RTHW LS26........45 H4
s Dr RTHW LS26.........45 G5
e Rd RTHW LS26.........45 G5
s Vw RTHW LS26.........44 A5
ttages HDGY LS6........24 A2
HDGY LS6.................19 F5
OSM LS9..................29 F4
...........................29 F4
RTHW LS26..............44 A5
Vw BHP/TINH LS16 *....12 A4
a SCFT LS14.............31 E2
ner Cha AL/HA/HU LS17.14 A2

Alwoodley Court Gdns
  AL/HA/HU LS17.........13 E1
Alwoodley Gdns
  AL/HA/HU LS17.........13 E2
Alwoodley Gates
  AL/HA/HU LS17.........14 A1
Amberley Gdns WOR/ARM LS12 .35 E2
Amberley Rd WOR/ARM LS12 ..35 E1
Amberley St WOR/ARM LS12 ...35 E2
Amberton Ap RHAY LS8 ....30 A1
Amberton Cl RHAY LS8 ....22 A5
Amberton Crs RHAY LS8 ....30 A1
Amberton Gdns RHAY LS8 .....30 A1
Amberton Garth RHAY LS8 .....30 A1
Amberton La RHAY LS8 ....30 A1
Amberton Mt RHAY LS8 ....30 A1
Amberton Pl RHAY LS8 ....29 H1
Amberton Rd OSM LS9 ....30 A2
  RHAY LS8 ....29 H1
Amberton St RHAY LS8 ....30 A2
Amberton Ter RHAY LS8 ....29 H1
Amblers Ct PDSY/CALV LS28 ...32 C2
Ambleside Gdns
  PDSY/CALV LS28..........32 A1
Ambleside Gv RTHW LS26 .....45 G5
America Moor La MOR LS27 ....46 C4
Amspool Ct EARD/LOFT WF5 ...50 A5
Ancaster Crs BHP/TINH LS16 ..18 D3
Ancaster Rd BHP/TINH LS16 ...18 D3
Anderson Av RHAY LS8 ....29 F5
Anderson Mt RHAY LS8 ....29 E5
Andrew Sq PDSY/CALV LS28 ...24 B2
Andrew St PDSY/CALV LS28 ...24 B3
Angel Ct BVRD LS2 ....2 A2
Annie St MOR LS27 ....46 D2
Apex Vw BEE/HOL LS11 ....36 B5
Apex Wy BEE/HOL LS11 ....36 C3
Apperley La IDLE BD10 ....8 B5
Appleby Pl MSTN/BAR LS15 ...30 C5
Appleby Wk MOR LS27 ....46 D1
Applegarth RTHW LS26 ....45 G4
Appleton Gv OSM LS9 ....29 H5
Appleton Wy OSM LS9 ....29 F5
Archery Pl LDSU LS2 ....28 B3
Archery St LDSU LS2 ....28 B3
Archery Ter LDSU LS2 ....28 B3
Argie Av BULY LS4 ....26 D2
Argie Gdns BULY LS4 ....27 E2
Argie Rd BULY LS4 ....27 E2
Argie Ter BULY LS4 ....27 E2
Argyle Rd OSM LS9 ....3 K3
Argyll Cl HORS LS18 ....10 B3
Arksey Pl WOR/ARM LS12 *....27 E5
Arksey Ter WOR/ARM LS12 *...27 E5
Arkwright Wk MOR LS27 ......40 C5
Arley Gv WOR/ARM LS12 .....27 E5
Arley Pl WOR/ARM LS12 ......27 E5
Arley Ter WOR/ARM LS12 .....27 E5
Arlington Gv RHAY LS8 ....30 B4
Arlington Rd RHAY LS8 ....30 B4
Armitage Sq PDSY/CALV LS28 .32 B2
Armitage St RTHW LS26 *.....50 C2
Armley Grange Av
  WOR/ARM LS12 *........26 B5
Armley Grange Crs
  WOR/ARM LS12..........26 B4
Armley Grange Dr
  WOR/ARM LS12..........26 B5
Armley Grange Mt
  WOR/ARM LS12..........26 B5
Armley Grange Ov
  WOR/ARM LS12..........26 B4
Armley Grange Ri
  WOR/ARM LS12..........26 B5
Armley Grange Vw
  WOR/ARM LS12..........26 B5
Armley Grange Wk
  WOR/ARM LS12..........26 C5
Armley Grove Pl
  WOR/ARM LS12..........35 F1
Armley Lodge Rd
  WOR/ARM LS12..........27 E4
Armley Park Rd WOR/ARM LS12 .26 C5
Armley Ridge Cl WOR/ARM LS12 .26 C5
Armley Ridge Rd
  WOR/ARM LS12..........26 B3
Armley Ridge Ter
  WOR/ARM LS12..........26 C5
Armley Rd WOR/ARM LS12 ....27 F5
Armouries Dr MID LS10 ....36 D2
Armouries Wy MID LS10 ......3 J6
Armstrong St PDSY/CALV LS28 .24 C3
Arncliffe Crs MOR LS27 ....47 E4
Arncliffe Garth PDSY/CALV LS28 .24 A3
Arncliffe Gra AL/HA/HU LS17 ..13 H5
Arncliffe Rd BHP/TINH LS16 ...18 C2
Arncliffe St PDSY/CALV LS28 ..24 C3
Arndale Centre HORS LS18 ....10 B5
Arran Wy RTHW LS26 ....50 D1
Arthington Av MID LS10 ......42 D1
Arthington Gv MID LS10 ......42 D1
Arthington Pl MID LS10 ....42 D1
Arthington St MID LS10 ......42 D1
Arthington Ter MID LS10 .....42 D1
Arthington Vw MID LS10 .....42 D1
Arthur St PDSY/CALV LS28 ...24 C3
Artist St WOR/ARM LS12 .....35 G1
Arundel St PDSY/CALV LS28 ..24 A3
Ascot Gdns MID LS10 ....48 D5
Ash Av HDGY LS6 ....19 F5
Ashbrooke Pk BEE/HOL LS11 *.42 C2
Ashby Av BRAM LS13 ....25 H3
Ashby Cl BRAM LS13 ....25 H3
Ashby Cres BRAM LS13 ......25 H3
Ashby Mt BRAM LS13 ....25 H3
Ashby Sq BRAM LS13 ....25 H3
Ashby Ter BRAM LS13 ....25 H3
Ashby Vw BRAM LS13 ....25 H3

Ash Crs HDGY LS6 ....19 E5
Ashdene WOR/ARM LS12 .....33 H5
Ashdene Cl PDSY/CALV LS28 ..32 C3
Ashdene Crs PDSY/CALV LS28 .32 C3
Ashdown St BRAM LS13 ......25 G5
Ashfield Av MOR LS27 ....46 B4
Ashfield Cl MSTN/BAR LS15 ...31 H2
  WOR/ARM LS12..........34 A4
Ashfield Crs PDSY/CALV LS28 *.24 B4
Ashfield Gv HDGY LS6 ....19 C5
Ashfield Pl MOR LS27 ....46 B4
  PDSY/CALV LS28..........24 B4
Ashfield Ter EARD/LOFT WF5 ..49 F4
  MSTN/BAR LS15..........31 H1
Ashfield Wy WOR/ARM LS12 ..34 B3
Ashford Dr PDSY/CALV LS28 ..32 D2
Ash Gdns HDGY LS6 ....19 F5
Ash Gv HORS LS18 ....10 C5
  PDSY/CALV LS28..........32 C2
Ashgrove Ms BRAM LS13 .....24 D1
Ash Hill Dr AL/HA/HU LS17 ...15 H3
Ash Hill Gdns AL/HA/HU LS17 .15 H3
Ash Hill La AL/HA/HU LS17 ...15 H3
Ashlea Ga BRAM LS13 ....25 G1
Ashlea Gn BRAM LS13 ....25 G2
Ashleigh Gdns RTHW LS26 ....45 G5
Ashleigh Rd BHP/TINH LS16 ..18 C2
Ashley Av RHAY LS8 ....29 G3
Ashley Rd RHAY LS8 ....29 G3
  WOR/ARM LS12..........34 D2
Ashley St OSM LS9 ....29 G3
Ash Rd HDGY LS6 ....19 E5
Ashroyd RTHW LS26 ....50 D2
Ash Ter HDGY LS6 ....19 F5
Ashtofts Mt GSLY LS20 ....5 E3
Ashton Av RHAY LS8 ....29 F3
Ashton Ct RHAY LS8 ....29 G2
Ashton Crs EARD/LOFT WF3...50 B3
Ashton Gv RHAY LS8 ....29 F3
Ashton Mt RHAY LS8 ....29 F3
Ashton Pl RHAY LS8 ....29 F3
Ashton Rd RHAY LS8 ....29 F3
Ashton St RHAY LS8 ....29 F2
Ashton Ter RHAY LS8 ....29 F3
Ashton Vw RHAY LS8 ....29 F3
Ashville Av HDGY LS6 ....27 F2
Ashville Gv HDGY LS6 ....27 F2
Ashville Rd HDGY LS6 ....27 F2
Ashville Ter HDGY LS6 ....27 F2
Ashville Vw HDGY LS6 ....27 G3
Ashwood SCFT LS14 ....23 F1
Ashwood Ter HDGY LS6 ......27 H1
Ashwood Vs HDGY LS6 ......27 H1
Asket Av SCFT LS14 ....22 C5
Asket Cl SCFT LS14 ....22 C4
Asket Crs SCFT LS14 ....22 C4
Asket Dr SCFT LS14 ....22 C4
Asket Gdns RHAY LS8 ....22 B4
Asket Garth SCFT LS14 ......22 C4
Asket Gn SCFT LS14 ....22 C5
Asket Hl RHAY LS8 ....22 B4
Asket Pl SCFT LS14 ....22 C4
Asket Wk SCFT LS14 ....22 C5
Askey Av WOR/ARM LS12 ....46 D4
Askey Crs MOR LS27 ....46 D4
Aspect Gdns PDSY/CALV LS28 .24 A5
Aspen Ct EARD/LOFT WF3 ....47 E5
Aspen Mt BHP/TINH LS16 ....11 E5
Asquith Av MOR LS27 ....40 B5
Asquith Cl MOR LS27 ....46 B1
Asquith Dr MOR LS27 ....46 B1
Assembly St LDSU LS2 ....3 H5
Aston Av BRAM LS13 * 26 A3
Aston Crs BRAM LS13 ....26 A3
Aston Dr BRAM LS13 ....26 A3
Aston Gv BRAM LS13 ....26 A3
Aston Mt BRAM LS13 ....25 H3
Aston Pl BRAM LS13 ....26 A3
Aston Rd BRAM LS13 ....25 H3
Aston St BRAM LS13 ....25 H3
Aston Ter BRAM LS13 ....26 A3
Aston Vw BRAM LS13 ....25 H3
Astor Gv BRAM LS13 ....25 E3
Astor St BRAM LS13 ....25 E3
Astra Pk BEE/HOL LS11 * 42 C1
Astura Ct CHAL LS7 ....20 B5
Atha Cl BEE/HOL LS11 ....42 A2
Atha Crs BEE/HOL LS11 ......42 A2
Atha St BEE/HOL LS11 ....42 A2
Athlone Gv WOR/ARM LS12 ..35 E1
Athlone St WOR/ARM LS12 ...35 E1
Athlone Ter WOR/ARM LS12 ..35 E1
Atkinson St MID LS10 ....37 E3
Atlanta St BRAM LS13 ....25 E3
Authorpe La MSTN/BAR LS15..31 H4
Authorpe Rd MSTN/BAR LS15 .31 H5
Authorpe Rd CHAL LS7 ......19 H4
Autumn Av HDGY LS6 ....27 G3
Autumn Crs HORS LS18 ......17 H3
Autumn Gv HDGY LS6 ....27 G3
Autumn Pl HDGY LS6 ....27 G3
Autumn St HDGY LS6 ....27 G3
Autumn Ter HDGY LS6 ......27 G3
Auty Sq MOR LS27 ....46 D3
Avenue Crs RHAY LS8 ....29 F1
Avenue Gdns AL/HA/HU LS17 .13 H2
Avenue Hl RHAY LS8 ....29 F1
Avenue Lawns AL/HA/HU LS17 .12 D2
The Avenue AL/HA/HU LS17 ..13 E2
  HORS LS18................16 D1
  IDLE BD10................8 A4
  MSTN/BAR LS15..........30 D4
  OSM LS9.................29 H3
  RHAY LS8................29 F1
Avenue Victoria RHAY LS8 ....21 G2
Aviary Gv WOR/ARM LS12 ....27 E5
Aviary Mt WOR/ARM LS12 ....27 E5
Aviary Pl WOR/ARM LS12 ....27 E5

Aviary Rd WOR/ARM LS12 * ..27 E4
Aviary Rw WOR/ARM LS12 ...27 E5
Aviary St WOR/ARM LS12 ....27 E5
Aviary Ter WOR/ARM LS12 ...27 E5
Aviary Vw WOR/ARM LS12 ...27 E5
Avocet Garth MID LS10 ....48 H3
Avon Cl AL/HA/HU LS17 ......15 H3
Avon Ct AL/HA/HU LS17 ......15 G2
Avondale St BRAM LS13 ......25 E3
Axis Ct MOR LS27 * 46 A1
Ayresome Av RHAY LS8 ......14 C5
Ayresome Ter RHAY LS8 .....14 B5
Aysgarth Cl OSM LS9 ....37 F1
Aysgarth Dr OSM LS9 ....37 F1
Aysgarth Fold MID LS10 ......48 C2
Aysgarth Pl OSM LS9 ....37 F1
Aysgarth Wk OSM LS9 ......37 F1

B

Bachelor La HORS LS18 * 10 C5
Back Airlie Av RHAY LS8 * 29 F1
Back Airlie Pl RHAY LS8 ......29 F1
Back Albert Gv HDGY LS6 ....19 F1
Back Albert Ter HDGY LS6 ....27 G5
Back Alcester Pl RHAY LS8 * ..29 F1
Back Alcester Rd RHAY LS8 ...29 F1
Back Alcester Ter RHAY LS8 * .29 F1
Back Archery Pl LDSU LS2 * ...28 B3
Back Archery Rd LDSU LS2 ...28 B3
Back Archery St LDSU LS2 ....28 B3
Back Archery Ter LDSU LS2 ...28 B3
Back Ash Gv HDGY LS6 ......27 H2
Back Ashley Av OSM LS9 * ...29 G3
Back Ashley St OSM LS9 .....29 G3
Back Ash Vw HDGY LS6 .....19 F5
Back Ashville Av HDGY LS6 ...27 F3
Back Ashville Gv HDGY LS6 ...27 F2
Back Ashville Rd HDGY LS6 ...27 F2
Back Ashville Ter HDGY LS6 ..27 F2
Back Ashwood Ter HDGY LS6 .27 H1
Back Aston St BRAM LS13 ....25 H3
Back Aston Ter BRAM LS13 ...25 H3
Back Aston Vw BRAM LS13 ...25 H3
Back Athlone Av
  WOR/ARM LS12 * 35 E1
Back Athlone Gv
  WOR/ARM LS12..........35 E1
Back Athlone Ter
  WOR/ARM LS12 * 35 E1
Back Atlanta St BRAM LS13 ...25 E3
Back Austhorpe Rd
  MSTN/BAR LS15..........31 H3
Back Autumn Rd HDGY LS6 * .27 G3
Back Baileys Pl HDGY LS6 ....19 F4
Back Baldovan Ter HDGY LS8 .29 F1
Back Bank Ter PDSY/CALV LS28 .24 C5
Back Banstead St RHAY LS8 ..29 F2
Back Barden Pl WOR/ARM LS12 .34 C1
Back Barkly Gv BEE/HOL LS11 .42 A1
Back Barkly Pde BEE/HOL LS11 .42 A1
Back Barkly Ter BEE/HOL LS11 *.42 A1
Back Bath Rd BRAM LS13 ....25 E5
Back Beamsley Gv HDGY LS6 *.27 G3
Back Beamsley Mt HDGY LS6 .27 G3
Back Beamsley Ter HDGY LS6 .27 G3
Back Beechwood Gv BULY LS4 *.27 F2
Back Beechwood Rd
  BULY LS4................27 F2
Back Bellbrooke Gv OSM LS9 ..29 G3
Back Belvedere Av
  BEE/HOL LS11............42 B1
Back Belvedere Mt
  BEE/HOL LS11............42 B1
Back Bentley Av HDGY LS6 ...19 H4
Back Bentley Gv HDGY LS6 ...19 H4
Back Berkeley Av RHAY LS8 ..29 G2
Back Berkeley Ter RHAY LS8 ..29 G2
Back Beverley Ter
  BEE/HOL LS11............36 B5
Back Blenheim Av LDSU LS2 * .28 B3
Back Blenheim Ter LDSU LS2 ..28 B3
Back Boundary Ter BVRD LS2 *.27 G4
Back Breary Av HORS LS18 ...17 H1
Back Breary Ter HORS LS18 *..17 H1
Back Bright St PDSY/CALV LS28 .24 D1
Back Broad La BRAM LS13 ...25 H1
Back Broomfield Crs HDGY LS6 .27 F2
Back Broomfield Pl HDGY LS6 *.27 F2
Back Brudenell Gv HDGY LS6 .27 H3
Back Brudenell Mt HDGY LS6 .27 H3
Back Brudenell Rd HDGY LS6 .27 H2
Back Brunswick St
  PDSY/CALV LS28..........24 B5
Back Burchett Gv HDGY LS6 ..28 A1
Back Burchett Pl HDGY LS6 ...28 A1
Back Burley Hl BULY LS4 .....26 D5
Back Burley Lodge Rd
  HDGY LS6................27 H4
Back Burley Lodge Ter
  BEE/HOL LS11............42 B1
Back Burley St BVRD LS2 * ...2 C4
Back Burlington Pl
  BEE/HOL LS11............42 B1
Back Burlington Rd
  BEE/HOL LS11............42 B1
Back Burton Crs HDGY LS6 ...19 F4
Back Burton Ter
  BEE/HOL LS11............36 C5
Back Camberley St
  BEE/HOL LS11............36 C5
Back Carberry Pl HDGY LS6 ...27 G3
Back Carberry Rd HDGY LS6 ..27 G3
Back Carberry Ter HDGY LS6 ..27 G3
Back Carter Ter
  MSTN/BAR LS15..........31 G4
Back Chapel La HDGY LS6 ....27 G2
Back Chatsworth Rd RHAY LS8 .29 G2
Back Chestnut Av HDGY LS6 *.27 G2
  MSTN/BAR LS15..........31 H3

Back Chiswick Ter HDGY LS6 *.27 G3
Back Christ Church Vw
  ....26 D5
Back Church La BHP/TINH LS16 .12 A2
  KSTL LS5................25 G4
Back Claremont Av BVRD LS3 *.27 G2
Back Clarence Rd HORS LS18 .17 F5
Back Clarkson Vw HDGY LS6 .28 A1
Back Clayton St RTHW LS26 ..50 D1
Back Cliff Mt HDGY LS6 ......27 H5
Back Clifton Ter OSM LS9 ....29 H3
Back Clipston Av HDGY LS6 ..19 H4
Back Coldcotes Av OSM LS9 ..29 H3
Back Colenso Mt BEE/HOL LS11 .35 H4
Back Colenso Rd BEE/HOL LS11 .35 H4
Back Cotton Rd WOR/ARM LS12 .35 E1
Back Colwyn Pl BEE/HOL LS11 *.42 B1
Back Colwyn Vw
  BEE/HOL LS11............42 B1
Back Conway St RHAY LS8 ...29 G2
Back Cowper Gv RHAY LS8 * .29 G2
Back Cowper St CHAL LS7 ...28 D2
Back Cranbrook Av
  BEE/HOL LS11............36 A5
Back Cranbrook Ter
  ....36 A5
Back Cromer Ter LDSU LS2 ...28 A3
Back Cross Flatts Av
  BEE/HOL LS11............42 A1
Back Cross Flatts Crs
  ....41 H1
Back Cross Flatts Gv
  ....42 A1
Back Cross Flatts Pl
  BEE/HOL LS11............42 A1
Back Cross Flatts Rw
  ....41 H1
Back Cross Green Crs OSM LS9 .37 F2
Back Cross Green La OSM LS9 .37 F2
Back Dalton Av BEE/HOL LS11 .42 A1
Back Dalton Rd BEE/HOL LS11 .42 A1
Back Dargai St CHAL LS7 ....28 C2
Back De Lacy Mt KSTL LS5 ..18 C5
Back Delph Mt HDGY LS6 ....27 H4
Back Dent St OSM LS9 ......37 F1
Back Devonshire La RHAY LS8 .14 C4
Back Dorset Mt RHAY LS8 ...29 G1
Back Dorset Rd RHAY LS8 ...29 G1
Back Dorset Ter RHAY LS8 ...29 G2
Back East Park Rd OSM LS9 * .37 G1
Back Ecclesburn Gv OSM LS9 *.37 H1
Back Ecclesburn St OSM LS9 .37 H1
Back Elford Pl RHAY LS8 .....29 F1
Back Ellers Gv RHAY LS8 ....29 F1
Back Ellers Rd RHAY LS8 ....29 F1
Back Elsworth St
  WOR/ARM LS12..........35 F1
Back Eric St BRAM LS13 .....25 G5
Back Eshald Pl RTHW LS26 ...45 H5
Back Esmond Ter
  WOR/ARM LS12..........34 D1
Back Estcourt Av HDGY LS6 ..19 E5
Back Estcourt Ter HDGY LS6 .27 E1
Back Fairford Pl
  BEE/HOL LS11 * 36 B5
Back Foundry Mill Dr SCFT LS14 .30 C1
Back Garton Rd OSM LS9 ....37 G1
Back Garton Ter OSM LS9 ....37 G1
Back Gathorne St RHAY LS8 * .29 E2
Back Gillett La RTHW LS26 ...50 D1
Back Glenthorpe Ter OSM LS9 .28 B1
Back Glossop St HDGY LS6 ..28 B1
Back Gordon Ter HDGY LS6 ..19 H4
Back Graham Gv BULY LS4 ...27 E2
Back Granby Gv HDGY LS6 ...27 F1
Back Grange Av CHAL LS7 ...29 E1
Back Grange Crs CHAL LS7 ..29 E1
Back Grange Ter CHAL LS7 ..28 D1
Back Grange Vw CHAL LS7 * .28 D1
Back Granville Ter GSLY LS20 .5 F2
Back Gt MOR LS27 ....41 E4
Back Greenmount Ter
  ....36 B5
Back Greenwood Mt HDGY LS6..19 G3
Back Grimthorpe St HDGY LS6 .19 E5
Back Grosvenor Ter HDGY LS6 .27 H1
Back Grovehall Av
  ....42 A1
Back Grovehall Dr
  ....42 A2
Back Haigh Av RTHW LS26 ...44 A5
Back Haigh St RTHW LS26 ...44 A5
Back Haigh Vw RTHW LS26 ..44 A5
Back Halliday Gv
  WOR/ARM LS12..........26 C5
Back Halliday Pl
  WOR/ARM LS12..........26 C5
Back Hamilton Av CHAL LS7 .29 E1
Back Hamilton Vw CHAL LS7 .29 E1
Back Harehills Av CHAL LS7 ..29 E1
Back Harehills Park Vw
  OSM LS9.................29 H3
Back Harehills Pl RHAY LS8 ..29 F2
Back Harehills Rd RHAY LS8 ..29 F2
Back Hares Av RHAY LS8 ....29 F1
Back Hares Mt RHAY LS8 ....29 E1
Back Hares Ter RHAY LS8 ....29 F1
Back Hares Vw RHAY LS8 ....29 F1
Back Harold Gv HDGY LS6 ...27 G5
Back Hartley Av HDGY LS6 ...28 A1
Back Hartley Gv HDGY LS6 ...28 A1
Back Hartley St MOR LS27 ...46 D3
Back Hawksworth Gv KSTL LS5 .17 H4
Back Headingley Av HDGY LS6 .19 E5
Back Headingley Mt HDGY LS6 .19 E5
Back Heddon St HDGY LS6 ...19 G4
Back Hessle Av HDGY LS6 ...27 G2
Back Hessle Mt HDGY LS6 ...27 G2
Back Hessle Rd HDGY LS6 ...27 G2
Back Hessle Ter HDGY LS6 ...27 G2
Back Hessle Vw HDGY LS6 ...27 G2
Back Highbury Ter HDGY LS6 .19 G4
Back Highfield Rd BRAM LS13 .25 H3

Back High St YEA LS19 .....5 H5
Back Highthorne Gv WOR/ARM LS12 * 26 C5
Back Highthorne St WOR/ARM LS12 .....26 C5
Back Hillcrest Av CHAL LS7 .....29 E1
Back Hill Top Av CHAL LS7 .....29 E1
Back Hill Top Mt RHAY LS8 .....29 F1
Back Hilton Gv RHAY LS8 * 29 F1
Back Hilton Pl RHAY LS8 * 29 F1
Back Hilton Rd RHAY LS8 * 29 F1
Back Kensluell La AL/HA/HU LS17 .....15 F2
Back Hovingham Gv RHAY LS8 .....29 G1
Back Hovingham Mt RHAY LS8 .....29 G2
Back Hovingham Ter RHAY LS8 .....29 G2
Back Hyde Ter LDSU LS2 .....2 C1
Back ibbetson Pl LDSU LS2 .....2 E1
Back Ivy Gv OSM LS9 * 37 H1
Back Ivy Mt OSM LS9 .....29 G5
Back Ivy St OSM LS9 .....29 G5
Back Karnac Rd RHAY LS8 .....29 F1
Back Kelso Rd LDSU LS2 * 27 H3
Back Kendal La BVRD LS5 * 2 C2
Back Kensington St HDGY LS6 .....27 H2
Back King's Av HDGY LS6 .....27 H3
Back Kitson St OSM LS9 * 37 F1
Back Lambton Gv RHAY LS8 * 29 F1
Back Landseer Av BRAM LS13 .....26 A2
Back Landseer Gv BRAM LS13 * 26 A2
Back Landseer Ter BRAM LS13 * 26 A2
Back La BEE/HOL LS11 .....41 H2
  BRAM LS13 .....24 B5
  GSLY LS20 .....4 D5
  HORS LS18 .....17 F2
  PDSY/CALV LS28 .....24 B2
  SCFT LS14 .....55 G5
  YEA LS19 .....8 C2
Back Langdale Gdns HDGY LS6 .....27 E1
Back Langdale Ter HDGY LS6 .....27 E1
Back Laurel Mt PDSY/CALV LS28 .....24 C5
Back Lodge La BEE/HOL LS11 .....36 B5
Back Lombard St YEA LS19 .....8 E5
Back Longroyd Ter BEE/HOL LS11 * 36 C1
Back Lucas St HDGY LS6 .....28 A1
Back Lunan Pl RHAY LS8 * 29 F1
Back Lunan Ter RHAY LS8 .....29 F1
Back Mafeking Av BEE/HOL LS11 .....42 A2
Back Mafeking Mt BEE/HOL LS11 .....42 A2
Back Manor Dr HDGY LS6 .....27 G2
Back Manor Gv CHAL LS7 .....20 D4
Back Manor Ter HDGY LS6 .....27 G2
Back Markham Av RHAY LS8 * 29 F1
Back Masham St WOR/ARM LS12 * 35 F1
Back Maud Av CHAL LS7 * 42 A1
Back Mayville Av HDGY LS6 .....27 G2
Back Mayville Pl HDGY LS6 .....27 G2
Back Mayville St HDGY LS6 .....27 G2
Back Mayville Ter HDGY LS6 .....27 G2
Back Meadow Vw HDGY LS6 .....27 G2
Back Melbourne Gv BRAM LS13 .....25 G3
Back Methley Dr CHAL LS7 .....20 D4
Back Mexborough Av CHAL LS7 .....28 D1
Back Mexborough Dr CHAL LS7 .....28 D1
Back Mexborough Gv CHAL LS7 .....28 D1
Back Mexborough St CHAL LS7 .....28 D1
Back Meynell Av RTHW LS26 .....50 C1
Back Middle Cross St WOR/ARM LS12 * 35 F1
Back Middleton Vw BEE/HOL LS11 .....36 A5
Back Midland Rd HDGY LS6 .....27 H2
Back Milan Av RHAY LS8 .....29 G2
Back Milan St RHAY LS8 .....29 G2
Back Mitford Rd WOR/ARM LS12 .....35 F1
Back Model Av WOR/ARM LS12 .....35 F1
Back Model Rd WOR/ARM LS12 .....35 F1
Back Model Ter WOR/ARM LS12 .....35 F1
Back Model Vw WOR/ARM LS12 .....35 F1
Back Monk Bridge Dr HDGY LS6 .....19 H4
Back Monk Bridge St HDGY LS6 .....19 G4
Back Moorfield Ter WOR/ARM LS12 .....26 C5
Back Moorland Ter LDSU LS2 .....2 E3
Back Morritt Dr MSTN/BAR LS15 .....30 D5
Back Mount Pleasant MID LS10 .....43 F2
Back Mount Vw HDGY LS6 .....27 H1
Back Nansen St BRAM LS13 .....25 E3
Back Newport Gdns HDGY LS6 .....27 F2
Back Newport Mt HDGY LS6 .....27 F2
Back Newport Pl HDGY LS6 .....27 F2
Back Newton Gv CHAL LS7 .....28 D1
Back Nice Vw RHAY LS8 * 29 F1
Back Norman Mt KSTL LS5 .....26 C1
Back Norman Pl RHAY LS8 .....14 C5
Back Norman Ter RHAY LS8 .....14 C5
Back Northbrook St CHAL LS7 .....20 D5
Back North Park Av RHAY LS8 .....20 D4
Back Norwood Gv HDGY LS6 .....27 G2
Back Norwood Pl HDGY LS6 .....27 G2
Back Norwood Rd HDGY LS6 .....27 G2
Back Nowell Crs OSM LS9 .....29 H4
Back Nowell Pl OSM LS9 .....29 H4
Back Nowell Ter OSM LS9 .....29 H4
Back Nunington St WOR/ARM LS12 .....27 F5
Back Nunington Vw WOR/ARM LS12 .....27 F5
Back Nunroyd Rd AL/HA/HU LS17 .....20 D1
Back Nursery Mt MID LS10 * 43 E2
Back Oakfield Ter HDGY LS6 .....19 G4
Back Oakley St EARD/LOFT WF3 .....49 E5
Back Oakley Ter BEE/HOL LS11 * 42 C1
Back Oak Rd CHAL LS7 * 20 D5
Back Oakwood Av RHAY LS8 .....21 H4

Back Oakwood Dr RHAY LS8 .....21 H4
Back Osmondthorpe La OSM LS9 .....30 A5
Back Outwood La HORS LS18 .....17 G3
Back Overdale Ter MSTN/BAR LS15 * 31 E5
Back Park Crs RHAY LS8 .....14 D5
Back Parkfield Rd BEE/HOL LS11 .....36 A5
Back Park Vw BEE/HOL LS11 .....36 A5
Back Park View Av BULY LS4 .....27 F2
Back Parkville Rd BRAM LS13 * 25 G2
Back Parnaby Av MID LS10 .....43 F2
Back Parnaby St MID LS10 .....43 F2
Back Parnaby Ter MID LS10 .....43 F2
Back Pasture Gv CHAL LS7 .....20 D3
Back Pasture Rd RHAY LS8 .....29 E1
Back Pollard La BRAM LS13 .....17 G5
Back Potternewton La CHAL LS7 .....20 C4
Back Potters St CHAL LS7 .....20 D4
Back Prospect Ter OSM LS9 * 37 F1
Back Providence Av HDGY LS6 .....28 A1
Back Ravenscar Av RHAY LS8 .....21 H5
Back Raynville Mt BRAM LS13 .....26 A2
Back Regent Park Ter HDGY LS6 .....27 H1
Back Regent Ter HDGY LS6 .....27 H3
Back Reginald Mt CHAL LS7 * 28 D1
Back Reginald Pl CHAL LS7 * 28 D1
Back Reginald St CHAL LS7 .....28 D1
Back Richardshaw La PDSY/CALV LS28 .....24 C5
Back Richmond Mt HDGY LS6 .....27 G2
Back Ridge Mount Ter HDGY LS6 .....27 H1
Back Ridge Vw CHAL LS7 .....20 A5
Back Roberts St RTHW LS26 * 45 G5
Back Rochester Ter HDGY LS6 .....27 F1
Back Rokeby Gdns HDGY LS6 .....19 E5
Back Roman Gv RHAY LS8 .....14 C5
Back Roman Pl RHAY LS8 .....14 C5
Back Roman St RHAY LS8 .....14 C5
Back Rosebank Crs HDGY LS6 * 27 H3
Back Rosemont Wk BRAM LS13 .....25 G3
Back Rossall Rd RHAY LS8 * 29 G2
Back Rossington Gv RHAY LS8 * 29 E1
Back Rossington Pl RHAY LS8 .....29 E1
Back Roundhay Av RHAY LS8 .....21 F5
Back Roundhay Crs RHAY LS8 .....21 F5
Back Roundhay Gv RHAY LS8 .....21 F5
Back Roundhay Pl RHAY LS8 .....21 F5
Back Roundhay Vw RHAY LS8 * 21 F5
Back Rowland Ter BEE/HOL LS11 .....36 C5
Back Ruthven Vw RHAY LS8 .....29 G2
Back St Alban Crs OSM LS9 .....30 A4
Back St Elmo Gv OSM LS9 .....29 G5
Back Saint Ives Mt WOR/ARM LS12 .....26 C5
Back St Luke's Crs BEE/HOL LS11 .....36 A4
Back Salisbury Gv WOR/ARM LS12 .....27 E5
Back Salisbury Ter WOR/ARM LS12 .....27 E5
Back Salisbury Vw WOR/ARM LS12 .....27 E5
Back Sandhurst Gv RHAY LS8 .....29 G2
Back Sandhurst Pl RHAY LS8 .....29 G2
Back Sandhurst Rd RHAY LS8 .....29 G2
Back Savile Dr CHAL LS7 .....28 D2
Back Savile Rd CHAL LS7 .....28 D2
Back School Vw HDGY LS6 .....27 G2
Back Seaforth Ter OSM LS9 * 29 G2
Back Sefton Av BEE/HOL LS11 .....36 A5
Back Sefton Ter BEE/HOL LS11 .....36 A5
Back Shaftesbury Av RHAY LS8 .....21 G1
Back Shepherd's La CHAL LS7 .....29 E1
Back Shepherd's Pl RHAY LS8 .....29 E1
Back Sholebroke Av CHAL LS7 .....20 D5
Back Sholebroke Mt CHAL LS7 .....28 D1
Back Sholebroke Pl CHAL LS7 .....28 D1
Back Sholebroke Rw CHAL LS7 * 28 D1
Back Sholebroke St CHAL LS7 .....20 D5
Back Sholebroke Vw CHAL LS7 .....28 D1
Back Sidlaw Ter RHAY LS8 .....29 F1
Back Somerset Rd PDSY/CALV LS28 .....24 B5
Back South End Gv BRAM LS13 .....26 A3
Back Springfield Mt WOR/ARM LS12 .....34 C1
Back Spring Grove Wk HDGY LS6 .....27 G3
Back Stanley St OSM LS9 * 29 F3
Back Stanmore Pl BULY LS4 .....27 E2
Back Stanmore St BULY LS4 .....27 E2
Back Storey Pl SCFT LS14 .....30 C4
Back Stratford Av BEE/HOL LS11 .....42 A1
Back Stratford St BEE/HOL LS11 * 36 C5
Back Stratford Ter BEE/HOL LS11 .....36 B5
Back Sunnybank Rd HORS LS18 .....17 F3
Back Sunnydene SCFT LS14 .....30 D4
Back Sutton Ap SCFT LS14 .....30 C4
Back Tempest Rd BEE/HOL LS11 .....36 B5
Back Temple Vw BEE/HOL LS11 * 36 A5
Back The Crs HDGY LS6 .....28 A2
Back Thornville Rd HDGY LS6 .....27 G3
Back Tower Gv WOR/ARM LS12 .....26 C5
Back Town St HORS LS18 .....17 F2
Back Trentham Pl BEE/HOL LS11 .....42 B1
Back Vicars Rd RHAY LS8 * 29 F1
Back Victoria Gv OSM LS9 .....37 H1
Back Walmsley Rd HDGY LS6 .....27 G3
Back Welton Av HDGY LS6 .....27 G2
Back Welton Mt HDGY LS6 .....27 G2

Back Welton Pl HDGY LS6 .....27 G2
Back Westbourne Ter LDSU LS2 .....28 A5
Back Westbury St MID LS10 .....43 F2
Back Westlock Av OSM LS9 .....29 G4
Back Westover Rd BRAM LS13 .....25 G2
Back Wetherby Gv BULY LS4 .....27 E3
Back Wetherby Rd RHAY LS8 .....21 H4
Back Wickham St BEE/HOL LS11 .....36 A5
Back William Av MSTN/BAR LS15 * 30 C5
Back Wilton Gv HDGY LS6 * 19 G4
Back Winfield Gv LDSU LS2 .....28 B3
Back Winston Gdns HDGY LS6 .....19 E5
Back Woodbine Ter BEE/HOL LS11 .....19 G4
Back Woodland Park Rd HDGY LS6 * 19 G5
Back Woodlands Av PDSY/CALV LS28 .....24 A4
Back Woodlands Gv PDSY/CALV LS28 .....24 A4
Back Woodlands Ter PDSY/CALV LS28 .....24 A4
Back Woodstock St LDSU LS2 * 28 B3
Back York Pl LDS LS1 .....2 E5
Back York St LDSU LS2 .....3 J5
Badminton Dr MID LS10 .....48 D3
Bagby Rd LDSU LS2 .....2 E4
Bagley La PDSY/CALV LS28 .....24 B1
Baildon Cl SCFT LS14 .....23 G4
Baildon Dr SCFT LS14 .....23 G4
Baildon Gn SCFT LS14 .....23 G4
Baildon Pl SCFT LS14 .....23 G4
Baildon Rd SCFT LS14 .....23 G4
Bailey's Cl SCFT LS14 .....23 E5
Bailey's Hl SCFT LS14 .....23 E5
Bailey's La SCFT LS14 .....23 E5
Baileys Lawn SCFT LS14 .....23 E5
Bainbrigge Rd HDGY LS6 .....27 F1
Baines St RTHW LS26 * 50 C1
Baker Crs MOR LS27 .....46 C3
Baker Rd MOR LS27 .....46 C3
Baker St MOR LS27 .....46 C3
Balbec Av HDGY LS6 .....19 G5
Balbec St HDGY LS6 .....19 G5
Baldovan Mt RHAY LS8 .....29 F1
Baldovan Pl RHAY LS8 .....29 F1
Baldovan Ter RHAY LS8 .....29 F1
Balkcliffe La MID LS10 .....42 A5
Balmoral Cha MID LS10 .....37 F5
Balmoral Wy YEA LS19 .....9 H1
Balm Pl BEE/HOL LS11 .....36 A3
Balm Rd BEE/HOL LS11 .....43 E1
Balm Wk BEE/HOL LS11 .....35 H5
Bangor Gv WOR/ARM LS12 .....34 C4
Bangor St WOR/ARM LS12 .....34 C4
Bangor Ter WOR/ARM LS12 .....34 C4
Bangor Vw WOR/ARM LS12 .....34 C4
Bank Av HORS LS18 .....17 F2
  MOR LS27 .....46 C1
Banker St BULY LS4 .....27 F4
Bankfield Gdns BULY LS4 .....27 E2
Bankfield Gv BULY LS4 .....27 E2
Bankfield Rd BULY LS4 .....27 E2
Bankfield Ter BULY LS4 .....27 E3
Bank Gdns HORS LS18 .....17 F2
Bankhouse PDSY/CALV LS28 .....32 B5
Bank House Cl PDSY/CALV LS28 .....32 B5
Bankhouse Ct PDSY/CALV LS28 .....32 B5
Bankhouse La PDSY/CALV LS28 .....32 B5
Banksfield Av YEA LS19 .....5 H4
Banksfield Cl YEA LS19 .....5 H4
Banksfield Crs YEA LS19 .....5 H4
Banksfield Gv YEA LS19 .....5 H4
Banksfield Mt YEA LS19 .....5 H4
Banksfield Rd YEA LS19 .....5 H4
Bank Side St RHAY LS8 .....29 F2
Bank Sq MOR LS27 .....46 C1
Bank St LDS LS1 .....3 G5
  MOR LS27 .....46 C1
Bank Ter MOR LS27 .....46 C1
Bank View Ter CHAL LS7 .....20 B3
Banstead St East RHAY LS8 .....29 F2
Banstead St West RHAY LS8 .....29 F2
Banstead Ter East RHAY LS8 .....29 F2
Banstead Ter West RHAY LS8 * 29 F2
Bantam Cl MID LS10 .....47 F2
Bantam Grove La MOR LS27 .....47 F2
Bantam Grove Vw MOR LS27 .....47 F2
Baptist Wy PDSY/CALV LS28 .....25 E5
Barclay St CHAL LS7 .....3 J1
Barcroft Gv YEA LS19 .....8 C1
Barden Cl WOR/ARM LS12 .....34 C1
Barden Gn WOR/ARM LS12 .....34 C1
Barden Mt WOR/ARM LS12 * 34 C1
Barden Pl WOR/ARM LS12 .....34 C1
Barden Ter WOR/ARM LS12 .....34 C1
Bardon Hall Gdns BHP/TINH LS16 .....19 E2
Dardon Hall Ms BHP/TINH LS16 * 19 E2
Barfield Av YEA LS19 .....8 C1
Barfield Dr YEA LS19 .....14 B2
Barfield Gv AL/HA/HU LS17 .....14 C2
Barfield Mt AL/HA/HU LS17 .....14 C2
Barker Pl BRAM LS13 .....25 H4
Barkers Well Fold 33 H4
Barkers Well Garth WOR/ARM LS12 * 34 A5
Barkers Well Ga 34 A5
Barkers Well Lawn WOR/ARM LS12 .....34 A5
Barkly Av BEE/HOL LS11 .....42 A2
Barkly Dr BEE/HOL LS11 * 42 A2
Barkly Gv BEE/HOL LS11 .....42 A2
Barkly Pde BEE/HOL LS11 .....42 A2
Barkly Pl BEE/HOL LS11 .....42 A2
Barkly Rd BEE/HOL LS11 .....41 H1
Barkly St BEE/HOL LS11 .....42 A2

Barkly Ter BEE/HOL LS11 .....42 A1
Bar La HORS LS18 .....16 C2
Barley Wy RHAY LS8 .....22 A4
Barley Field Ct MSTN/BAR LS15 * 31 E5
Barley Ms EARD/LOFT WF3 .....49 H3
Barnbrough St BULY LS4 .....27 E3
Barncroft Cl SCFT LS14 .....22 D5
Barncroft Dr SCFT LS14 .....22 C4
Barncroft Gdns SCFT LS14 .....22 D4
Barncroft Gv SCFT LS14 .....22 C4
Barncroft Mt SCFT LS14 .....22 C4
Barncroft Ri SCFT LS14 .....22 C4
Barncroft Rd SCFT LS14 .....22 C4
Barnet Gv MOR LS27 .....46 C4
Barnet Rd WOR/ARM LS12 .....35 F1
Barnswick Vw BHP/TINH LS16 .....11 E3
Baron Cl BEE/HOL LS11 .....36 A4
Baronscourt MSTN/BAR LS15 .....31 H5
Baronsmead MSTN/BAR LS15 .....31 H5
Baronsway MSTN/BAR LS15 .....31 G5
Barrack Rd CHAL LS7 .....28 D2
Barrack St CHAL LS7 .....28 D3
Barras Garth Pl WOR/ARM LS12 .....34 D2
Barras Garth Rd WOR/ARM LS12 .....34 D2
Barras Pl WOR/ARM LS12 .....34 D2
Barras St WOR/ARM LS12 .....34 D2
Barras Ter WOR/ARM LS12 .....34 D2
Barthorpe Crs CHAL LS7 .....20 D2
Barton Ct MSTN/BAR LS15 .....39 G1
Barton Gv BEE/HOL LS11 .....36 A4
Barton Hl BEE/HOL LS11 .....36 A4
Barton Mt BEE/HOL LS11 .....36 A4
Barton Pl BEE/HOL LS11 .....36 A4
Barton Rd BEE/HOL LS11 .....36 A4
Barton Ter BEE/HOL LS11 .....36 A4
Barton Vw BEE/HOL LS11 .....36 A4
Barwick Rd SCFT LS14 .....31 F2
Batcliffe Dr HDGY LS6 .....19 E4
Batcliffe Mt HDGY LS6 .....19 E5
Bath Cl BRAM LS13 .....25 G3
Bath Gv BRAM LS13 * 25 G3
Bath La BRAM LS13 .....25 G3
Bath Rd BEE/HOL LS11 .....36 A2
  BRAM LS13 .....25 G3
Batter La YEA LS19 .....9 E5
Bawn Ap WOR/ARM LS12 .....34 A3
Bawn Av WOR/ARM LS12 .....34 A2
Bawn Dr WOR/ARM LS12 .....34 A2
Bawn Gdns WOR/ARM LS12 .....34 A2
Bawn La WOR/ARM LS12 .....34 A2
Bayswater Crs RHAY LS8 .....29 F2
Bayswater Gv RHAY LS8 .....29 F2
Bayswater Mt RHAY LS8 .....29 F2
Bayswater Pl RHAY LS8 .....29 F2
Bayswater Rd RHAY LS8 .....29 E2
Bayswater Row RHAY LS8 .....29 E2
Bayswater Ter RHAY LS8 .....29 F2
Bayswater Vw RHAY LS8 .....29 F2
Bayton La YEA LS19 .....9 G1
Beacon Av MOR LS27 .....46 B4
Deacon Gv MOR LS27 .....46 B4
Beamsley Gv HDGY LS6 * 27 G3
Beamsley Mt HDGY LS6 * 27 G3
Beamsley Pl HDGY LS6 .....27 G3
Beamsley Ter HDGY LS6 * 27 G3
Bear Pit Gdns HDGY LS6 .....27 G3
Beaumont Av RHAY LS8 .....14 C5
Beckbury Cl PDSY/CALV LS28 .....24 B5
Beckbury St PDSY/CALV LS28 .....24 B5
Beckett's Park Dr HDGY LS6 .....19 F5
Beckett's Park Rd HDGY LS6 .....19 F5
Beckett St LS9 .....29 E4
Beckhill Ap CHAL LS7 .....20 A4
Beckhill Av CHAL LS7 .....20 A4
Beckhill Cha CHAL LS7 .....20 A4
Beckhill Cl CHAL LS7 * 20 A3
Beckhill Dr CHAL LS7 .....20 A3
Beckhill Fold CHAL LS7 .....20 A3
Beckhill Gdns CHAL LS7 .....20 A4
Beckhill Garth CHAL LS7 .....20 A4
Beckhill Ga CHAL LS7 .....20 A4
Beckhill Gn CHAL LS7 .....20 A4
Beckhill Gv CHAL LS7 .....20 A4
Beckhill Lawn CHAL LS7 * 20 A3
Beckhill Pl CHAL LS7 .....20 A3
Beckhill Rw CHAL LS7 .....20 A3
Beckhill Vw CHAL LS7 .....20 A4
Beckhill Wk CHAL LS7 .....20 A3
Beck Rd RHAY LS8 .....29 F1
Beckside Gdns BHP/TINH LS16 .....19 F3
Beckside Vw MOR LS27 .....47 E2
Bedale Ct MOR LS27 .....46 B4
Bedford Cl BHP/TINH LS16 .....11 E4
Bedford Ct HORS LS18 .....17 F1
  RHAY LS8 .....11 E4
Bedford Dr BHP/TINH LS16 .....11 E4
Bedford Gdns BHP/TINH LS16 .....11 E4
Bedford Garth BHP/TINH LS16 .....11 E4
Bedford Gn BHP/TINH LS16 .....11 E4
Bedford Gv BHP/TINH LS16 .....11 E4
Bedford Mt BHP/TINH LS16 .....11 E4
Bedford Rw MID LS10 .....36 D4
Bedford St LDS LS1 .....3 G5
Bedford Vw BHP/TINH LS16 .....11 E4
Beech Av HORS LS18 .....17 G3
  MOR LS27 .....50 B5
Beech Crs OSM LS9 .....30 B2
Beechcroft Cl BEE/HOL LS11 .....41 E2
Beechcroft Mt BEE/HOL LS11 .....14 C3
Beechcroft Vw BEE/HOL LS11 .....41 E2
Beech Dr WOR/ARM LS12 .....27 E5
Beechfield WOR/ARM LS12 .....33 E5
Beech Gv RTHW LS26 .....44 D5
Beech Lees PDSY/CALV LS28 .....24 A1
Beech Mt OSM LS9 .....30 B2
Beech St EARD/LOFT WF3 .....49 H5
Beech Wk BHP/TINH LS16 .....12 B5
  OSM LS9 .....30 B2
Beechwood RTHW LS26 .....45 G4
Beechwood Cl HORS LS18 .....10 A4

Beechwood Ct BHP/TINH LS16 LS1...
  SCFT LS14
Beechwood Crs BULY LS4 .....27 E2
Beechwood Gv BULY LS4 .....27 E2
Beechwood Mt BULY LS4 .....27 E2
Beechwood Pl BULY LS4 * 27 E2
Beechwood Rd BULY LS4 .....27 E2
Beechwood Row BULY LS4 .....27 E2
Beechwood St BULY LS4 .....27 E2
  PDSY/CALV LS28
Beechwood Ter BULY LS4 .....27 E2
Beechwood Vw BULY LS4 .....27 E2
Beecroft Cl BRAM LS13
Beecroft Crs BRAM LS13
Beecroft Gdns BRAM LS13
Beecroft Mt BRAM LS13
Beecroft St KSTL LS5
Beeston Park Cft BEE/HOL LS11
Beeston Park Ter BEE/HOL LS11
Beeston Rd BEE/HOL LS11
Belford Ct HDGY LS6
Belfry Rd OSM LS9
The Belfry YEA LS19
Belgrave Ms YEA LS19 *
Belgrave St LDSU LS2
Belgravia Gdns RHAY LS8 *
Belinda St MID LS10
Bellbrooke Av OSM LS9
Bellbrooke Gv OSM LS9
Bellbrooke Pl OSM LS9
Bellbrooke St OSM LS9
Belle Isle Cl MID LS10
Belle Isle Pde MID LS10
Belle Isle Rd MID LS10
Belle Vue Av RHAY LS8
Belle Vue Ct BVRD LS3 *
Belle Vue Gv PDSY/CALV LS28
Belle Vue Rd BVRD LS3
Bell La BRAM LS13
Bellmount Cl BRAM LS13
Bellmount Gdns BRAM LS13 *
Bellmount Gn BRAM LS13
Bellmount Pl BRAM LS13
Bellmount Vw BRAM LS13
Bell Rd BRAM LS13
Bell St OSM LS9
Belmont Gv LDSU LS2
Belvedere Av EARD/LOFT WF3
Belvedere Av AL/HA/HU LS17
Belvedere Ct AL/HA/HU LS17
Belvedere Gv AL/HA/HU LS17
Belvedere Mt BEE/HOL LS11
Belvedere Rd AL/HA/HU LS17
Belvedere Ter BEE/HOL LS11
Belvedere Vw AL/HA/HU LS17
Bennet Ct MSTN/BAR LS15
Bennett Rd HDGY LS6
Benson Gdns WOR/ARM LS12
Benson St CHAL LS7
Bentcliffe Av AL/HA/HU LS17
Bentcliffe Cl AL/HA/HU LS17
Bentcliffe Ct AL/HA/HU LS17
Bentcliffe Dr AL/HA/HU LS17
Bentcliffe Gdns AL/HA/HU LS17
Bentcliffe Gv AL/HA/HU LS17
Bentcliffe La AL/HA/HU LS17
Bentcliffe Mt AL/HA/HU LS17
Bentley Gdns CHAL LS7
Bentley Gv HDGY LS6
Bentley La HDGY LS6
Bentley Mt HDGY LS6 *
Bentley Pde HDGY LS6
Benton Park Av YEA LS19
Benton Park Crs YEA LS19
Benton Park Dr YEA LS19
Benton Park Rd YEA LS19
Benyon Park Wy WOR/ARM LS12
Berkeley Av RHAY LS8
Berkeley Crs RHAY LS8
Berkeley Gv RHAY LS8
Berkeley Mt RHAY LS8 *
Berkeley Rd RHAY LS8
Berkeley St RHAY LS8
Berkeley Ter RHAY LS8
Berking Av OSM LS9
Bernard St RTHW LS26
Bertha St PDSY/CALV LS28
Bertrand St BEE/HOL LS11
Beulah Mt HDGY LS6
Beulah St HDGY LS6
Beulah Ter HDGY LS6
Beulah Vw HDGY LS6
Bevedere Gdns AL/HA/HU LS17
Beverley Av BEE/HOL LS11
Beverley Mt BEE/HOL LS11
Beverley Ter BEE/HOL LS11
Bewick Gv MID LS10
Bexley Av RHAY LS8
Bexley Gv RHAY LS8
Bexley Mt RHAY LS8
Bexley Pl RHAY LS8
Bexley Rd RHAY LS8
Bexley Ter RHAY LS8
Bexley Vw RHAY LS8
#623 St MID LS10
Bidder Dr EARD/LOFT WF3
Bideford Av RHAY LS8
Bilsey La WOR/ARM LS12
Billingbauk Dr BRAM LS13
Billing Ct YEA LS19
Billing Dr YEA LS19
Billing Vw YEA LS19
Billingwood Dr YEA LS19
Bingley Lands GSLY LS20
Bingley St BVRD LS3
Birch Av MSTN/BAR LS15
Birch Crs MSTN/BAR LS15

Garth SCFT LS14......23 G3
Av SCFT LS14......23 G2
Ct SCFT LS14......23 G3
Crs SCFT LS14......23 G2
Ri SCFT LS14......23 G2
li HORS LS18......18 A2
RTHW LS26......50 D2
OR LS27......46 D4
Wy BHP/TINH LS16 *......11 E5
d Av AL/HA/HU LS17......14 C4
d HI AL/HA/HU LS17......14 C3
H ML AL/HA/HU LS17......14 C3
BULY LS4......26 D2
l AL/HA/HU LS17......13 F3
ar AL/HA/HU LS17......13 E3
n AL/HA/HU LS17......13 E3
Gv AL/HA/HU LS17......13 E3
l AL/HA/HU LS17......13 E3
t AL/HA/HU LS17......13 E3
Wk AL/HA/HU LS17......13 E3
OR LS27......46 A2
l SCFT LS14......23 F2
St LDS LS1 *......5 G6
Ct BEE/HOL LS11......36 B4
Or Rd AL/HA/HU LS17......36 B4
St BEE/HOL LS11......36 B4
MOR LS27......47 E5
on Rd BRAM LS13......25 H3
St MID LS10......38 D2
Ct RTHW LS26......50 D1
La LDSU LS2......28 B3
Vr Rd AL/HA/HU LS17......12 D4
Gv WOR/ARM LS12......34 C4
St WOR/ARM LS12......34 C4
Ter WOR/ARM LS12......34 C4
Vw WOR/ARM LS12......34 C4
Ms EARD/LOFT WF3 ...49 H3
n Ct MID LS10......42 D3
d Av BHP/TINH LS16 ...10 D4
d Gdns
NH LS16......10 D4
od Gv BHP/TINH LS16...10 D4
od Mt BHP/TINH LS16...10 D4
od Ri BHP/TINH LS16...10 D4
Gdns BRAM LS13......25 F1
Gv BRAM LS13......25 F1
GSLY LS20......5 F4
HAL LS7......20 D4
Rd MID LS10......42 D2
d Gdns LDSU LS2 *......28 B3
rth RTHW LS26......50 C1
s LDS LS1......3 G6
OSM LS9......37 F1
l LDS LS1......3 G6
Cl SCFT LS14......30 D1
arth SCFT LS14......30 D1
Rd SCFT LS14......30 D1
Vw SCFT LS14......30 D1
Cr LDSU LS2 *......28 B3
Gv LDSU LS2......28 B3
Sq LDSU LS2......28 B3
Ter LDSU LS2......28 B3
Vw LDSU LS2......28 B2
Wk LDSU LS2......28 B3
/HA/HU LS17......15 G3
crs WOR/ARM LS12......34 C2
ra WOR/ARM LS12......34 C3
a WOR/ARM LS12......34 C3
LDS LS1......2 E2
DS LS1......3 G3
r BULY LS4......27 F4
p MID LS10......48 A1
St MID LS10......48 A1
t MID LS10......48 A2
dns MID LS10......48 A2
arth MID LS10......48 A2
l MID LS10......48 A2
d MID LS10......47 H1
St SCFT LS14......22 C4
Hill Crs SCFT LS14......22 C4
Hill Dr SCFT LS14......22 C4
Hill Gdns SCFT LS14......22 C4
Hill Rd SCFT LS14......22 C4
dr MSTN/BAR LS15......38 C1
a YEA LS19......9 E1
l LS19......3 F4
DS LS1......3 F4
St PDSY/CALV LS28 *...24 C4
Dr HDGY LS6......19 E5
Av RHAY LS8......21 E2
Rd RHAY LS8......21 E2
le Cl WOR/ARM LS12 ...26 B3
le Crs WOR/ARM LS12...26 B3
le Ter WOR/ARM LS12...30 D2
KSTL LS6......28 B2
's Buildings
S6......28 B2
evard BEE/HOL LS11...35 F5
CAL LS28......24 B3
y Farm Rd
HU LS17......13 E4
l LS11......36 A3
Av CHAL LS7......20 A3
CHAL LS7......20 A3
Gv CHAL LS7......20 A3
St CHAL LS7......37 E1
St AL/HA/HU LS17......20 A3
LS12......35 G5

Bracken Edge RHAY LS8......21 F5
Bracken Hl AL/HA/HU LS17......20 C1
Brackenhurst Pl AL/HA/HU LS17.13 C5
Brackenwood Cl RHAY LS8......21 E2
Brackenwood Dr RHAY LS8......21 E2
Brackenwood Gn RHAY LS8......21 E2
Bradbury Rd EARD/LOFT WF3...49 G3
Bradford Rd EARD/LOFT WF3...47 G5
GSLY LS20......4 C3
PDSY/CALV LS28......24 A4
Bradstock Gdns MOR LS27......40 C5
Braithwaite Rw MID LS10 *......43 E1
Braithwaite St MID LS10......35 H2
Brambling Ms MOR LS27......47 E2
Bramham Park Ct MID LS10......48 A2
Bramleigh Dr MOR LS27......40 C5
Bramleigh Gv MOR LS27......40 C5
Bramley St BRAM LS13......25 G4
Bramstan Av BRAM LS13......25 E2
Bramstan Cl BRAM LS13......25 E2
Bramstan Gdns BRAM LS13......25 E2
Brancepeth Pl WOR/ARM LS12...35 G1
Branch Cl WOR/ARM LS12......34 C4
Branch Pl WOR/ARM LS12......34 C4
Branch Rd WOR/ARM LS12......27 E5
WOR/ARM LS12......34 C4
Branch St WOR/ARM LS12......34 C4
Brander Ap OSM LS9......30 A4
Brander Cl OSM LS9......30 B4
Brander Dr OSM LS9......30 A4
Brander Gv OSM LS9......30 A4
Brander Rd OSM LS9......30 A4
Brander St OSM LS9......30 B3
Brandling Ct MID LS10......48 C1
Brandon Cl AL/HA/HU LS17 *...12 C4
Brandon Crs AL/HA/HU LS17...15 H1
Brandon Rd BVRD LS3......2 C1
Brandon St WOR/ARM LS12......2 A3
Brandon Wy CHAL LS7......20 D5
Bransome St HDGY LS6 *......27 G3
Branksome Ter HDGY LS6 *......27 G3
Bransby Cl PDSY/CALV LS28...24 C3
Bransby Ct PDSY/CALV LS28...24 C3
Bransby Ri PDSY/CALV LS28...24 C3
Bransdale Av GSLY LS20......5 E4
Bransdale Cl GSLY LS20......5 E4
Bransdale Garth GSLY LS20......5 E4
Brantford St CHAL LS7......20 D4
Brathay Gdns SCFT LS14......31 E2
Brayton Ap SCFT LS14......23 G5
Brayton Cl SCFT LS14......23 G5
Brayton Gn SCFT LS14......23 H5
Brayton Gv SCFT LS14......23 G5
Brayton Wk SCFT LS14......23 G5
Breary Av HORS LS18......17 H1
Breary Ter HORS LS18......17 H1
Breary Wk HORS LS18......17 H1
Brecon Ap OSM LS9......30 C2
Brentford Gv WOR/ARM LS12 *.35 E1
Brentwood St WOR/ARM LS12 *.35 E1
Brentwood Ter WOR/ARM LS12.35 E1
Bret Gdns BEE/HOL LS11......36 A2
Brian Crs MSTN/BAR LS15......31 F5
Brian Pl MSTN/BAR LS15......31 F5
Briardene RTHW LS26 *......51 G1
Briarlea Cl YEA LS19......8 B1
Briarsdale Ct RHAY LS8 *......30 A2
Briarsdale Garth RHAY LS8......29 H2
Briarsdale Hts OSM LS9......29 H2
Briarsdale Ms OSM LS9......29 H2
Brick St OSM LS9......3 J6
Bridge Ct MOR LS27......46 D3
Bridge End LDS LS1......3 H6
Bridge Fold KSTL LS6......26 C1
Bridge Rd BEE/HOL LS11......36 A2
BRAM LS13......16 C5
KSTL LS5......28 B2
Bridge St LDSU LS2......3 J3
MOR LS27......46 D4
Bridge Vw BRAM LS13......16 C5
Bridgewater HDGY LS6......19 G4
Bridgewater Rd OSM LS9......36 D1
Bridle Av WOR/ARM LS12 *...10 D5
Bridle Pth MSTN/BAR LS15......31 E3
Bridle Path Rd SCFT LS14......31 F2
Bridle Path Wk MSTN/BAR LS15.31 F2
Briggate LDS LS1......3 G5
Brighton Av MOR LS27......46 B1
Brighton Cliff BRAM LS13......25 G4
Brighton Gv BRAM LS13......25 H4
Bright St WOR/ARM LS12......2 A2
PDSY/CALV LS28......24 C4
Brignall Cft WOR/ARM LS12......29 F4
Brignall Gdns OSM LS9......29 F4
Brignall Wy OSM LS9......29 F4
Bristol St CHAL LS7......3 K1
Britannia Cl PDSY/CALV LS28...24 D5
Britannia Rd MOR LS27......46 B3
Britannia St LDS LS1......2 D5
PDSY/CALV LS28......24 D5
Broadgate Av HORS LS18......17 H2
Broadgate Ct HORS LS18......17 H2
Broadgate Dr HORS LS18......17 G1
Broadgate La HORS LS18......17 G1
Broadgate Ms HORS LS18......17 H2
Broadgate Ri HORS LS18......17 H2
Broadgate Wk HORS LS18......17 H2
Broad La BRAM LS13......25 E3
Broad Lane Cl AL/HA/HU LS17...13 E5
Broad La BRAM LS13......26 A1
Broadlea Av BRAM LS13......26 A1
Broadlea Cl BRAM LS13......26 A1
Broadlea Crs BRAM LS13......26 A1
Broadlea Gdns BRAM LS13......26 A1
Broadlea Hl BRAM LS13......26 A1
Broadlea Mt BRAM LS13......26 B2
Broadlea Pl BRAM LS13......26 A1
Broadlea Rd BRAM LS13......26 A1

Broadlea St BRAM LS13......26 A1
Broadlea Ter BRAM LS13......26 A1
Broadlea Vw BRAM LS13......25 H1
Broad St PDSY/CALV LS28......24 A2
Broadway GSLY LS20......4 C4
HORS LS18......16 D3
KSTL LS5......18 B2
Broadway Dr HORS LS18......17 F2
Brodrick Ct HDGY LS6......19 F5
Brompton Gv BEE/HOL LS11......42 B1
Brompton Mt BEE/HOL LS11......42 B1
Brompton Rw BEE/HOL LS11 *...42 B1
Brompton Ter BEE/HOL LS11......42 B1
Brompton Vw BEE/HOL LS11......42 B1
Brookfield Av BRAM LS13......16 B4
RHAY LS8......29 F1
Brookfield Gdns BRAM LS13......16 B4
Brookfield Rd HDGY LS6......19 G4
Brookfield St MID LS10......36 D3
Brookhill Av AL/HA/HU LS17......14 A3
Brookhill Cl AL/HA/HU LS17......14 A3
Brookhill Cr AL/HA/HU LS17......14 A3
Brookhill Dr AL/HA/HU LS17......14 A3
Brookhill Gv AL/HA/HU LS17......14 A3
Brooklands Av SCFT LS14......30 D1
Brooklands Cl SCFT LS14......30 C1
Brooklands Crs SCFT LS14......30 C1
YEA LS19......8 C1
Brooklands Ct SCFT LS14......30 C1
YEA LS19......8 D1
Brooklands Dr SCFT LS14......30 C1
Brooklands Garth SCFT LS14...30 D1
Brooklands La SCFT LS14......30 D1
Brooklands Vw SCFT LS14......30 D1
Brooklyn Av WOR/ARM LS12......35 E1
Brooklyn Pl WOR/ARM LS12......35 E1
Brooklyn St WOR/ARM LS12......35 E1
Brooklyn Ter WOR/ARM LS12...35 E1
Brooksbank Dr MSTN/BAR LS15.31 E5
Brookside AL/HA/HU LS17......14 A2
Broom Crs MID LS10......43 E4
Broom Cross MID LS10......43 E4
Broomfield BHP/TINH LS16......11 H5
Broomfield Crs HDGY LS6 *......27 F2
Broomfield Pl HDGY LS6 *......27 F2
Broomfield Rd HDGY LS6......27 F2
Broomfield St HDGY LS6 *......27 F2
Broomfield Ter HDGY LS6 *......27 F2
Broomfield Vw HDGY LS6 *......27 F2
Broom Gdns MID LS10......43 E4
Broom Garth MID LS10......43 E4
Broom Gv MID LS10......43 F5
Broomhill Av AL/HA/HU LS17......13 H5
Broomhill Crs AL/HA/HU LS17...13 H5
Broomhill Dr AL/HA/HU LS17 *...13 H5
Broom Mt MID LS10......43 F5
Broom Nook MID LS10......43 E4
Broom Pl MID LS10......43 E4
Broom Rd MID LS10......43 E4
Broom Ter MID LS10......43 E4
Broom Vw MID LS10......43 F5
Broughton Av OSM LS9......29 G3
Broughton Ter PDSY/CALV LS28.24 C5
Brown Av BEE/HOL LS11......35 G4
Brownberrie Av HORS LS18......10 B4
Brownberrie Crs HORS LS18......10 B4
Brownberrie Dr HORS LS18......10 B4
Brownberrie Gdns HORS LS18...10 A4
Brownberrie La HORS LS18......10 A4
Brownberrie Wk HORS LS18......10 C4
Brown Hill Av OSM LS9......29 G3
Brown Hill Crs OSM LS9......29 G3
Brown Hill Ter OSM LS9 *......29 G3
Brown La East WOR/ARM LS11...35 H5
Brown La West WOR/ARM LS11.35 G4
Brown Rd BEE/HOL LS11......35 G4
Bruce Gdns WOR/ARM LS12......35 G1
Bruce Lawn WOR/ARM LS12 *...35 G1
Brudenell Av HDGY LS6......27 H2
Brudenell Gv HDGY LS6......27 H2
Brudenell Mt HDGY LS6......27 H2
Brudenell Rd HDGY LS6......27 G2
Brudenell St HDGY LS6 *......27 H2
Brudenell Vw HDGY LS6......27 H2
Brunswick Ct LDSU LS2......3 J2
Brunswick Pl PDSY/CALV LS28...24 A4
Brunswick Rw LDSU LS2......3 J3
Brunswick St MOR LS27......46 C1
Brunswick Ter LDSU LS2......3 G3
Bruntcliffe Av MOR LS27......46 A2
Bruntcliffe Cl MOR LS27......46 B2
Bruntcliffe Dr MOR LS27......46 B2
Bruntcliffe La MOR LS27......46 A2
Bruntcliffe Rd MOR LS27......46 A3
Bruntcliffe Wy MOR LS27......46 B2
Brussels St LDS LS9......3 K5
Bryan St PDSY/CALV LS28......24 B1
Bryan St North PDSY/CALV LS28.24 B1
Bryngate RTHW LS26......45 G5
Bryony Ct MID LS10......49 E1
Buckingham Av HDGY LS6......27 G1
Buckingham Dr HDGY LS6......27 G1
Buckingham Gv HDGY LS6......27 G1
Buckingham Mt HDGY LS6......27 G1
Buckingham Rd HDGY LS6......27 G2
Buckley Av BEE/HOL LS11......36 B5
Buck Stone Av AL/HA/HU LS17...12 D3
Buck Stone Cl AL/HA/HU LS17...13 E3
Buck Stone Cr AL/HA/HU LS17...12 D3
Buck Stone Dr YEA LS19......12 D3
Buck Stone Gdns
AL/HA/HU LS17......13 E3
Buck Stone Gn AL/HA/HU LS17...12 D3
Buck Stone Gv AL/HA/HU LS17...12 D3
Buck Stone Mt AL/HA/HU LS17...12 D3
Buck Stone Oval AL/HA/HU LS17.12 D3
Buck Stone Ri AL/HA/HU LS17...12 D3
Buck Stone Rd AL/HA/HU LS17...12 D3
Buck Stone Vw
AL/HA/HU LS17 *......12 D3
Buck Stone Wy AL/HA/HU LS17...12 D3
Buckton Cl BEE/HOL LS11......36 A4

Buckton Mt BEE/HOL LS11......36 A4
Buckton Vw BEE/HOL LS11......36 A4
Bude Rd BEE/HOL LS11......42 B1
Buller Cl OSM LS9......30 A4
Buller Gv OSM LS9......29 H4
Buller St RTHW LS26......30 A4
Bullough La RTHW LS26......44 D4
Burchett Gv HDGY LS6......28 A1
Burchett Pl HDGY LS6......28 A1
Burchett Ter HDGY LS6......28 A1
Burdett Ter BULY LS4......27 E3
Burghley Ms MID LS10......48 D2
Burley Hill Crs BULY LS4......26 D2
Burley Hill Dr BULY LS4......26 D2
Burley La HORS LS18......17 F3
Burley Lodge Pl HDGY LS6 *......27 G4
Burley Lodge Rd HDGY LS6......27 G4
Burley Lodge St HDGY LS6 *......27 G4
Burley Lodge Ter HDGY LS6......27 G3
Burley Rd BULY LS4......27 E2
BVRD LS3......2 A2
Burley St BVRD LS3......2 D4
Burlington Pl BEE/HOL LS11......42 B1
Burlington Rd BEE/HOL LS11......42 B1
Burmantofts St OSM LS9......29 E5
Burnsall Ct WOR/ARM LS12......34 D5
Burnsall Gdns WOR/ARM LS12...26 D5
Burnsall Gra WOR/ARM LS12...26 D5
Burnsall Ms WOR/ARM LS12 *...34 D5
Burnshaw Ms MID LS10......48 C3
Burr Tree Dr MSTN/BAR LS15...31 H1
Burr Tree Garth
MSTN/BAR LS15 *......39 H1
Burr Tree V MSTN/BAR LS15 *...39 H1
Burton Av BEE/HOL LS11......36 C5
Burton Crs HDGY LS6......19 F4
Burton Ms AL/HA/HU LS17......13 H2
Burton Rw BEE/HOL LS11......36 C5
Burtons Ar LDS LS1......3 G5
Burton St BEE/HOL LS11......36 C4
PDSY/CALV LS28......24 A4
Burton Ter BEE/HOL LS11......36 C5
Busely Ct MOR LS27......46 B1
Buslingthorpe Gn CHAL LS7......28 C2
Buslingthorpe La CHAL LS7......28 C2
Bussey Ct HDGY LS6 *......27 H3
Butcher Hl BHP/TINH LS16......18 B2
Butcher La RTHW LS26......50 C1
Butcher St BEE/HOL LS11......36 C2
Butterbowl Gdns
WOR/ARM LS12......34 A3
Butterbowl Gv WOR/ARM LS12...34 A3
Butterbowl Lawn
WOR/ARM LS12......34 A3
Butterbowl Mt WOR/ARM LS12...34 B3
Butterbowl Rd WOR/ARM LS12...34 B3
Butterfield St OSM LS9......37 F1
Butterley St MID LS10......36 C2
Butt La WOR/ARM LS12......33 H2
Button Hl CHAL LS7......28 C2
Butts Ct LDS LS1......3 G4
Butts Mt WOR/ARM LS12......35 F1
Byeway GSLY LS20......4 C3
Byron St LDSU LS2......3 J2

C

Cabbage Hl WOR/ARM LS12......34 D2
Cad Beeston Ms
BEE/HOL LS11 *......36 A5
Cain Cl OSM LS9......37 F1
Cairn Av GSLY LS20......4 C3
Calgary Pl CHAL LS7......20 D4
California Ms MOR LS27 *......46 D2
Cali La LDS LS1......3 H5
The Calls LDS LS1......3 J5
Calverley Av BRAM LS13......25 F2
Calverley Ct BRAM LS13......25 F1
YEA LS19......5 H5
Calverley Dr BRAM LS13......25 F2
Calverley Gdns BRAM LS13......25 E1
Calverley Garth BRAM LS13......25 E1
Calverley Gv BRAM LS13......25 E1
Calverley La BRAM LS13......25 E1
BRAM LS13......17 E5
PDSY/CALV LS28......16 A4
Calverley St LDS LS1......2 D3
Calverley Ter BRAM LS13......25 F2
Camberley Cl PDSY/CALV LS28...32 C2
Camberley St BEE/HOL LS11 *...36 A4
Cambrian St BEE/HOL LS11......36 A4
Cambrian Ter BEE/HOL LS11......36 A4
Cambridge Cl MOR LS27......46 D1
Cambridge Dr BRAM LS13......25 F2
Cambridge Gdns BRAM LS13......25 F2
Cambridge Rd BRAM LS13......28 C2
Campbell St PDSY/CALV LS28...24 A4
Camp Rd BHP/TINH LS16......7 H3
Canada Crs YEA LS19......9 E3
Canada Dr YEA LS19......9 E3
Canada Rd YEA LS19......9 E3
Canada Ter YEA LS19......9 E3
Canal Pl WOR/ARM LS12......2 B5
Canal Rd BRAM LS13......16 C5
WOR/ARM LS12......2 B5
Canal St WOR/ARM LS12......35 F2
Canal Whf BEE/HOL LS11......2 E6
Cancel St MID LS10......36 D3

Canonbury Ter BEE/HOL LS11...35 G5
Canterbury Dr HDGY LS6......27 E1
Canterbury Rd HDGY LS6......27 E1
The Canter MID LS10......48 D3
Capitol Bvd EARD/LOFT WF3...47 E5
Capitol Pde HDGY LS6......19 G5
Caraway Dr HDGY LS6......19 H1
Carberry Pl HDGY LS6......27 G3
Carberry Rd HDGY LS6......27 G3
Carberry Ter HDGY LS6......27 G3
Carden Av MSTN/BAR LS15......30 D5
Cardigan Ct HDGY LS6 *......46 C4
Cardigan Crs HDGY LS6......27 G1
Cardigan Fields Rd BULY LS4...27 F4
Cardigan La BULY LS4......27 F3
Cardigan Rd HDGY LS6......27 F1
Cardinal Av BEE/HOL LS11......41 H3
Cardinal Crs BEE/HOL LS11......41 H3
Cardinal Gdns BEE/HOL LS11...41 G3
Cardinal Gv BEE/HOL LS11......41 G3
Cardinal Rd BEE/HOL LS11......41 G2
Cardinal Sq BEE/HOL LS11......41 G2
Cardinal Wk BEE/HOL LS11 *...41 G2
Carisbrooke Rd BHP/TINH LS16 .19 E3
Cariss St MID LS10......36 D5
Carlisle Av YEA LS19......9 G3
Carlisle Dr PDSY/CALV LS28......32 B2
Carlisle Gv PDSY/CALV LS28......32 B2
Carlisle Rd MID LS10......36 D2
PDSY/CALV LS28......32 B2
Carlton Av PDSY/CALV LS28......32 C1
Carlton Cl CHAL LS7 *......28 C3
Carlton Ct WOR/ARM LS12......35 C4
Carlton Cft CHAL LS7 *......28 C3
Carlton Dr GSLY LS20......5 F2
Carlton Garth AL/HA/HU LS17...14 C2
CHAL LS7 *......28 C3
Carlton Ga CHAL LS7......28 C3
Carlton Gdns CHAL LS7......28 C3
Carlton Gv BEE/HOL LS11......36 C5
CHAL LS7......28 C3
Carlton Hl CHAL LS7......28 C3
Carlton La EARD/LOFT WF3......50 A5
GSLY LS20......5 F2
RTHW LS26......50 B2
Carlton Moor Ms MID LS10......48 D3
Carlton Mt YEA LS19......6 A4
Carlton Ri PDSY/CALV LS28......32 C1
Carlton Rw WOR/ARM LS12......34 C1
Carlton St CHAL LS7......28 C3
Carlton Vw CHAL LS7......28 C3
Carr Bridge Av BHP/TINH LS16...10 D4
Carr Bridge Cl BHP/TINH LS16...10 D4
Carr Bridge Vw BHP/TINH LS16...10 D4
Carr Cl YEA LS19......9 F4
Carr Crofts WOR/ARM LS12......34 D1
Carr Crofts Dr WOR/ARM LS12...34 C1
Carrholm Crs CHAL LS7......20 B3
Carrholm Dr CHAL LS7......20 B3
Carrholm Gn CHAL LS7......20 B3
Carrholm Mt CHAL LS7......20 B3
Carrholm Rd CHAL LS7......20 B3
Carrholm Vw CHAL LS7......20 B3
Carrington Ter GSLY LS20......4 D4
Carr La EARD/LOFT WF3......50 C3
YEA LS19......9 F4
Carr Manor Av
AL/HA/HU LS17......20 B2
Carr Manor Crs AL/HA/HU LS17...20 B2
Carr Manor Cft CHAL LS7......20 B2
Carr Manor Dr AL/HA/HU LS17...20 B2
Carr Manor Gdns
AL/HA/HU LS17......20 B2
Carr Manor Garth
AL/HA/HU LS17......20 B1
Carr Manor Gv AL/HA/HU LS17...20 B1
Carr Manor Mt AL/HA/HU LS17...20 B2
Carr Manor Pde
AL/HA/HU LS17......20 C2
Carr Manor Pl AL/HA/HU LS17...20 B2
Carr Manor Rd AL/HA/HU LS17...20 B2
Carr Manor Vw AL/HA/HU LS17...20 B1
Carr Manor Wk CHAL LS7......20 B2
Carr Moor Side BEE/HOL LS11...36 C5
Carter La MSTN/BAR LS15......31 G4
Carter Mt MSTN/BAR LS15......31 G4
Carter Ter MSTN/BAR LS15......31 G4
Cartmell Dr MSTN/BAR LS15......38 C1
Casson Av EARD/LOFT WF3......48 B5
Casson Dr EARD/LOFT WF3......48 B5
Casson Gv EARD/LOFT WF3......48 B5
Castlefields RTHW LS26......49 H1
Castle Gra YEA LS19......9 F1
Castle Grove Av HDGY LS6......19 F3
Castle Grove Dr HDGY LS6......19 F3
Castle Head Cl EARD/LOFT WF3 .50 A5
Castle Ings Cl WOR/ARM LS12...33 H5
Castle Ings Dr WOR/ARM LS12...33 H5
Castle Ings Gdns WOR/ARM LS12.33 H5
Castle Lodge Av RTHW LS26......44 A4
Castle Lodge Garth RTHW LS26..44 A4
Castle Lodge Ms RTHW LS26......44 A4
Castle Rd RTHW LS26......50 B1
Castle St LDS LS1......2 D4
Castleton Cl WOR/ARM LS12......27 G5
Castleton Rd WOR/ARM LS12...27 G5
Castle Vw AL/HA/HU LS17......20 E1
Cathcart St HDGY LS6......27 G2
Catherine Gv BEE/HOL LS11 *...36 B5
Cautley Rd OSM LS9......37 F2
Cavalier Ap OSM LS9......37 F2
Cavalier Cl OSM LS9 *......37 F2
Cavalier Ct OSM LS9......37 F2
Cavalier Gdns OSM LS9 *......37 F2
Cavalier Ga OSM LS9......37 F2
Cavalier Ms OSM LS9......37 F2
Cavalier Vw OSM LS9......37 F2
Cavendish Dr GSLY LS20......4 D4
Cavendish Gv GSLY LS20......4 D4
Cavendish Ri PDSY/CALV LS28...33 E1
Cavendish Rd GSLY LS20......4 D4
LDSU LS2......28 B3
Cavendish St BVRD LS3......2 B5
PDSY/CALV LS28......33 E1
YEA LS19......6 A5

Caythorpe Rd BHP/TINH LS16 ......18 D3
Cecil Gv WOR/ARM LS12 .....27 E5
Cecil Mt WOR/ARM LS12 .....27 E5
Cecil Rd WOR/ARM LS12 .....27 E5
Cecil St WOR/ARM LS12 .....27 E5
Cedar Av WOR/ARM LS12 .....34 D1
Cedar Cl WOR/ARM LS12 .....35 E1
Cedar Mt WOR/ARM LS12 .....34 D1
Cedar Rd WOR/ARM LS12 .....34 D1
Cedar St WOR/ARM LS12 .....34 D1
Cedar Ter WOR/ARM LS12 .....34 D1
Cemetery La EARD/LOFT WF3 ...50 A5
Cemetery Rd BEE/HOL LS11 .....36 A4
  PDSY/CALV LS28 ...24 B5
  YEA LS19 ......6 A5
Central St LDS LS1 ......2 E4
Chaddlewood Cl HORS LS18 .....17 G1
Chadwick St MID LS10 ......3 K7
Chadwick St South MID LS10 ....48 C3
Chalfont Rd BHP/TINH LS16 * ...18 D3
Chalice Cl MID LS10 .....43 E4
Chalner Av WOR/ARM LS12 .....46 B4
Chalner Cl MOR LS27 .....46 B4
Chancellor St HDGY LS6 .....28 C2
The Chandlers MID LS10 ......3 J6
Chandos Fold RHAY LS8 .....21 E2
Chandos Gdns RHAY LS8 .....21 E3
Chandos Garth RHAY LS8 .....21 E2
Chandos Gn RHAY LS8 .....21 E2
Chandos Pl RHAY LS8 .....21 F2
Chandos Ter RHAY LS8 .....21 E3
Chandos Wk RHAY LS8 .....21 E3
Chantrell Ct LDSU LS2 ......3 J5
Chantry Cft MSTN/BAR LS15 .....39 H1
Chantry Garth MSTN/BAR LS15 ..39 H1
Chapel Ct MSTN/BAR LS15 .....31 E5
Chapel Fold MSTN/BAR LS15 ....31 E5
  PDSY/CALV LS28 * ...
Chapel Hl MOR LS27 .....46 C1
  YEA LS19 ......5 H5
Chapel La HDGY LS6 .....27 F1
  WOR/ARM LS12 ...33 H3
  YEA LS19 .....35 E1
Chapel Pl HDGY LS6 .....19 F5
Chapel Rd CHAL LS7 .....20 D5
Chapel St EARD/LOFT WF3 .....47 H5
  EARD/LOFT WF3 ...50 B3
  HDGY LS6 * ...
  MSTN/BAR LS15 ...31 G4
  PDSY/CALV LS28 ...24 C4
  YEA LS19 ......5 E4
Chapel Ter HDGY LS6 .....19 F5
Chapeltown PDSY/CALV LS28 ...32 E2
Chapeltown Rd CHAL LS7 ...20 D?
Chapel Yd MSTN/BAR LS15 .....39 H2
Chapman St OSM LS9 .....29 E4
Charles Av OSM LS9 .....37 G1
Charles Gdns BEE/HOL LS11 .....36 A4
Charles Gv RTHW LS26 .....45 G5
Charles St HORS LS18 .....17 F2
  PDSY/CALV LS28 ...
Charlton Gv OSM LS9 .....37 G1
Charlton Mt OSM LS9 .....37 F1
Charlton Pl OSM LS9 .....37 F1
Charlton Rd OSM LS9 .....37 F1
Charlton St OSM LS9 .....37 F1
Charnley Dr CHAL LS7 .....21 E4
Chartists Wy MOR LS27 .....46 C5
Chartwell Ct AL/HA/HU LS17 ....14 D2
Charville Gdns AL/HA/HU LS17 ..15 H4
The Chase YEA LS19 ......8 C3
Chatswood Av BEE/HOL LS11 ...41 H5
Chatswood Cl BEE/HOL LS11 ...41 H5
Chatswood Dr BEE/HOL LS11 ...41 H2
Chatsworth Cl RHAY LS8 .....29 G2
Chatsworth Ms MOR LS27 * 47 E3
Chatsworth Rd RHAY LS8 .....29 G2
Chaucer Av PDSY/CALV LS28 ...32 D2
Chaucer Gdns PDSY/CALV LS28 .32 D2
Chaucer Gv PDSY/CALV LS28 ...32 D2
Chelsea Cl WOR/ARM LS12 .....35 E2
Cheltenham St WOR/ARM LS12 ..35 F2
Chelwood Av RHAY LS8 .....14 B4
Chelwood Crs RHAY LS8 .....14 B5
Chelwood Dr RHAY LS8 .....14 B4
Chelwood Gv RHAY LS8 .....14 B4
Chelwood Mt RHAY LS8 .....14 B4
Chelwood Pl RHAY LS8 .....14 A4
Chenies Cl SCFT LS14 .....30 A4
Chepstow Dr MID LS10 .....48 D3
Cherry Ct LDS LS1 .....19 H4
  OSM LS9 .....29 E4
Cherry Gv HDGY LS6 .....19 H4
Cherry Lea Ct YEA LS19 ......8 D3
Cherry Pl OSM LS9 .....29 E4
Cherry Ri SCFT LS14 .....23 G2
Cherry Rw OSM LS9 .....29 E4
Cherry Tree Crs
  PDSY/CALV LS28 ...24 B2
Cherry Tree Dr
Cherry Tree Wk LDS LS1 * 3 F5
Cherrywood Cl SCFT LS14 .....23 F1
Cherrywood Gdns SCFT LS14 ...23 F1
Chesney Av MID LS10 .....36 D4
Chester St WOR/ARM LS12 .....27 E5
Chesterton Ct MSTN/BAR LS15 ..31 G2
Chestnut Av HDGY LS6 .....27 G2
  MSTN/BAR LS15 ...31 H2
Chestnut Dr BHP/TINH LS16 .....11 H2
Chestnut Gdns MOR LS27 .....54 D2
  WOR/ARM LS12 ...
Chestnut Gv HDGY LS6 * 27 G2
Chestnut Pl HDGY LS6 * 27 G2
Chestnut Ri WOR/ARM LS12 .....34 D2
Chestnut Rd HDGY LS6 * 27 G2
Chestnut Wy BHP/TINH LS16 ...11 H2
Chevington Ct YEA LS19 * 8 C4
Chichester St WOR/ARM LS12 ..27 E5
Chiltern Ct BRAM LS13 .....16 C5
Chirton Gv RHAY LS8 .....21 G5

Chiswick St HDGY LS6 .....27 G4
Chiswick Ter HDGY LS6 .....27 G3
Chorley La BVRD LS3 ......2 D3
Christ Church Av
  WOR/ARM LS12 ...26 D5
Christ Church Mt
  WOR/ARM LS12 ...26 D5
Christ Church Pde
  WOR/ARM LS12 ...26 D5
Christ Church Pl
  WOR/ARM LS12 ...26 D5
Christ Church Rd
  WOR/ARM LS12 ...26 D5
Christ Church Ter
  WOR/ARM LS12 ...26 D5
Christ Church Vw
  WOR/ARM LS12 ...26 D5
Christopher Rd HDGY LS6 .....28 A2
Church Av HDGY LS6 .....19 H5
  HORS LS18 .....17 F1
Church Ct SCFT LS14 .....31 F1
Church Crs YEA LS19 ......8 C1
Church Farm Ct
  EARD/LOFT WF3 ...50 A5
Churchfarm Garth
  AL/HA/HU LS17 ...15 H3
Churchfield Cft RTHW LS26 .....50 C1
Churchfield Gv RTHW LS26 .....50 C1
Churchfield La RTHW LS26 .....44 C5
Churchfield Rd RTHW LS26 .....50 C1
Church Gdns AL/HA/HU LS17 ...13 H4
Churchgate BHP/TINH LS16 ......7 H1
Church Ga HORS LS18 .....17 F1
Church Gv HDGY LS6 .....19 G5
  HORS LS18 .....17 F1
Church Hl BHP/TINH LS16 ......7 H1
Church Hill Gdns
  PDSY/CALV LS28 ...24 D3
Church Hill Gn PDSY/CALV LS28 .24 D3
Church Hill Mt PDSY/CALV LS28 .24 D3
Churchill Gdns LDSU LS2 * 28 B3
Church La BHP/TINH LS16 .....12 A3
  CHAL LS7 ...
  HDGY LS6 .....19 H5
  HORS LS18 .....17 F1
  MSTN/BAR LS15 ...31 G3
  PDSY/CALV LS28 ...32 C1
Church Mt HORS LS18 .....17 F1
Church Rd HORS LS18 .....17 F2
  WOR/ARM LS12 ...35 E1
Church Rw LDSU LS2 ......3 J5
Church St GSLY LS20 ......5 E3
  KSTL LS5 .....26 C1
  MID LS10 .....36 D4
  MID LS10 .....3 H7
  RTHW LS26 .....45 G4
  RTHW LS26 .....50 C1
  YEA LS19 ......8 C1
Church Vw KSTL LS5 .....26 D1
Church Wk LDSU LS2 ......3 J5
Church Wy MOR LS27 * 46 C1
Church Wood Av
  BHP/TINH LS16 ...19 E4
Church Wood Mt HDGY LS6 .....19 E4
Church Wood Rd
  BHP/TINH LS16 ...19 E4
City La LDS LS1 ......3 F5
City Wk BEE/HOL LS11 .....36 B2
Clapham Dene Rd
  MSTN/BAR LS15 ...31 F4
Clara St PDSY/CALV LS28 .....24 B3
Claremont PDSY/CALV LS28 ...32 D1
Claremont Av BVRD LS3 ......2 C2
Claremont Crs HDGY LS6 .....19 G4
Claremont Dr HDGY LS6 .....19 G4
Claremont Gv BVRD LS3 * 2 C2
  PDSY/CALV LS28 ...32 C1
Claremont Pl WOR/ARM LS12 ..34 C1
Claremont St RTHW LS26 * 45 G5
  WOR/ARM LS12 ...
Claremont Ter WOR/ARM LS12 ..34 C1
Claremont Vw BVRD LS3 * 2 C2
Claremont Vls BVRD LS3 * 2 C2
Claremount HDGY LS6 .....19 G4
Claremount Rd HDGY LS6 .....19 G4
Clarence Dr HORS LS18 .....17 F3
Clarence Gdns HORS LS18 .....17 F3
Clarence Rd HORS LS18 .....17 F3
  MID LS10 ...
Clarence St RTHW LS26 .....45 G4
Clarence Ter PDSY/CALV LS28 ..24 B5
Clarendon Pl LDSU LS2 .....28 A3
Clarendon Rd LDSU LS2 ......2 C1
Clarendon Ter PDSY/CALV LS28 .32 C2
Clarendon Wy LDSU LS2 ......2 D2
Clark Av OSM LS9 .....37 F2
Clark Crs OSM LS9 .....37 F2
Clark Gv OSM LS9 .....37 F2
Clark La OSM LS9 .....37 F1
Clark Mt OSM LS9 .....37 F1
Clark Rd OSM LS9 .....37 F2
Clark Rw OSM LS9 .....37 F2
Clarkson Vw HDGY LS6 .....28 A1
Clark Spring Ri MOR LS27 .....40 D4
Clark Ter OSM LS9 .....37 F2
Clark Vw OSM LS9 .....37 F2
Clay Pit La CHAL LS7 ......3 F1
Clayton Cl MID LS10 .....43 E1
Clayton Ct MID LS10 .....43 F1
Clayton Dr MID LS10 .....43 F1
Clayton Gv YEA LS19 ......8 C4
Clayton Rd MID LS10 .....43 F1
Clayton St RTHW LS26 * 50 D1
Clayton Wy MID LS10 .....43 F1
Clayton Wood Bank
  BHP/TINH LS16 ...18 B1
Clayton Wood Cl
  BHP/TINH LS16 ...18 B1
Clayton Wood Ri
  BHP/TINH LS16 ...18 B1

Clayton Wood Rd
  BHP/TINH LS16 ...18 B1
The Clearings MID LS10 .....42 D3
Cleasby Rd ILK LS29 ......4 A1
Cleeve Hl YEA LS19 ......8 D3
Clement Ter RTHW LS26 .....50 C2
Cleopatra Pl BRAM LS13 .....25 E2
Cleveleys Av BEE/HOL LS11 ...35 H4
Cleveleys Ct BEE/HOL LS11 * ...35 H4
Cleveleys Mt BEE/HOL LS11 * ...35 H4
Cleveleys Rd BEE/HOL LS11 ...35 H4
Cleveleys St BEE/HOL LS11 * ...35 H4
Cleveleys Ter BEE/HOL LS11 * ..35 H4
Cliffdale Rd CHAL LS7 .....28 B1
Cliffe Dr YEA LS19 ......8 D5
Cliffe La YEA LS19 ......9 E4
Cliffe Park Cha WOR/ARM LS12 .34 C2
Cliffe Park Cl WOR/ARM LS12 ..34 C2
Cliffe Park Crs WOR/ARM LS12 .34 C2
Cliffe Park Dr WOR/ARM LS12 ..34 C2
Cliffe Park Mt WOR/ARM LS12 .34 C2
Cliffe Park Ri WOR/ARM LS12 ..34 B2
Cliff La HDGY LS6 .....27 H1
Cliff Mt HDGY LS6 .....28 A1
Cliff Mount St HDGY LS6 * 28 A1
Clifford Hodgson Pl
  MOR LS27 * ...40 D4
Clifford Pl MOR LS27 .....40 D4
Cliff Rd HDGY LS6 .....28 A1
Cliff Side Gdns HDGY LS6 .....28 A1
Cliff Ter HDGY LS6 .....28 A1
Clifton Av OSM LS9 .....29 G4
Clifton Ct PDSY/CALV LS28 ...24 C5
Clifton Gv OSM LS9 .....29 G4
Clifton Hl PDSY/CALV LS28 .....24 C5
Clifton Mt OSM LS9 .....29 G4
Clifton Pl PDSY/CALV LS28 .....24 C5
Clifton Rd PDSY/CALV LS28 ...24 C5
Clifton Ter OSM LS9 .....29 G4
Clipston Av HDGY LS6 .....19 H4
Clipston St HDGY LS6 .....19 H4
Clipston Ter HDGY LS6 * 19 H4
The Close AL/HA/HU LS17 .....13 J2
  GSLY LS20 ......4 C4
  OSM LS9 .....37 E1
Cloth Hall St LDS LS1 ......3 H5
Clough St MOR LS27 .....46 D2
Clovelly Av BEE/HOL LS11 .....36 B5
Clovelly Gv BEE/HOL LS11 .....36 B5
Clovelly Pl BEE/HOL LS11 .....36 B5
Clovelly Rw BEE/HOL LS11 .....36 B5
Clovelly Ter BEE/HOL LS11 .....36 B5
Club La BRAM LS13 .....16 C5
Club Rw CHAL LS7 .....20 C3
  YEA LS19 ......6 A5
Clyde Ap WOR/ARM LS12 * ...35 G2
Clyde Cha WOR/ARM LS12 .....35 G2
Clyde Ct WOR/ARM LS12 * ...35 G2
Clyde Gdns WOR/ARM LS12 ...35 G2
Clyde Gra WOR/ARM LS12 .....35 G2
Clyde Vw WOR/ARM LS12 .....35 G2
Clyde Wk WOR/ARM LS12 .....35 G2
Coach Rd GSLY LS20 ......4 D5
  WOR/ARM LS12 ...34 A5
Coal Hill Dr BRAM LS13 .....24 D1
Coal Hill Fold BRAM LS13 .....24 D1
Coal Hill Gdns BRAM LS13 .....24 D1
Coal Hill Gn BRAM LS13 .....24 D1
Coal Hill La PDSY/CALV LS28 ...24 C1
Coal Rd SCFT LS14 .....23 F4
Cobden Av WOR/ARM LS12 ...34 B4
Cobden Gv WOR/ARM LS12 ...34 B4
Cobden Ms MOR LS27 .....46 C1
Cobden Pl WOR/ARM LS12 .....34 C4
Cobden Rd WOR/ARM LS12 ...34 B4
Cobden St WOR/ARM LS12 * ...34 C4
Cobden Ter WOR/ARM LS12 ...34 B4
Cockburn Cl BEE/HOL LS11 ...36 C5
Cockburn Wy BEE/HOL LS11 ...36 C5
Cockshott Dr WOR/ARM LS12 ..26 A4
Cockshott La WOR/ARM LS12 ..26 B4
Coggil St MID LS10 .....43 G1
Colby St MSTN/BAR LS15 .....38 C1
Coldcotes Av OSM LS9 .....29 H3
Coldcotes Crs OSM LS9 .....30 B3
Coldcotes Dr OSM LS9 .....30 B3
Coldcotes Garth OSM LS9 .....30 B3
Coldcotes Vw OSM LS9 .....30 A3
Coldcotes Wk OSM LS9 .....30 B3
Cold Well Rd MSTN/BAR LS15 ..31 F4
Cold Well Sq MSTN/BAR LS15 ..31 F4
Coleman St WOR/ARM LS12 .....2 A7
Colenso Gdns BEE/HOL LS11 ...35 H4
Colenso Gv BEE/HOL LS11 .....35 H4
Colenso Mt BEE/HOL LS11 .....35 H4
Colenso Pl BEE/HOL LS11 .....35 H4
Colenso Rd BEE/HOL LS11 .....35 H4
Colenso Ter BEE/HOL LS11 .....35 H4
Coleridge Cl RTHW LS26 .....51 G2
Coleridge La PDSY/CALV LS28 ..32 C1
College Lawns WOR/ARM LS12 .26 C5
College Vw WOR/ARM LS12 * ...
Colliers La AL/HA/HU LS17 .....15 G3
Collin Rd SCFT LS14 .....30 D4
Colmore Gv WOR/ARM LS12 ...34 D4
Colmore Rd WOR/ARM LS12 ...34 D5
Colton Ct MSTN/BAR LS15 .....39 H1
Colton Cft MSTN/BAR LS15 .....39 H1
Colton Garth MSTN/BAR LS15 ..39 H1
Colton La MSTN/BAR LS15 .....39 H2
Colton Rd MSTN/BAR LS15 .....39 H2
  WOR/ARM LS12 ...35 E1
Colton St WOR/ARM LS12 .....35 E1
Colville Ter BEE/HOL LS11 .....36 A3
  EARD/LOFT WF3 ...49 E5
Colwyn Av BEE/HOL LS11 .....42 B3
Colwyn Mt BEE/HOL LS11 .....42 B3
Colwyn Pl BEE/HOL LS11 .....42 B3
Colwyn Rd BEE/HOL LS11 .....42 B3
Colwyn Ter BEE/HOL LS11 .....42 B3
Colwyn Vw BEE/HOL LS11 .....42 B3
Commercial Ct LDS LS1 ......3 G6

Commercial Rd KSTL LS5 .....26 C2
Commercial St LDS LS1 ......3 G4
  MOR LS27 .....46 C2
  RTHW LS26 .....45 G4
Commercial Vls
Common La EARD/LOFT WF3 ...48 C5
Compton Av OSM LS9 .....29 G3
Compton Crs OSM LS9 .....29 G3
Compton Gv OSM LS9 .....29 G3
Compton Mt OSM LS9 .....29 G3
Compton Pl OSM LS9 .....29 G3
Compton Rd OSM LS9 .....29 G3
Compton Rw OSM LS9 .....29 G3
Compton St OSM LS9 .....29 G3
Compton Ter OSM LS9 .....29 G3
Concordia St LDS LS1 ......3 G6
Concord St LDSU LS2 ......3 J2
Conference Pl WOR/ARM LS12 ..34 C1
Conference Rd WOR/ARM LS12 .34 C1
Conference Ter WOR/ARM LS12 .34 C1
Congress Mt WOR/ARM LS12 ...34 C1
Congress St WOR/ARM LS12 ...34 C1
Coniston Av HDGY LS6 .....19 G5
Coniston Gdns MSTN/BAR LS15 .38 C2
Coniston Wy RTHW LS26 .....45 G4
Consort St BVRD LS3 ......2 B2
Consort Ter BVRD LS3 ......2 B2
Consort Vw BVRD LS3 ......2 B2
Consort Wk BVRD LS3 ......2 B2
Constance Gdns LDSU LS2 .....28 B3
Constance Wy CHAL LS7 .....28 B3
Conway Av OSM LS9 .....29 F2
Conway Dr RHAY LS8 .....29 F2
Conway Gv RHAY LS8 .....29 F2
Conway Mt RHAY LS8 .....29 F2
Conway Pl RHAY LS8 .....29 F2
Conway Rd RHAY LS8 .....29 F2
Conway St OSM LS9 .....29 F2
  RHAY LS8 .....29 F2
Conway Ter RHAY LS8 .....29 F2
Conway Vw RHAY LS8 .....29 F2
Cookridge Av BHP/TINH LS16 ...11 E1
Cookridge Dr BHP/TINH LS16 ...11 E1
Cookridge Gv BHP/TINH LS16 ...11 E1
Cookridge St LDSU LS2 ......3 F3
Cooperative Rd MOR LS27 .....46 B4
Co-operative St
  EARD/LOFT WF3 ...50 A5
  MOR LS27 .....46 C2
Copgrove Rd RHAY LS8 .....21 G5
Copley Hill Wy WOR/ARM LS12 .35 G2
Copley La AL/HA/HU LS17 .....15 H2
Copley St WOR/ARM LS12 * ...35 G2
Copley Yd WOR/ARM LS12 .....35 G2
Copperfield Crs OSM LS9 .....37 F2
Copperfield Dr OSM LS9 .....37 F2
Copperfield Gv OSM LS9 .....37 F2
Copperfield Mt OSM LS9 .....37 F2
Copperfield Pl OSM LS9 .....37 F2
Copperfield Rw OSM LS9 .....37 F2
Copperfield Ter OSM LS9 .....37 F2
Copperfield Vw OSM LS9 .....37 F2
Coppice La SCFT LS14 ......5 H4
The Coppice YEA LS19 ......8 B2
Coppice Wy RHAY LS8 .....21 G4
Coppice Wood Gv GSLY LS20 ....5 G3
Coppice Wood Crs GSLY LS20 ...5 G4
Coppice Wood Ri GSLY LS20 ....5 G4
Coppy La BRAM LS13 .....25 G1
Copt Royd Gv YEA LS19 ......5 G4
Corn Mill Ct WOR/ARM LS12 ...33 H1
Cornstone Fold
  WOR/ARM LS12 ...34 A5
Cornus Gdns MID LS10 .....42 D5
Cornwall Cl RTHW LS26 .....44 B5
Cornwall Crs RTHW LS26 .....44 B5
Coronation Pde
  MSTN/BAR LS15 ...38 C2
Coronation St
  EARD/LOFT WF3 ...50 B3
Corporation St WOR/ARM LS12 .46 C2
Cotefields Av PDSY/CALV LS28 ..24 A3
Cote La PDSY/CALV LS28 .....24 A3
Coteroyd Av MOR LS27 .....41 E3
Coteroyd Dr MOR LS27 .....41 E4
The Cote PDSY/CALV LS28 .....44 B5
Cotswold Dr RTHW LS26 .....44 B5
Cotswold Rd RTHW LS26 .....44 B5
Cottage Rd HDGY LS6 .....19 F4
Cotterdale Vw MSTN/BAR LS15 .38 C2
Cottingley Cha BEE/HOL LS11 ...41 E1
Cottingley Crs BEE/HOL LS11 ...41 E2
Cottingley Dr BEE/HOL LS11 ...41 E1
Cottingley Fold BEE/HOL LS11 ..41 E2
Cottingley Gdns BEE/HOL LS11 .41 E2
Cottingley Gn BEE/HOL LS11 ...41 E2
Cottingley Gv BEE/HOL LS11 ...41 E2
Cottingley V BEE/HOL LS11 ...41 E2
Cotton St LDS LS1 ......3 K6
County Ar LDS LS1 ......3 H4
Coupland Pl BEE/HOL LS11 .....36 A4
Coupland Rd BEE/HOL LS11 ...36 A4
Coupland St BEE/HOL LS11 .....36 B5
Court Dr KSTL LS5 .....18 B5
Courtenays SCFT LS14 .....31 F1
The Court AL/HA/HU LS17 .....12 D2
The Courtyards SCFT LS14 .....23 F5
Coverley Ri YEA LS19 ......8 D3
Cow Close Gv WOR/ARM LS12 ..34 B4
Cow Close Rd WOR/ARM LS12 ..34 A4
Cowley Rd BRAM LS13 .....16 D5
Cowper Av OSM LS9 .....29 G2
Cowper Crs OSM LS9 .....29 G2
Cowper Gv OSM LS9 .....29 G2
Cowper Mt OSM LS9 .....29 G2

Cowper Rd OSM LS9 .....29 G2
Cowper St CHAL LS7 ...
Cowper Ter OSM LS9 .....29 G2
Crab La WOR/ARM LS12 ...
Cragg Av HORS LS18 ...
Cragg Rd HORS LS18 ...
Cragg Ter HORS LS18 ...
Cragg Wood Dr YEA LS19 ...
Craggwood Rd HORS LS18 ...
Crag Hill Vw BHP/TINH LS16 ...
Crag La AL/HA/HU LS17 ...
Cragside Cl KSTL LS5 ...
Cragside Crs KSTL LS5 ...
Cragside Gdns KSTL LS5 ...
Cragside Gv KSTL LS5 ...
Cragside Mt KSTL LS5 ...
Cragside Pl KSTL LS5 ...
Cragside Wk KSTL LS5 ...
Cranbrook Av BEE/HOL LS11 ...
Cranbrook Vw PDSY/CALV LS28 ...
Cranewells Dr MSTN/BAR LS15 ...
Cranewells Gn MSTN/BAR LS15 ...
Cranewells Garth MID LS10 ...
Cranewells V MSTN/BAR LS15 ...
Cranmer Bank AL/HA/HU LS17 ...
Cranmer Cl AL/HA/HU LS17 ...
Cranmer Gdns AL/HA/HU LS17 ...
Cranmer Ri AL/HA/HU LS17 ...
Cranmer Rd AL/HA/HU LS17 ...
Cranmore Crs MID LS10 ...
Cranmore Dr MID LS10 ...
Cranmore Gdns MID LS10 ...
Cranmore Garth MID LS10 ...
Cranmore Gn MID LS10 ...
Cranmore Gv MID LS10 ...
Cranmore La MID LS10 ...
Cranmore Ri MID LS10 ...
Cranmore Rd MID LS10 ...
Craven Rd RHAY LS8 ...
Crawshaw Av PDSY/CALV LS28 ...
Crawshaw Gdns
  PDSY/CALV LS28 ...
Crawshaw Hl PDSY/CALV LS28 ...
Crawshaw Pk PDSY/CALV LS28 ...
Crawshaw Ri PDSY/CALV LS28 ...
Crawshaw Rd PDSY/CALV LS28 ...
Crescent Av RTHW LS26 ...
Crescent Gdns AL/HA/HU LS17 ...
Crescent Gra BEE/HOL LS11 * ...
The Crescent AL/HA/HU LS17 ...
  BHP/TINH LS16 ...
  GSLY LS20 ...
  MSTN/BAR LS15 ...
  PDSY/CALV LS28 ...
Crescent Towers
  BEE/HOL LS11 * ...
Crescent Vw AL/HA/HU LS17 ...
Creskell Rd BEE/HOL LS11 ...
Cricketers Fold AL/HA/HU LS17 ...
Cricketers Gn YEA LS19 ...
Cricketers Ter WOR/ARM LS12 ...
The Cricketers BULY LS4 ...
Cricketers Vw AL/HA/HU LS17 ...
Cricklegate MSTN/BAR LS15 ...
Crimbles Ct PDSY/CALV LS28 ...
Crimbles Pl PDSY/CALV LS28 ...
Crimbles Rd PDSY/CALV LS28 ...
Crimbles Ter PDSY/CALV LS28 ...
Croft Av PDSY/CALV LS28 ...
Croft Ct HORS LS18 ...
Croftdale Gv MSTN/BAR LS15 ...
Crofters Lea YEA LS19 ...
Croft House Av MOR LS27 ...
Croft House La MOR LS27 ...
Croft House Ct
  PDSY/CALV LS28 * ...
Croft House Dr MOR LS27 ...
Croft House Gdns MOR LS27 ...
Croft House La MOR LS27 ...
Croft House Ms MOR LS27 ...
Croft House Mt MOR LS27 ...
Croft House Rd MOR LS27 ...
Croft House Vw MOR LS27 ...
Croft House Wy MOR LS27 ...
Croft's Ct LDS LS1 ...
Croftside Cl SCFT LS14 ...
The Croft MSTN/BAR LS15 ...
  RTHW LS26 ...
Cromack Vw PDSY/CALV LS28 ...
Cromer Pl LDSU LS2 ...
Cromer Rd LDSU LS2 ...
Cromer St LDSU LS2 ...
Cromer Ter LDSU LS2 ...
Crompton Dr MOR LS27 ...
Cromwell Hts OSM LS9 ...
Cromwell Ms OSM LS9 ...
Cromwell Mt MID LS10 ...
Cromwell St OSM LS9 ...
Cropper Ga LDS LS1 ...
Crosby Av BEE/HOL LS11 ...
Crosby Pl BEE/HOL LS11 ...
Crosby Rd BEE/HOL LS11 ...
Crosby St BEE/HOL LS11 ...
Crosby Ter BEE/HOL LS11 ...
Crosby Vw BEE/HOL LS11 ...
Cross Albert Pl WOR/ARM LS12 ...
Cross Alcester Rd RHAY LS8 ...
Cross Alma St OSM LS9 ...
Cross Ar LDS LS1 * ...
Cross Aston Gv BRAM LS13 ...
Cross Av RTHW LS26 ...
Cross Aysgarth St OSM LS9 ...
Cross Banstead St RHAY LS8 ...
Cross Bath Rd BRAM LS13 ...
Cross Beck Rd RHAY LS8 ...
Cross Belgrave St LDSU LS2 ...
Cross Bellbrooke Av OSM LS9 ...
Cross Bell St OSM LS9 ...

ıtley La HDGY LS6 .... 19 H4
:h St MOR LS27 .... 46 D4
ley Lodge Rd
S6 .... 27 G3
digan Ter BULY LS4 .... 27 E4
herine St OSM LS9 .... 37 E1
ancellor St HDGY LS6 .... 28 C2
apel St HDGY LS6 .... 19 F5
f Rd HDGY LS6 .... 27 H1
wlish Gv OSM LS9 .... 29 H5
y Rd OSM LS9 * 37 F2
ord St RHAY LS8 * 29 F2
: St BRAM LS13 .... 17 G5
ald Pl RTHW LS26 .... 45 H5
anston Av BULY LS4 .... 27 E3
d St LDSU LS2 .... 28 A2
tts BEE/HOL LS11 .... 36 A5
tts Av BEE/HOL LS11 .... 42 A1
tts Crs BEE/HOL LS11 .... 41 H1
tts Dr BEE/HOL LS11 .... 35 H5
tts Gv BEE/HOL LS11 .... 42 A1
tts Mt BEE/HOL LS11 .... 42 A1
tts Pde BEE/HOL LS11 .... 41 H1
tts Pl BEE/HOL LS11 .... 41 H1
tts Rd BEE/HOL LS11 .... 41 H1
tts Rw BEE/HOL LS11 .... 41 H1
tts St BEE/HOL LS11 .... 41 H1
tts Ter BEE/HOL LS11 .... 41 H1
untaine St LDS LS1 * 3 F4
ancis St CHAL LS7 .... 28 D2
tes Av MSTN/BAR LS15 .... 31 G2
tes La MSTN/BAR LS15 .... 31 F2
tes Rd MSTN/BAR LS15 .... 31 E3
en Rd BHP/TINH LS16 .... 19 E3
anby Ter HDGY LS6 * 19 F5
ange Av RHAY LS8 .... 29 E2
asmere St
ARM LS12 .... 35 F1
een Ap OSM LS9 .... 37 G3
een Av OSM LS9 * 37 F2
een Cl OSM LS9 .... 37 G3
een Crs OSM LS9 .... 37 F2
een Dr OSM LS9 .... 37 G3
een Gv OSM LS9 .... 37 F2
een La MSTN/BAR LS15 .... 31 F5
LS9 .... 37 F2
een Ri OSM LS9 .... 37 G3
een Rd OSM LS9 .... 37 F2
een Rw HDGY LS6 .... 19 G3
een V OSM LS9 .... 37 G3
een Wy OSM LS9 .... 37 G3
rtley Av HDGY LS6 .... 28 A1
eath Gv BEE/HOL LS11 .... 35 G5
enley Rd BRAM LS13 .... 25 G3
lton Gv RHAY LS8 .... 29 F1
gledew Crs RHAY LS8 .... 14 D5
gram Rd BEE/HOL LS11 .... 35 H3
y Mt OSM LS9 .... 29 G5
elso Rd LDSU LS2 .... 2 B1
ld Ct BEE/HOL LS11 * 36 A3
ld Rd MOR LS27 .... 40 D4
ld Ter BEE/HOL LS11 .... 36 C5
GSLY LS20 .... 5 F1
/ARM LS12 .... 34 A3
/ARM LS12 .... 34 D1
a Farm Rd KSTL LS5 .... 18 B3
dgett Pl RHAY LS8 .... 21 F2
uis St CHAL LS7 .... 28 D2
aude St LDSU LS2 * 3 J5
lan Rd RHAY LS8 .... 29 G2
smondthorpe La
LS9 .... 30 A5
ark St MSTN/BAR LS15 .... 31 E5
eel St MOR LS27 .... 46 D2
uarry St HDGY LS6 * 28 A1
eginald Mt CHAL LS7 * 28 D1
d HORS LS18 .... 17 E2
oseville Rd RHAY LS8 * 29 E2
oundhay Av RHAY LS8 .... 21 F5
t Michael's La
LS6 * 27 F1
peedwell St HDGY LS6 .... 28 B2
tamford St CHAL LS7 .... 3 K1
: MSTN/BAR LS15 .... 31 E5
/ LS26 .... 50 C1
er RTHW LS26 .... 50 C1
alley Dr MSTN/BAR LS15 .... 31 E4
Vestfield Rd BVRD LS3 * 2 A1
ingham St CHAL LS7 * 28 D3
ork St LDSU LS2 .... 3 J5
est La BEE/HOL LS11 .... 41 F1
est Ms BEE/HOL LS11 .... 41 G1
Point Rd MID LS10 .... 3 J7
St LDSU LS2 .... 3 H5
er Pl HDGY LS6 .... 28 B2
ees Ct YEA LS19 .... 8 D4
rees Pk YEA LS19 .... 8 D3
n St BEE/HOL LS11 .... 35 H3
ır St MID LS10 .... 3 J7
rland Ct HDGY LS6 .... 27 F2
rland Rd HDGY LS6 .... 27 H1
Ri MOR LS27 .... 47 F3
BEE/HOL LS11 .... 36 A3

D

Av MOR LS27 .... 40 D4
Grange Ms MOR LS27 * 40 D4
Grange Wy MOR LS27 .... 40 D4
Gv MOR LS27 .... 40 D4
Rd MOR LS27 .... 40 D4
eld Rd BRAM LS13 * 25 H4
Hl MOR LS27 .... 47 E1
Hill Av MOR LS27 .... 41 E5
Hill Cl MOR LS27 * 41 E5
Vale Ms EARD/LOFT WF3 .... 49 E5
Vale Ter EARD/LOFT WF3 .... 49 E5
GSLY LS20 .... 4 B4
ark Av BHP/TINH LS16 .... 10 D3
ark Cl BHP/TINH LS16 .... 10 D3
ark Gdns BHP/TINH LS16 .... 10 D3
ark Ri BHP/TINH LS16 .... 10 D3
Dale Park Wk BHP/TINH LS16 .... 10 D3
Dales Dr GSLY LS20 .... 4 B4
Dales Wy BHP/TINH LS16 .... 12 C1
BHP/TINH LS16 .... 19 F2
GSLY LS20 .... 4 B4
Dales Way Link BHP/TINH LS16 .... 12 C2
HDGY LS6 .... 19 G3
Dalmeny Ter BRAM LS13 * 16 C5
Dalton Av BEE/HOL LS11 .... 42 A1
Dalton Gv BEE/HOL LS11 .... 42 A1
Dalton Rd BEE/HOL LS11 .... 42 A1
Dam La YEA LS19 .... 6 A5
Danby Wk OSM LS9 .... 37 F1
Darfield Av RHAY LS8 .... 29 G2
Darfield Crs RHAY LS8 .... 29 G2
Darfield Gv RHAY LS8 .... 29 F2
Darfield Pl RHAY LS8 .... 29 G2
Darfield Rd RHAY LS8 .... 29 G2
Darfield St RHAY LS8 .... 29 G2
Darkwood Cl AL/HA/HU LS17 .... 14 C3
Darkwood Wy AL/HA/HU LS17 .... 14 C3
Darley Av MID LS10 .... 42 D4
Darnell Ter BEE/HOL LS11 .... 3 G7
Darnley La MSTN/BAR LS15 .... 39 G2
Dartmouth Av MOR LS27 .... 46 C4
Dartmouth Ms MOR LS27 .... 46 B3
David St BEE/HOL LS11 .... 2 E7
Davies Av RHAY LS8 .... 21 G2
Dawlish Av OSM LS9 .... 29 H5
Dawlish Crs OSM LS9 .... 29 G5
Dawlish Gv OSM LS9 .... 37 H1
Dawlish Mt OSM LS9 .... 29 H5
Dawlish Pl OSM LS9 .... 29 H5
Dawlish Rd OSM LS9 .... 29 H5
Dawlish Rw OSM LS9 .... 29 H5
Dawlish St OSM LS9 .... 29 H5
Dawlish Ter OSM LS9 .... 29 H5
Dawson Hl MOR LS27 .... 46 C1
Dawson Rd BEE/HOL LS11 .... 36 A5
Dawsons Meadow
PDSY/CALV LS28 .... 24 A3
Dawson St EARD/LOFT WF3 .... 47 F5
PDSY/CALV LS28 * 24 B4
Dean Av RHAY LS8 .... 21 G3
Dean Ct RHAY LS8 .... 21 G4
Deanfield Av MOR LS27 .... 46 B1
Dean Hall Cl MOR LS27 * 46 B2
Dean Head HORS LS18 .... 7 E4
Dean La HORS LS18 .... 7 E4
Deansway MOR LS27 .... 40 B5
Deanswood Cl AL/HA/HU LS17 .... 13 E4
Deanswood Dr AL/HA/HU LS17 .... 12 D4
Deanswood Gn AL/HA/HU LS17 .... 12 D4
Deanswood Hl AL/HA/HU LS17 .... 12 D4
Deanswood Pl AL/HA/HU LS17 .... 13 E4
Deanswood Ri AL/HA/HU LS17 .... 12 D4
Deanswood Vw AL/HA/HU LS17 .... 13 E4
Deighton Vw HDGY LS6 .... 19 G1
De Lacies Ct RTHW LS26 .... 45 E4
De Lacies Rd RTHW LS26 .... 45 E4
De Lacy Mt KSTL LS5 .... 26 C1
Delph Ct HDGY LS6 .... 28 A1
Delph Hl PDSY/CALV LS28 .... 24 C5
Delph Mt HDGY LS6 .... 28 A1
Delph Vw HDGY LS6 .... 28 A2
Dence Pl MSTN/BAR LS15 .... 30 C5
Dene House Ct LDSU LS2 .... 28 B3
Deneway PDSY/CALV LS28 .... 24 A3
Denham Av MOR LS27 .... 46 C4
Denison Rd BVRD LS3 .... 2 C3
Denison St YEA LS19 .... 5 H5
Dennil Crs MSTN/BAR LS15 .... 31 H1
Dennil Rd MSTN/BAR LS15 .... 31 H2
Dennistead Crs HDGY LS6 .... 19 F5
Denshaw Dr MOR LS27 .... 47 E2
Denshaw Gv MOR LS27 .... 47 E2
Denshaw La EARD/LOFT WF3 .... 47 G3
Denton Av RHAY LS8 .... 21 F2
Denton Gv RHAY LS8 * 21 F2
Dent St OSM LS9 .... 37 F1
Derby Rd YEA LS19 .... 8 D3
Derbyshire St MID LS10 .... 37 F5
Derwent Av RTHW LS26 .... 45 H5
Derwent Dr BHP/TINH LS16 .... 12 B3
Derwent Pl BEE/HOL LS11 .... 36 A2
Derwentwater Gv HDGY LS6 .... 27 E1
Derwentwater Ter HDGY LS6 .... 19 F5
Detroit Av MSTN/BAR LS15 .... 31 H5
Devon Cl LDSU LS2 .... 28 B3
Devon Rd CHAL LS7 .... 28 B2
Devonshire Av RHAY LS8 .... 14 C5
Devonshire Cl RHAY LS8 .... 14 C5
Devonshire Crs RHAY LS8 .... 21 F1
Devonshire Gdns LDSU LS2 .... 28 B2
Devonshire La RHAY LS8 .... 14 C5
Dewsbury Rd BEE/HOL LS11 .... 41 H3
MOR LS27 .... 47 G1
Diadem Dr SCFT LS14 .... 30 C4
Dial St OSM LS9 .... 37 F2
Dibb La YEA LS19 .... 5 F5
Dib Cl RHAY LS8 .... 22 B5
Dib La RHAY LS8 .... 22 B5
Dickinson St HORS LS18 .... 10 C5
Disraeli Gdns BEE/HOL LS11 .... 36 B4
Disraeli Ter BEE/HOL LS11 .... 36 B4
Dixon La WOR/ARM LS12 .... 35 E3
Dixon Lane Rd WOR/ARM LS12 .... 35 E3
Dobson Av BEE/HOL LS11 .... 36 C5
Dobson Gv BEE/HOL LS11 .... 36 C5
Dobson Pl BEE/HOL LS11 .... 36 C5
Dobson Ter BEE/HOL LS11 .... 36 C5
Dobson Vw BEE/HOL LS11 .... 36 C5
Dock St MID LS10 .... 3 H6
Dodgson Av CHAL LS7 .... 29 E2
Dolly La OSM LS9 .... 29 E4
Dolphin Ct OSM LS9 .... 37 E1
Dolphin La EARD/LOFT WF3 .... 49 E4
Dolphin Rd MID LS10 .... 49 E1
Dolphin St OSM LS9 .... 37 E1
Dolphin Ct BRAM LS13 .... 25 F3
Domestic Rd BEE/HOL LS11 .... 35 G3
Domestic St BEE/HOL LS11 .... 35 H3
Dominion Av CHAL LS7 .... 20 D4
Dominion Cl CHAL LS7 * 20 D4
Donald St PDSY/CALV LS28 .... 24 B3
Donisthorpe St MID LS10 .... 37 E3
Dorchester Dr YEA LS19 .... 9 E1
Dorset Av RHAY LS8 .... 29 G1
Dorset Gv PDSY/CALV LS28 * 24 C5
Dorset Mt RHAY LS8 .... 29 G2
Dorset Rd RHAY LS8 .... 29 G1
Dorset St RHAY LS8 * 29 G1
Dorset Ter RHAY LS8 .... 29 G2
Dotterel Gln MOR LS27 .... 47 E3
Dragon Ct WOR/ARM LS12 * 2 B7
Dragon Crs WOR/ARM LS12 .... 35 F3
Dragon Dr WOR/ARM LS12 .... 35 E3
Dragon Rd WOR/ARM LS12 .... 35 E3
Drayton Manor Yd
BEE/HOL LS11 * 36 C4
Driver Pl WOR/ARM LS12 .... 35 G2
Driver St WOR/ARM LS12 .... 2 A7
Driver Ter WOR/ARM LS12 .... 35 G2
The Drive AL/HA/HU LS17 .... 13 E1
BHP/TINH LS16 .... 11 G3
MSTN/BAR LS15 .... 31 H3
OSM LS9 .... 37 E1
RHAY LS8 .... 21 G2
Drummond Av BHP/TINH LS16 .... 19 E4
Drummond Ct BHP/TINH LS16 .... 19 E4
Drummond Rd BHP/TINH LS16 .... 19 E4
Drury Av HORS LS18 .... 17 G2
Drury Cl HORS LS18 .... 17 F2
Drury La HORS LS18 .... 17 F2
Dufton Ap SCFT LS14 .... 31 E2
Dulverton Cl BEE/HOL LS11 .... 41 F2
Dulverton Gdns BEE/HOL LS11 .... 41 E1
Dulverton Garth BEE/HOL LS11 .... 41 E2
Dulverton Gn BEE/HOL LS11 .... 41 F2
Dulverton Gv BEE/HOL LS11 .... 41 E2
Dulverton Pl BEE/HOL LS11 .... 41 E2
Dulverton Sq BEE/HOL LS11 .... 41 F2
Duncan St LDS LS1 .... 3 G5
Duncombe St LDS LS1 .... 2 C3
Dungeon La RTHW LS26 .... 51 E5
Dunhill Crs OSM LS9 .... 30 C5
Dunhill Ri OSM LS9 .... 30 C5
Dunlin Cl MOR LS27 .... 47 E3
Dunlin Ct MID LS10 .... 48 D1
Dunlin Cft MID LS10 .... 48 D1
Dunlin Dr MID LS10 .... 48 D1
Dunlin Fold MID LS10 .... 48 D1
Dunningley La EARD/LOFT WF3 .... 47 H4
Dunnock Cft MOR LS27 .... 47 E3
Dunstarn Dr BHP/TINH LS16 .... 12 B4
Dunstarn Gdns BHP/TINH LS16 .... 12 C4
Dunstarn La BHP/TINH LS16 .... 12 B5
Durban Av BEE/HOL LS11 .... 41 H1
Durban Crs BEE/HOL LS11 .... 41 H1
Dutton Gn SCFT LS14 .... 23 E2
Dutton Wy SCFT LS14 .... 23 E3
Dyehouse La PDSY/CALV LS28 .... 32 C4
Dyers Ct HDGY LS6 .... 27 H1
Dyer St LDSU LS2 .... 3 J4

E

Earlsmere Dr MOR LS27 .... 46 B1
Earlswood Av RHAY LS8 .... 14 B5
Earlswood Cha PDSY/CALV LS28 .... 32 C2
Earlswood Md PDSY/CALV LS28 .... 32 C3
Easdale Cl SCFT LS14 .... 30 D1
Easdale Crs SCFT LS14 .... 23 E5
Easdale Mt SCFT LS14 .... 30 D1
Easdale Rd SCFT LS14 .... 30 D1
East Cswy BHP/TINH LS16 .... 12 B2
East Causeway Cl
BHP/TINH LS16 .... 12 B2
East Causeway Crs
BHP/TINH LS16 .... 12 B3
East Causeway V
BHP/TINH LS16 .... 12 C3
Eastdean Bank SCFT LS14 .... 23 E4
Eastdean Dr SCFT LS14 .... 23 E4
Eastdean Gdns SCFT LS14 .... 23 F4
Eastdean Ga SCFT LS14 .... 23 F4
Eastdean Gv SCFT LS14 .... 23 F4
Eastdean Ri SCFT LS14 .... 23 F4
Eastdean Rd SCFT LS14 .... 23 E4
Easterly Av RHAY LS8 .... 29 G1
Easterly Cl RHAY LS8 .... 29 H2
Easterly Crs RHAY LS8 .... 29 G1
Easterly Cross RHAY LS8 .... 29 H1
Easterly Garth RHAY LS8 .... 29 H1
Easterly Gv RHAY LS8 .... 29 G1
Easterly Mt RHAY LS8 .... 29 H1
Easterly Rd RHAY LS8 .... 22 B5
Easterly Sq RHAY LS8 .... 29 H1
Easterly Vw RHAY LS8 .... 29 H1
Eastfield Crs RTHW LS26 .... 45 F5
Eastfield Dr RTHW LS26 .... 45 E5
East Field St OSM LS9 .... 37 E1
Eastgate BHP/TINH LS16 .... 7 H1
LDSU LS2 .... 3 H4
Eastgate Cl BHP/TINH LS16 .... 7 H1
East Grange Cl MID LS10 * 43 E2
East Grange Dr MID LS10 .... 43 E2
East Grange Garth MID LS10 .... 43 E2
East Grange Ri MID LS10 .... 43 E2
East Grange Rd MID LS10 .... 43 E2
East Grange Sq MID LS10 .... 43 E2
East Grange Vw MID LS10 .... 43 E2
East King St OSM LS9 .... 37 E1
Eastland Wk BRAM LS13 .... 26 A4
East Moor Crs RHAY LS8 .... 14 B5
East Moor Dr RHAY LS8 .... 21 G1
East Moor La BHP/TINH LS16 .... 12 B3
East Moor Rd RHAY LS8 .... 14 B5
East Pde LDS LS1 .... 3 F4
East Parade Wk LDS LS1 .... 3 F4
East Park Dr OSM LS9 * 37 G1
East Park Gv OSM LS9 .... 37 G1
East Park Mt OSM LS9 .... 37 G1
East Park Pde OSM LS9 .... 37 G2
East Park Pl OSM LS9 .... 37 G1
East Park Rd OSM LS9 .... 37 F1
East Park St MOR LS27 .... 46 B3
OSM LS9 .... 37 G1
East Park Ter OSM LS9 .... 37 G1
East Park Vw OSM LS9 .... 37 G1
East Side Ct PDSY/CALV LS28 .... 33 F3
East St OSM LS9 .... 3 K6
East Vw MSTN/BAR LS15 * 31 G3
PDSY/CALV LS28 .... 32 C3
RTHW LS26 .... 51 G1
YEA LS19 .... 9 E1
East View Rd YEA LS19 .... 9 E1
Eastwood Crs SCFT LS14 .... 31 H1
Eastwood Dr SCFT LS14 .... 23 G5
Eastwood Gdns SCFT LS14 .... 31 G1
Eastwood Garth SCFT LS14 .... 31 H1
Eastwood La SCFT LS14 .... 31 H1
Eastwood Nook SCFT LS14 .... 31 H1
Easy Rd OSM LS9 .... 37 F2
Eaton Hl BHP/TINH LS16 .... 11 F4
Eaton Ms MID LS10 .... 48 C1
Eaton Sq MID LS10 .... 48 C2
Ebberston Gv HDGY LS6 .... 27 H2
Ebberston Pl HDGY LS6 .... 27 H2
Ebenezer St EARD/LOFT WF3 .... 49 H3
PDSY/CALV LS28 .... 24 B2
Ebor Mt HDGY LS6 .... 27 H3
Ebor Pl HDGY LS6 .... 27 H3
Ebor St HDGY LS6 .... 27 H3
Ecclesburn Av OSM LS9 .... 37 G1
Ecclesburn Rd OSM LS9 .... 37 G1
Ecclesburn St OSM LS9 .... 37 G1
Ecclesburn Ter OSM LS9 .... 37 G1
Eccup La BHP/TINH LS16 .... 12 B1
Edale Wy BHP/TINH LS16 .... 11 F4
Eddison Cl BHP/TINH LS16 .... 12 B2
Eddison St PDSY/CALV LS28 .... 24 B3
Eden Crs BULY LS4 .... 26 D1
Eden Dr BULY LS4 .... 26 D1
Eden Gdns BULY LS4 .... 26 D2
Eden Gv BULY LS4 .... 26 D2
Eden Mt BULY LS4 .... 26 D2
Eden Rd BULY LS4 .... 26 D1
Eden Wk BULY LS4 .... 26 D2
Eden Wy BULY LS4 .... 26 D2
Edgbaston Cl AL/HA/HU LS17 .... 13 E1
Edgbaston Wk AL/HA/HU LS17 .... 13 E1
Edgerton Rd BHP/TINH LS16 .... 18 D3
Edgware Av RHAY LS8 .... 29 F3
Edgware Gv RHAY LS8 .... 29 F3
Edgware Mt RHAY LS8 .... 29 F3
Edgware Pl RHAY LS8 .... 29 F3
Edgware Rw RHAY LS8 * 29 F3
Edgware St RHAY LS8 .... 29 F3
Edgware Ter RHAY LS8 .... 29 F3
Edgware Vw RHAY LS8 .... 29 F3
Edinburgh Av WOR/ARM LS12 .... 26 C5
Edinburgh Gv WOR/ARM LS12 .... 26 C5
Edinburgh Pl WOR/ARM LS12 .... 26 C5
Edinburgh Rd WOR/ARM LS12 .... 26 C5
Edinburgh Ter WOR/ARM LS12 .... 26 C5
Edmonton Pl CHAL LS7 .... 20 D4
Edroyd Pl PDSY/CALV LS28 .... 24 B2
Edroyd St PDSY/CALV LS28 .... 24 B2
Education Rd CHAL LS7 .... 28 C2
Edward St LDSU LS2 .... 3 H4
Edwin Av GSLY LS20 .... 4 D3
Edwin Rd HDGY LS6 .... 27 H3
Eggleston St BRAM LS13 .... 16 D5
Eighth Av RTHW LS26 .... 45 E4
WOR/ARM LS12 .... 35 F2
Eightlands Av BRAM LS13 .... 25 H3
Eightlands La BRAM LS13 .... 25 H3
Ekota Pl RHAY LS8 .... 29 F1
Elder Cft BRAM LS13 .... 25 G4
Elder Mt BRAM LS13 * 25 G4
Elder Pl BRAM LS13 .... 25 G4
Elder Ri RTHW LS26 .... 45 H5
Elder Rd BRAM LS13 .... 25 G4
Elder St BRAM LS13 .... 25 G4
Elford Gv RHAY LS8 .... 29 F2
Elford Pl East RHAY LS8 .... 29 F2
Elford Pl West RHAY LS8 .... 29 F2
Elford Rd RHAY LS8 * 29 F2
Eliot Gv GSLY LS20 .... 5 F4
Elizabeth Gv MOR LS27 .... 47 E1
Elizabeth Pl SCFT LS14 .... 23 E5
Elizabeth St HDGY LS6 .... 27 G2
Elland Rd BEE/HOL LS11 .... 35 H5
MOR LS27 .... 40 D4
Elland Wy BEE/HOL LS11 .... 41 F1
Ellerby La OSM LS9 .... 37 E2
Ellerby Rd OSM LS9 .... 37 E1
Ellers Gv RHAY LS8 .... 29 F1
Ellers Rd RHAY LS8 .... 29 F1
Ellis Fold WOR/ARM LS12 .... 34 D1
Ellis Pl BEE/HOL LS11 .... 36 A5
Ellis Ter HDGY LS6 .... 19 F3
Ellwood Cl CHAL LS7 .... 19 H3
Elm Cft SCFT LS14 .... 23 G2
Elmete Av RHAY LS8 .... 22 A4
Elmete Cl RHAY LS8 .... 22 B4
Elmete Ct RHAY LS8 .... 22 A4
Elmete Dr RHAY LS8 .... 22 B3
Elmete Gv RHAY LS8 .... 22 A3
Elmete Hl RHAY LS8 .... 22 B4
Elmete La AL/HA/HU LS17 .... 15 G5
RHAY LS8 .... 22 B2
Elmete Mt RHAY LS8 .... 22 B4
Elmete Wk RHAY LS8 .... 22 A4
Elmete Wy RHAY LS8 .... 22 C4
Elmfield Ct MOR LS27 .... 46 C3
Elmfield Gv WOR/ARM LS12 * 35 F2
Elmfield Pl WOR/ARM LS12 .... 35 F2
Elmfield Rd MOR LS27 .... 46 D4
Elmfield Wy BRAM LS13 .... 25 H4
Elmhurst Cl AL/HA/HU LS17 .... 14 C3
Elmhurst Gdns AL/HA/HU LS17 .... 14 C3
Elmroyd RTHW LS26 .... 50 D2
The Elms GSLY LS20 .... 5 E3
Elm St HDGY LS6 * 28 B1
Elmton Cl MID LS10 .... 43 E4
Elmtree La MID LS10 .... 36 D4
The Elm Wk MSTN/BAR LS15 .... 39 F3
Elmwood La LDSU LS2 .... 3 H1
Elmwood Rd LDSU LS2 .... 3 G1
Elsham Ter BULY LS4 .... 27 E3
Elsworth St WOR/ARM LS12 .... 35 F1
Eltham Cl HDGY LS6 .... 28 B2
Eltham Ct HDGY LS6 .... 28 B2
Eltham Dr HDGY LS6 .... 28 B2
Eltham Gdns HDGY LS6 .... 28 B2
Eltham Ri HDGY LS6 .... 28 B2
Elvaston Rd MOR LS27 .... 46 C4
Elwell St EARD/LOFT WF3 .... 49 E5
Emmott Dr YEA LS19 .... 9 F4
Emsley Pl MID LS10 .... 37 E3
Emville Av AL/HA/HU LS17 .... 15 E2
Enfield YEA LS19 .... 8 D1
Enfield Av CHAL LS7 .... 29 E3
Enfield St CHAL LS7 .... 28 D3
Enfield Ter CHAL LS7 .... 29 E3
Enterprise Pk BEE/HOL LS11 * 41 H2
Enterprise Wy MID LS10 .... 43 F2
Envoy St BEE/HOL LS11 * 36 C4
Epworth Pl MID LS10 .... 37 E4
Eric St BRAM LS13 .... 17 G5
Eshald La RTHW LS26 .... 51 H1
Eshald Pl RTHW LS26 .... 45 H5
Esholt Av GSLY LS20 .... 4 D5
Eskdale Mt SCFT LS14 .... 30 D1
Esmond St WOR/ARM LS12 .... 35 E1
Esmond Ter WOR/ARM LS12 .... 34 D1
Estcourt Av HDGY LS6 .... 19 E5
Estcourt Ter HDGY LS6 .... 19 E5
Esthwaite Gdns
MSTN/BAR LS15 * 38 C2
Euston Gv BEE/HOL LS11 .... 35 H4
Euston Mt BEE/HOL LS11 .... 35 H4
Euston Ter BEE/HOL LS11 .... 35 H4
Evanston Av BULY LS4 .... 27 E4
Evelyn Pl WOR/ARM LS12 .... 35 E2
Everleigh St OSM LS9 .... 29 G5
Exeter Dr MID LS10 .... 42 D4
Exton Pl MSTN/BAR LS15 .... 38 C1
Eyres Av WOR/ARM LS12 .... 27 E5
Eyres Gv WOR/ARM LS12 .... 27 E5
Eyres Mill Side WOR/ARM LS12 .... 26 D5
Eyres St WOR/ARM LS12 .... 27 E5
Eyres Ter WOR/ARM LS12 .... 27 E5
Eyrie Ap MOR LS27 .... 47 E3

F

Fairfax Cl SCFT LS14 .... 31 F2
Fairfax Ct BEE/HOL LS11 .... 36 A5
Fairfax Gv YEA LS19 .... 5 F5
Fairfax Rd BEE/HOL LS11 .... 36 A5
Fairfax Vw HORS LS18 .... 10 B3
Fairfield Av BRAM LS13 .... 25 E3
PDSY/CALV LS28 .... 24 D5
Fairfield Cl BRAM LS13 .... 25 F3
RTHW LS26 .... 49 H2
Fairfield Crs BRAM LS13 .... 25 E3
Fairfield Dr RTHW LS26 .... 49 H2
Fairfield Gdns RTHW LS26 .... 49 H2
Fairfield Gv BRAM LS13 .... 25 F3
RTHW LS26 * 49 H2
Fairfield Hl BRAM LS13 .... 25 F3
Fairfield La RTHW LS26 .... 49 H2
Fairfield Mt BRAM LS13 .... 25 F3
Fairfield Rd BRAM LS13 .... 25 E3
Fairfield Sq BRAM LS13 .... 25 F2
Fairfield St BRAM LS13 .... 25 F3
Fairfield Ter BRAM LS13 .... 25 F3
Fairford Av BEE/HOL LS11 .... 36 C5
Fairford Mt HDGY LS6 .... 19 G1
Fairford Ter BEE/HOL LS11 .... 36 C5
Fairway GSLY LS20 .... 4 C3
Fairway Cl GSLY LS20 .... 4 C4
The Fairway AL/HA/HU LS17 .... 13 G1
Falcon Ms MOR LS27 .... 47 E3
Falkland Ct AL/HA/HU LS17 .... 20 C1
Falkland Crs AL/HA/HU LS17 .... 20 C1
Falkland Gv AL/HA/HU LS17 .... 20 C1
Falkland Mt AL/HA/HU LS17 .... 20 C1
Falkland Ri AL/HA/HU LS17 .... 20 C1
Falkland Rd AL/HA/HU LS17 .... 20 C1
Fall Park Ct BRAM LS13 .... 17 H5
Fallswood Gv BRAM LS13 .... 25 H1
Farfield Av PDSY/CALV LS28 .... 24 A2
Farfield Ct AL/HA/HU LS17 .... 14 A2
Farfield Dr PDSY/CALV LS28 .... 24 A3
Farfield Gv PDSY/CALV LS28 .... 24 A2
Farfield Ri PDSY/CALV LS28 .... 24 A2
Farm Ct MSTN/BAR LS15 .... 31 F3
Farm Hill Crs CHAL LS7 .... 20 A5
Farm Hl North CHAL LS7 .... 20 A4
Farm Hill Ri CHAL LS7 .... 20 A5
Farm Hill Rd MOR LS27 .... 46 A1
Farm Hl South CHAL LS7 .... 20 A5
Farm Hill Wy CHAL LS7 .... 20 A5
Farm Mt MSTN/BAR LS15 .... 31 G3
Far Moss AL/HA/HU LS17 .... 13 E2
Farm Rd MSTN/BAR LS15 .... 31 F3
Farndale Ap SCFT LS14 .... 23 G5
Farndale Cl SCFT LS14 .... 23 G5
Farndale Garth SCFT LS14 .... 23 G4
Farndale Pl SCFT LS14 .... 23 G4
Farnham Cl BHP/TINH LS16 .... 19 E3
SCFT LS14 .... 23 F1
Farnham Cft SCFT LS14 .... 23 F1
Farnley Crs WOR/ARM LS12 .... 34 A2
Farrar Ct BRAM LS13 .... 25 G2
Farrar Cft BHP/TINH LS16 .... 11 G3
Farrar Gv BHP/TINH LS16 .... 11 G3
Farrar La BHP/TINH LS16 .... 11 G3
Far Reef Cl HORS LS18 .... 10 C5
Farrer La RTHW LS26 .... 51 G1
Farrier Wy EARD/LOFT WF3 .... 49 H3
Farrow Bank WOR/ARM LS12 .... 34 A1
Farrow Gn WOR/ARM LS12 .... 34 A1
Farrow Hl WOR/ARM LS12 .... 34 B1
Farrow Rd WOR/ARM LS12 .... 34 A1
Farrow V WOR/ARM LS12 .... 34 A1
Fartown PDSY/CALV LS28 .... 32 C3
Fartown Cl PDSY/CALV LS28 .... 32 C3
Far Well Fold YEA LS19 .... 9 F4
Fawcett Av WOR/ARM LS12 .... 34 D3

Fawcett Bank *WOR/ARM* LS12 ......34 C3
Fawcett Cl *WOR/ARM* LS12 ....34 C3
Fawcett Dr *WOR/ARM* LS12 ....34 C3
Fawcett Gdns *WOR/ARM* LS12 ....34 C3
Fawcett La *WOR/ARM* LS12 ....34 C3
Fawcett Rd *WOR/ARM* LS12 ....34 C3
Fawcett V *WOR/ARM* LS12 ....34 C3
Fawcett Wy *WOR/ARM* LS12 ....34 C3
Fearnley Cl *WOR/ARM* LS12 ....35 F1
Fearnley Pl *WOR/ARM* LS12 ....35 F1
Fearnville Av *RHAY* LS8 ....30 B1
Fearnville Cl *RHAY* LS8 ....22 B5
Fearnville Dr *RHAY* LS8 ....30 B1
Fearnville Gv *RHAY* LS8 ....30 B1
Fearnville Pl *RHAY* LS8 ....22 C5
Fearnville Rd *RHAY* LS8 ....30 B1
Fearnville Ter *RHAY* LS8 ....30 B1
Fearnville Vw *RHAY* LS8 ....30 B1
Feast Fld *HORS* LS18 ....17 F3
Featherbank Av *HORS* LS18 ....17 F3
Featherbank Gv *HORS* LS18 ....17 F3
Featherbank Ter *HORS* LS18 ....17 F3
Featherbank Wk *HORS* LS18 ....17 F3
Felnex Rd *OSM* LS9 ....38 A3
Felnex Wy *OSM* LS9 ....38 A3
Fenton Av *RTHW* LS26 ....45 F4
Fenton Cl *RTHW* LS26 ....45 F4
Fentonsgate *EARD/LOFT* WF5 .....50 A5
Fenton St *EARD/LOFT* WF3 ....47 H5
LDSU LS2 ....2 C4
Fernbank Av *BRAM* LS13 ....24 D2
Fernbank Cl *BRAM* LS13 ....24 D2
Fernbank Dr *BRAM* LS13 ....24 D2
Fernbank Gdns *BRAM* LS13 ....24 D2
Fernbank Pl *BRAM* LS13 ....24 D2
Fernbank Rd *BRAM* LS13 ....24 D2
Ferncliffe Ter *BRAM* LS13 ....25 F3
Fern Gv *KSTL* LS5 ....26 C1
Fernlea *RTHW* LS26 ....44 D5
Fern Lea Vw *PDSY/CALV* LS28 .....24 C3
Fernwood *RHAY* LS8 ....21 G1
Fewston Av *OSM* LS9 ....37 F2
Fewston Ct *OSM* LS9 ....37 F2
Field End *MSTN/BAR* LS15 ....39 E1
Field End Cl *MSTN/BAR* LS15 ....39 E1
Field End Crs *MSTN/BAR* LS15 .....39 E1
Field End Gdns *MSTN/BAR* LS15 ..39 E1
Field End Garth *MSTN/BAR* LS15 .39 E1
Field End Gv *MSTN/BAR* LS15 ....39 E1
Field End Mt *MSTN/BAR* LS15 ....39 E1
Field End Rd *MSTN/BAR* LS15 * 31 F5
Fieldhead Dr *GSLY* LS20 ....4 C4
Fieldhouse Cl *AL/HA/HU* LS17 .....13 G5
Fieldhouse Dr *AL/HA/HU* LS17 ....13 G5
Fieldhouse Gv *PDSY/CALV* LS28 ..24 A3
Fieldhouse Lawn
AL/HA/HU LS17 ....13 G5
Fieldhouse Wk *AL/HA/HU* LS17 ..13 G5
Fielding Ct *MOR* LS27 ....46 A1
Fielding Ga *WOR/ARM* LS12 ....27 F5
Fields Rd *BEE/HOL* LS11 ....27 H1
The Fields *EARD/LOFT* WF3 ....50 B5
Field Ter *MSTN/BAR* LS15 ....31 E5
Fieldway Av *BRAM* LS13 ....25 E1
Fieldway Cha *RTHW* LS26 ....51 H1
Fieldway Cl *BRAM* LS13 ....25 E1
Fieldway Ri *BRAM* LS13 ....24 D1
Fifth Av *RTHW* LS26 ....45 F5
Fillingfir Dr *BHP/TINH* LS16 ....18 D2
Fillingfir Rd *BHP/TINH* LS16 ....18 D2
Fillingfir Wk *BHP/TINH* LS16 ....18 D2
Finch Mt *MOR* LS27 ....46 C3
Fink Hl *HORS* LS18 ....17 H4
Finsbury Rd *LDS* LS1 ....2 E1
Firbank Gv *MSTN/BAR* LS15 ....38 C2
First Av *PDSY/CALV* LS28 ....24 C4
RTHW LS26 ....44 D4
WOR/ARM LS12 ....35 F1
YEA LS19 ....5 G3
Firth Av *BEE/HOL* LS11 ....42 A1
Firth Gv *BEE/HOL* LS11 ....42 A1
Firth Mt *BEE/HOL* LS11 ....42 A1
Firth Rd *BEE/HOL* LS11 ....42 A1
Firth St *CHAL* LS7 ....3 K1
Firth Ter *OSM* LS9 ....29 E4
Firth Vw *BEE/HOL* LS11 ....42 A1
Fir Tree Ap *AL/HA/HU* LS17 ....13 F4
Fir Tree Cl *AL/HA/HU* LS17 ....13 G3
Fir Tree Gdns *AL/HA/HU* LS17 .....13 G3
Fir Tree Gn *AL/HA/HU* LS17 ....13 G3
Fir Tree Gv *AL/HA/HU* LS17 ....13 G4
Fir Tree La *AL/HA/HU* LS17 ....13 G4
Fir Tree Ri *AL/HA/HU* LS17 ....13 G4
Fir Tree V *AL/HA/HU* LS17 ....13 G3
Fish St *LDS* LS1 ....3 H4
Fitzroy Dr *RHAY* LS8 ....21 G4
Flax Pl *OSM* LS9 ....37 E1
Flaxton Gn *BFF/HOL* LS11 ....36 B5
Flaxton Gdns *BEE/HOL* LS11 * 36 B5
Flaxton St *BEE/HOL* LS11 ....36 B5
Flaxton Vw *BEE/HOL* LS11 ....36 B5
Fleet La *RTHW* LS26 ....51 H1
Fleet Thro Rd *HORS* LS18 ....17 H4
Flexbury Av *MOR* LS27 ....46 A4
Floral Av *CHAL* LS7 ....20 C4
Florence Av *OSM* LS9 ....29 G3
Florence Gv *RHAY* LS8 ....29 G3
Florence Mt *OSM* LS9 * 29 G3
Florence Pl *OSM* LS9 ....29 G3
Florence St *OSM* LS9 ....29 G3
Florence Ter *MOR* LS27 ....46 D2
Flower Cl *LS19 ....5 G5
Folly La *BEE/HOL* LS11 ....36 B4
Football *YEA* LS19 ....9 E1
Forber Pl *MSTN/BAR* LS15 ....38 C1
Forest Rdg *EARD/LOFT* WF3 ....48 C5
Forge La *WOR/ARM* LS12 ....27 F5
Forge Rw *WOR/ARM* LS12 ....33 F3

Forman's Dr *EARD/LOFT* WF3 .....49 G3
Forster Pl *WOR/ARM* LS12 ....34 C4
Forster St *OSM* LS9 ....37 E3
Foster Cl *MOR* LS27 ....46 C1
Foster Crs *MOR* LS27 ....46 C1
Foster Sq *MID* LS10 ....42 D3
Foster St *MOR* LS27 * 46 C2
Foundry Ap *OSM* LS9 ....29 H3
Foundry Av *RHAY* LS8 ....29 H2
Foundry Dr *RHAY* LS8 ....29 H2
Foundry La *OSM* LS9 ....30 C2
Foundry Mill Crs *SCFT* LS14 ....30 C2
Foundry Mill Dr *SCFT* LS14 ....30 C2
Foundry Mill Gdns *SCFT* LS14 .....22 C5
Foundry Mill Mt *SCFT* LS14 ....30 D2
Foundry Mill St *SCFT* LS14 ....30 D2
Foundry Mill Ter *SCFT* LS14 ....30 D2
Foundry Mill Vw *SCFT* LS14 ....30 D2
Foundry Mill Wk *SCFT* LS14 ....30 C2
Foundry Pl *OSM* LS9 ....29 H2
Foundry St *BEE/HOL* LS11 ....2 E7
OSM LS9 ....37 E1
Foundry Wk *RHAY* LS8 ....29 H2
Fountain St *LDS* LS1 ....2 D3
MOR LS27 ....46 B4
Fourteenth Av *WOR/ARM* LS12 ...35 G2
Fourth Av *RTHW* LS26 ....45 E4
Fourth Ct *BEE/HOL* LS11 ....36 A2
Fowler's Pl *PDSY/CALV* LS28 ....24 C3
Foxcroft Cl *HDGY* LS6 ....18 D5
Foxcroft Gn *HDGY* LS6 ....18 D5
Foxcroft Mt *HDGY* LS6 ....18 D5
Foxcroft Rd *HDGY* LS6 ....18 D5
Foxcroft Wk *HDGY* LS6 ....18 D5
Foxcroft Wy *HDGY* LS6 ....18 D5
Foxglove Av *RHAY* LS8 ....22 A4
Foxhill Av *BHP/TINH* LS16 ....19 E1
Foxhill Cl *BHP/TINH* LS16 ....19 F1
Foxhill Crs *BHP/TINH* LS16 ....19 F1
Foxhill Dr *BHP/TINH* LS16 ....19 F1
Foxhill Gn *BHP/TINH* LS16 ....19 F1
Foxhill Gv *BHP/TINH* LS16 ....19 F1
The Foxhills *BHP/TINH* LS16 ....10 D3
Foxton Gdns *MOR* LS27 ....46 B3
Fox Wy *MID* LS10 ....37 E3
Fox Wood Av *RHAY* LS8 ....22 C5
Fox Wood Cl *RHAY* LS8 ....22 C5
Foxwood Farm Wy *RHAY* LS8 .....22 C5
Fox Wood Gv *RHAY* LS8 ....22 C5
Fox Wood Ri *RHAY* LS8 ....22 C5
Fox Wood Wk *RHAY* LS8 ....22 C5
Frances St *PDSY/CALV* LS28 ....24 B3
Francis Gv *BEE/HOL* LS11 ....36 B5
Francis St *CHAL* LS7 ....28 D2
Frankland Gv *CHAL* LS7 ....28 D2
Frankland Pl *CHAL* LS7 ....29 E2
CHAL LS7 ....17 J2
Fraser St *OSM* LS9 ....29 F4
Frederick Av *OSM* LS9 ....37 G2
Frederick St *PDSY/CALV* LS28 .....24 A2
Freemont St *BRAM* LS13 ....25 E5
Freestone Ms *WOR/ARM* LS12 .....33 G1
Fremantle Pl *MSTN/BAR* LS15 .....38 C1
Frensham Av *MOR* LS27 ....46 B3
Frontline Cl *RHAY* LS8 ....21 G4
Front Rw *BEE/HOL* LS11 ....2 E7
Front Vw *BEE/HOL* LS11 ....2 E7
Fulham Pl *BEE/HOL* LS11 * 36 B5
Fulham St *BEE/HOL* LS11 ....36 B5
Fulmar Ct *MID* LS10 ....48 D1
Fulneck *PDSY/CALV* LS28 ....32 C3
Fulton St *BHP/TINH* LS16 ....19 E3

The Gables *HORS* LS18 ....10 C5
Gainsborough Av
BHP/TINH LS16 ....11 H2
Gainsborough Dr
BHP/TINH LS16 ....11 H2
Gaitskell Ct *BEE/HOL* LS11 ....36 A3
Gaitskell Gra *BEE/HOL* LS11 ....36 A3
Gaitskell Wk *BEE/HOL* LS11 ....36 A3
Gamble Hl *BRAM* LS13 ....25 H5
Gamble Hill Dr *BRAM* LS13 ....25 H5
Gamble Hill Gn *BRAM* LS13 ....25 H5
Gamble Hill Lawn *BRAM* LS13 .....25 H5
Gamble Hill Pl *BRAM* LS13 ....25 H5
Gamble Hill Ri *BRAM* LS13 ....25 H5
Gamble Hill Vw *BRAM* LS13 ....25 H5
Gamble La *WOR/ARM* LS12 ....33 G2
The Gang *WOR/ARM* LS12 ....27 E5
Ganners Cl *BRAM* LS13 ....25 H1
Ganners Gn *BRAM* LS13 ....25 G1
Ganners Gv *BRAM* LS13 * 25 H1
Ganners Hl *BRAM* LS13 ....25 H1
Ganners Mt *BRAM* LS13 ....25 G1
Ganners Ri *BRAM* LS13 ....25 H1
Ganners Rd *BRAM* LS13 ....25 G1
Ganners Wk *BRAM* LS13 ....25 G1
Ganners Wy *BRAM* LS13 ....25 H1
Ganton Cl *HDGY* LS6 ....28 B1
Gardeners Ct *MID* LS10 ....48 C2
The Gardens *MID* LS10 ....48 C2
MOR LS27 ....46 B4
PDSY/CALV LS28 ....24 C3
Gargrave Ap *OSM* LS9 ....29 F5
Gargrave Ct *OSM* LS9 * 29 H4
Gargrave Pl *OSM* LS9 ....29 G5
Garmont Ms *CHAL* LS7 * 20 D4
Garmont Rd *CHAL* LS7 ....20 D4
Garnet Av *BEE/HOL* LS11 * 36 C5
Garnet Crs *BEE/HOL* LS11 * 36 C5
Garnet Gv *BEE/HOL* LS11 * 36 C5
Garnet Pde *BEE/HOL* LS11 * 36 C5
Garnet Pl *BEE/HOL* LS11 * 36 C5
Garnet Rd *BEE/HOL* LS11 ....42 C1

Garnet Ter *BEE/HOL* LS11 ....42 C1
Garnet Vw *BEE/HOL* LS11 ....36 C5
Garth Av *AL/HA/HU* LS17 ....20 B1
Garth Dr *AL/HA/HU* LS17 ....20 B1
Garth Rd *AL/HA/HU* LS17 ....20 B1
The Garth *OSM* LS9 ....37 E1
Garth Wk *AL/HA/HU* LS17 ....20 B1
Garth Willow Av *SCFT* LS14 ....23 F2
Garth Willow Cl *SCFT* LS14 ....23 F2
Garton Av *OSM* LS9 ....37 G1
Garton Gv *OSM* LS9 ....37 G1
Garton Rd *OSM* LS9 ....37 G1
Garton Ter *OSM* LS9 ....37 G1
Garton Vw *OSM* LS9 ....37 G1
Gascoigne Rd *EARD/LOFT* WF3 ...49 E5
Gate House Ct *RTHW* LS26 ....45 H1
Gateland Dr *AL/HA/HU* LS17 ....15 G3
Gateland La *AL/HA/HU* LS17 ....15 G3
Gate Way Dr *YEA* LS19 ....8 C1
Gathorne Cl *RHAY* LS8 ....29 F2
Gathorne St *RHAY* LS8 ....29 E2
Gathorne Ter *RHAY* LS8 ....29 E2
Gelderd Cl *WOR/ARM* LS12 ....35 F4
Gelderd La *WOR/ARM* LS12 ....35 F4
Gelderd Pl *BEE/HOL* LS11 ....35 F5
Gelderd Rd *BEE/HOL* LS11 ....35 F5
MOR LS27 ....40 A4
Gelder Rd *WOR/ARM* LS12 ....34 D1
Genista Dr *MID* LS10 ....42 D3
George Mann Rd *MID* LS10 ....37 G5
George Mann Wy *MID* LS10 ....43 H1
George St *LDS* LS1 ....3 H4
YEA LS19 ....5 G5
Gerard Av *MOR* LS27 ....46 B3
Ghyll Beck Dr *YEA* LS19 ....9 G4
Ghyll Mt *YEA* LS19 ....8 B1
Ghyll Rd *HDGY* LS6 ....19 F5
Ghyll Royd *GSLY* LS20 ....5 E5
Gibraltar Island Rd *MID* LS10 ......37 F4
Gibson Dr *MSTN/BAR* LS15 ....31 G1
Gilbert Cha *KSTL* LS5 ....26 C2
Gilbert Cl *KSTL* LS5 ....26 C2
Gilbert Mt *BULY* LS4 ....26 D2
Gilbert St *PDSY/CALV* LS28 * 24 B3
Gillett Dr *RTHW* LS26 ....50 B1
Gillett La *RTHW* LS26 ....50 D1
Gill La *BAIL* BD17 ....8 A3
Gillroyd Pl *MOR* LS27 ....46 D3
Gilpin St *WOR/ARM* LS12 ....35 F2
Gilpin Ter *WOR/ARM* LS12 ....35 F2
Gilpin Vw *WOR/ARM* LS12 ....35 F2
Gipsy La *BEE/HOL* LS11 ....42 A3
RTHW LS26 ....45 F5
Gipsy Md *RTHW* LS26 ....45 F5
Gipton Ap *OSM* LS9 ....29 H4
Gipton Ga East *OSM* LS9 ....30 A2
Gipton Ga West *OSM* LS9 ....29 H2
Gipton Sq *OSM* LS9 ....30 B4
Gipton St *RHAY* LS8 ....29 F2
Gipton Wood Av *RHAY* LS8 ....21 H5
Gipton Wood Crs *RHAY* LS8 ....21 H5
Gipton Wood Gv *RHAY* LS8 ....21 H5
Gipton Wood Pl *RHAY* LS8 ....21 H5
Gipton Wood Rd *RHAY* LS8 ....21 H5
Glebe Av *KSTL* LS5 ....26 D1
Glebe Ct *RTHW* LS26 ....49 H1
Glebelands Dr *HDGY* LS6 ....19 H4
Glebe Mt *PDSY/CALV* LS28 ....24 C3
Glebe Pl *KSTL* LS5 ....26 D1
Glebe Ter *HDGY* LS6 ....19 F3
Gledhow Av *RHAY* LS8 ....21 F3
Gledhow Ct *CHAL* LS7 ....21 E3
Gledhow Dr *RHAY* LS8 ....21 F3
Gledhow Mt *RHAY* LS8 ....29 F2
Gledhow Park Av *CHAL* LS7 ....21 E4
Gledhow Park Crs *CHAL* LS7 * 21 E4
Gledhow Park Dr *CHAL* LS7 ....20 D4
Gledhow Park Gv *CHAL* LS7 ....21 E4
Gledhow Park Rd *CHAL* LS7 ....21 E4
Gledhow Park Vw *CHAL* LS7 ....21 E4
Gledhow Pl *RHAY* LS8 ....29 F2
Gledhow Ri *RHAY* LS8 ....21 H4
Gledhow Rd *RHAY* LS8 ....29 F2
Gledhow Ter *RHAY* LS8 ....29 F2
Gledhow Towers *RHAY* LS8 ....21 F4
Gledhow Vale Rd *CHAL* LS7 ....21 E4
RHAY LS8 ....21 F4
Gledhow Valley Rd *CHAL* LS7 ......20 D1
Gledhow Wood Av *RHAY* LS8 ......21 G3
Gledhow Wood Cl *RHAY* LS8 ....21 G3
Gledhow Wood Ct *RHAY* LS8 ....21 G4
Gledhow Wood Gv *RHAY* LS8 ......21 G3
Gledhow Wood Rd *RHAY* LS8 ....21 G3
Gledow Lane End *CHAL* LS7 ....20 D3
Glencoe Vw *OSM* LS9 ....37 F1
Glendower Pk *BHP/TINH* LS16 .....12 B5
Gleneagles Rd *AL/HA/HU* LS17 ...13 H3
Glen Gv *MOR* LS27 ....46 D3
Glenholme Rd *PDSY/CALV* LS28 ..24 A3
Glenlea Cl *BRAM* LS13 ....25 G2
Glenlea Gdns *BRAM* LS13 ....25 G2
Glen Mt *ILK* LS29 ....4 B1
MOR LS27 ....46 D3
Glenmere Mt *YEA* LS19 ....9 H5
Glenroyd Cl *PDSY/CALV* LS28 .....32 A1
Glensdale Est *MOR* LS27 ....47 E4
Glensdale Mt *OSM* LS9 ....37 F1
Glensdale Rd *OSM* LS9 ....37 F1
Glensdale St *OSM* LS9 ....37 F1

Glensdale Ter *OSM* LS9 ....37 F1
Glenthorpe Av *OSM* LS9 ....29 G5
Glenthorpe Crs *OSM* LS9 ....29 G5
Glenthorpe Ter *OSM* LS9 ....29 G5
Global Av *BEE/HOL* LS11 ....41 G2
Globe Rd *WOR/ARM* LS12 ....2 C6
Glossop Gv *HDGY* LS6 ....28 B1
Glossop Mt *HDGY* LS6 ....28 B1
Glossop Vw *HDGY* LS6 * 28 B1
Gloucester Ct *WOR/ARM* LS12 * ..22 G5
Gloucester Ter *WOR/ARM* LS12 ..35 G1
Glover Wy *BEE/HOL* LS11 ....42 C1
Golden Ter *WOR/ARM* LS12 ....34 C4
Goldsmith Dr *EARD/LOFT* WF3 ...49 H4
Goodman St *MID* LS10 ....36 D1
Goodwin Rd *WOR/ARM* LS12 ....35 G2
Goodwood *MID* LS10 ....48 D3
Gordon Dr *HDGY* LS6 ....19 G4
Gorse Lea *MID* LS10 ....42 D5
Gotts Park Av *WOR/ARM* LS12 ....26 B4
Gotts Park Crs *WOR/ARM* LS12 ...26 B4
Gotts Park Vw *WOR/ARM* LS12 ...26 B3
Gotts Rd *WOR/ARM* LS12 ....2 B5
Gower St *LDSU* LS2 ....3 J3
Grace St *LDS* LS1 ....2 C2
Grafton St *CHAL* LS7 ....3 H2
Gragwood Ct *HORS* LS18 ....17 G3
Graham Av *BULY* LS4 ....27 F2
Graham Gv *BULY* LS4 ....27 F2
Graham Mt *BULY* LS4 ....27 F2
Graham St *BULY* LS4 ....27 F2
Graham Ter *BULY* LS4 ....27 F2
Graham Vw *BULY* LS4 ....27 F2
Graingers Wy *WOR/ARM* LS12 ....2 B6
Granary Whf *LDS* LS1 * 3 F6
Granby Av *HDGY* LS6 ....19 F5
Granby Gv *HDGY* LS6 ....19 F5
Granby Mt *HDGY* LS6 ....19 F5
Granby Pl *HDGY* LS6 ....19 F5
Granby Rd *HDGY* LS6 ....19 F5
Granby St *HDGY* LS6 ....19 F5
Granby Vw *HDGY* LS6 ....27 F1
Grand Ar *LDS* LS1 * 3 H3
Grange Av *CHAL* LS7 ....29 E1
Grange Cl *HORS* LS18 ....16 D2
Grange Crs *AL/HA/HU* LS17 ....13 G2
MID LS10 ....36 D4
Grange Crs *AL/HA/HU* LS17 ....29 E1
RHAY LS8 ....22 C5
Grange Park Cl *RHAY* LS8 ....22 B5
Grange Park Crs *RHAY* LS8 ....22 B5
Grange Park Ct *MOR* LS27 ....40 D4
Grange Park Dr *MOR* LS27 ....40 D4
Grange Park Gv *RHAY* LS8 ....22 C5
Grange Park Ms *MOR* LS27 ....40 D4
Grange Park Pl *RHAY* LS8 ....22 C5
Grange Park Ri *RHAY* LS8 ....22 B5
Grange Park Ter *RHAY* LS8 ....22 C5
Grange Park Wk *RHAY* LS8 ....22 C5
Grange Park Wy *MOR* LS27 * 40 D4
Grange Rd *MID* LS10 ....36 D4
YEA LS19 ....9 E1
The Grange Rd *BHP/TINH* LS16 ...18 D1
Grange Ter *CHAL* LS7 ....29 E1
MOR LS27 ....40 D4
The Grange *EARD/LOFT* WF3 ....50 B3
Grange Vw *CHAL* LS7 ....29 E1
MID LS10 ....39 H2
PDSY/CALV LS28 ....24 C5
Grange View Gdns
AL/HA/HU LS17 ....13 G2
Grangewood Gdns
BHP/TINH LS16 ....18 D1
Granhamthorpe *BRAM* LS13 ....25 G3
Granny Av *MOR* LS27 ....41 E5
Granny La *WOR/ARM* LS12 ....34 C3
Grant Av *CHAL* LS7 ....20 D5
Granton Rd *CHAL* LS7 ....29 E4
Granville Rd *OSM* LS9 ....29 F4
Granville Ter *YEA* LS19 ....6 A5
Grape St *MID* LS10 ....36 D3
Grasmere Cl *WOR/ARM* LS12 ....35 F2
Grasmere Ct *WOR/ARM* LS12 * 35 F2
Grasmere Rd *WOR/ARM* LS12 .....35 F2
Graveleythorpe Ri
MSTN/BAR LS15 ....31 F4
Graveleythorpe Rd
MSTN/BAR LS15 ....31 F4
Gray Ct *MSTN/BAR* LS15 ....31 H5
Grayrigg Cl *MSTN/BAR* LS15 ....38 C1
Grayrigg Ct *MSTN/BAR* LS15 ....38 B1
Grayson Crest *BULY* LS4 ....26 D2
Grayson Hts *BULY* LS4 ....26 D2
Great George St *LDS* LS1 ....2 D3
Great Northern St *MOR* LS27 ....46 C3
Great Wilson St *BEE/HOL* LS11 ....3 G7
Greek St *LDS* LS1 ....2 D3
Greenacre Pk *YEA* LS19 ....8 E3
Greenacre Park Av *YEA* LS19 ....8 D2
Greenacre Park Ms *YEA* LS19 * 8 D2
Greenacre Park Ri *YEA* LS19 ....8 D2
Green Bank *EARD/LOFT* WF3 ....50 B5
Greenbanks Av *HORS* LS18 ....10 D5
Greenbanks Cl *HORS* LS18 ....10 D5
Greenbanks Dr *HORS* LS18 ....10 D5
Green Cha *HDGY* LS6 * 19 G3
Green Cl *HDGY* LS6 * 19 H3
Green Crs *HDGY* LS6 ....19 G3
Greenfield Av *GSLY* LS20 ....5 G5
Greenfield Ct *BHP/TINH* LS16 ......11 H3

Greenfield La *GSLY* LS20 ....5 G5
Greenfield Rd *OSM* LS9 ....37 F1
Greengate *RTHW* LS26 ....51 H1
Greenhead Rd *BHP/TINH* LS16 ....11 G5
Green Hill Cha *WOR/ARM* LS12 ...34 A2
Greenhill Crs *WOR/ARM* LS12 .....34 A2
Green Hill Cl *WOR/ARM* LS12 ......34 A1
Green Hill Dr *BRAM* LS13 ....25 G5
Green Hill Gdns *WOR/ARM* LS12 .34 A1
Green Hill Holt *WOR/ARM* LS12 ..34 A2
Green Hill Mt *BRAM* LS13 ....25 G5
Green Hill Pl *BRAM* LS13 ....25 G5
Green Hill Rd *BRAM* LS13 ....25 G5
Greenhills *YEA* LS19 ....5 J5
Green Hill Wy *BRAM* LS13 ....25 G5
Greenhow Cl *BULY* LS4 ....26 D3
Greenhow Gdns *BULY* LS4 ....26 D3
Greenhow Rd *BULY* LS4 ....26 D3
Greenhow Wk *BULY* LS4 ....26 D3
Green La *BEE/HOL* LS11 ....35 H4
BHP/TINH LS16 ....11 F5
EARD/LOFT WF3 ....50 C1
HORS LS18 ....16 D1
MSTN/BAR LS15 ....31 H3
PDSY/CALV LS28 ....24 A4
WOR/ARM LS12 ....34 B2
YEA LS19 ....5 G3
Green Lea *RTHW* LS26 ....44 D5
Greenlea Av *YEA* LS19 ....8 A4
Greenlea Cl *YEA* LS19 ....8 A4
Greenlea Rd *YEA* LS19 ....8 A4
Greenmoor Av *EARD/LOFT* WF3 ..49 E3
WOR/ARM LS12 ....34 A1
Greenmoor Cl *EARD/LOFT* WF3 ..49 E3
Greenmount La *BEE/HOL* LS11 * ..41 H1
Greenmount Pl *BEE/HOL* LS11 * ..41 H1
Greenmount St *BEE/HOL* LS11 ....41 H1
Greenmount Ter *BEE/HOL* LS11 ..41 H1
Greenock Pl *WOR/ARM* LS12 ....33 G1
Greenock Rd *WOR/ARM* LS12 * ...33 G1
Greenock St *WOR/ARM* LS12 ....33 G1
Greenock Ter *WOR/ARM* LS12 .....33 G1
Green Pasture Cl *OSM* LS9 ....30 B5
Green Rd *HDGY* LS6 ....19 H3
Greenshank Ms *MOR* LS27 ....46 D4
Greenside *PDSY/CALV* LS28 ....32 B1
Greenside Av *WOR/ARM* LS12 .....34 B1
Greenside Dr *WOR/ARM* LS12 .....34 B1
Greenside Gv *PDSY/CALV* LS28 ...32 B1
Greenside Rd *WOR/ARM* LS12 .....34 B1
Greenside Wk *WOR/ARM* LS12 ....34 B1
Green Ter *BEE/HOL* LS11 ....35 H4
The Green *AL/HA/HU* LS17 ....15 F2
GSLY LS20 ....5 E4
HORS LS18 ....16 D2
PDSY/CALV LS28 ....24 A3
Greenthorpe Hl *BRAM* LS13 ....25 F4
Greenthorpe Mt *BRAM* LS13 ....25 F4
Greenthorpe Rd
WOR/ARM LS12 ....25 F4
Greenthorpe St *BRAM* LS13 ....25 F4
Greenthorpe Wk *BRAM* LS13 ....25 F4
Greentop *PDSY/CALV* LS28 ....32 B1
Green Top *WOR/ARM* LS12 ....34 B2
Green Top Gdns *WOR/ARM* LS12 .34 A2
Green Vw *HDGY* LS6 ....19 G3
Greenview Cl *OSM* LS9 ....30 A5
Green View Ct *RHAY* LS8 ....21 F3
Greenville Av *WOR/ARM* LS12 .....33 G1
Greenville Dr *WOR/ARM* LS12 .....33 G1
Greenville Gdns *WOR/ARM* LS12 .33 G1
Greenway *GSLY* LS20 ....5 F4
MSTN/BAR LS15 ....31 F4
Greenway Cl *MSTN/BAR* LS15 ......31 F4
Greenwood Ct *HDGY* LS6 * 19 H4
Greenwood Mt *HDGY* LS6 ....19 H4
Green Wood Pk *HDGY* LS6 ....19 H4
Greenwood Rw
PDSY/CALV LS28 ....24 B3
Greyshiels Av *HDGY* LS6 ....27 F1
Greyshiels Cl *HDGY* LS6 ....27 F1
Greystone Mt *MSTN/BAR* LS15 ....31 F5
Greystones Ct *RHAY* LS8 ....22 A5
Grimthorpe Av *HDGY* LS6 * 27 F1
Grimthorpe Pl *HDGY* LS6 ....27 F1
Grimthorpe Ter *HDGY* LS6 ....27 F1
Grosmont Rd *BRAM* LS13 ....24 D3
Grosmont Ter *BRAM* LS13 ....24 D3
Grosvenor Hl *CHAL* LS7 ....21 E5
Grosvenor Mt *HDGY* LS6 ....27 G1
Grosvenor Park Gdns *HDCY* LS6 ..20 D5
Grosvenor Rd *CHAL* LS7 ....21 E5
Grosvenor Ter *HDGY* LS6 ....20 D5
Grove Av *HDGY* LS6 ....19 G3
Grove Cl *HDGY* LS6 ....19 H3
PDSY/CALV LS28 ....32 B1
Grove Farm Cl *BHP/TINH* LS16 ....11 G5
Grove Farm Crs *BHP/TINH* LS16 ..11 G5
Grove Farm Cft *BHP/TINH* LS16 ..11 G5
Grove Farm Dr *BHP/TINH* LS16 ....11 G5
Grove Gdns *HDGY* LS6 ....19 G3
Grovehall Av *BEE/HOL* LS11 ....41 H2
Grovehall Dr *BEE/HOL* LS11 ....41 H2
Grovehall Pde *BEE/HOL* LS11 * ...41 H2
Grovehall Rd *BEE/HOL* LS11 ....41 H2
Grove La *HDGY* LS6 ....19 G4
Grove Ri *AL/HA/HU* LS17 ....13 H2
Grove Rd *HDGY* LS6 ....19 G4
HORS LS18 ....17 F3
MID LS10 ....42 C4
MSTN/BAR LS15 ....31 H2
PDSY/CALV LS28 ....32 B1
Grove St *LDS* LS1 ....2 D2
PDSY/CALV LS28 * 24 A3

PDSY/CALV LS28 ....32 B1
AL/HA/HU LS17 ....12 D2
S18 ....17 F2
ALV LS28 ....32 B1
9 ....8 D1
od HDGY LS6 ....19 F4
ea HDGY LS6 ....19 F5
St HDGY LS6 ....19 F5
Ap MOR LS27 ....47 F5
Dr ILK LS29 ....4 B2
ood Cl MSTN/BAR LS15 ..39 H1
ood Crest
BAR LS15 ....39 H1

H

Av BULY LS4 ....27 E3
Pl BULY LS4 ....27 E3
BR BULY LS4 ....27 E3
Ct AL/HA/HU LS17 ....15 H5
n RTHW LS26 ....44 A4
ns RTHW LS26 ....44 A4
e RTHW LS26 ....44 A5
Cl RTHW LS26 ....44 A5
Wy RTHW LS26 ....44 A4
r RTHW LS26 ....44 A4
nd CHAL LS7 ....20 D3
ARM LS12 * 35 E2
n CHAL LS7 ....20 C2
WOR/ARM LS12 ....34 D3
BRAM LS13 ....24 C3
Cl PDSY/CALV LS28 ..24 D3
ct PDSY/CALV LS28 ..24 D3
Gdns BRAM LS13 ....24 D3
Gn PDSY/CALV LS28 ..24 D3
La BRAM LS13 ....24 D2
HDGY LS6 ....27 H3
e WOR/ARM LS12 ....26 C5
Dr WOR/ARM LS12 ....26 C5
e WOR/ARM LS12 ....26 C5
WOR/ARM LS12 * 26 C5
Pl WOR/ARM LS12 ....26 C5
Rd WOR/ARM LS12 ....26 C5
st PDSY/CALV LS28 ..24 C5
HP/TINH LS16 ....11 F1
S18 ....17 E1
ARM LS12 ....33 C2
ARM LS12 ....35 F1
Av HORS LS18 ....17 F4
Cl HORS LS18 ....17 E1
Garth HORS LS18 ....17 E1
Mt HORS LS18 * 17 F1
HORS LS18 ....17 E1
SM LS9 ....37 F1
WOR/ARM LS12 ....35 E1
Moor Av OSM LS9 ....31 E5
Moor Rd OSM LS9 ....38 A2
n CHAL LS7 ....29 E1
n Gdns CHAL LS7 ....28 D2
n Pl CHAL LS7 ....29 E1
n Ter CHAL LS7 ....29 E1
n Vw CHAL LS7 ....29 E1
ton Gv
CALV LS28 ....32 D1
ton St PDSY/CALV LS28 ..32 C1
nd St OSM LS9 ....37 E2
Pl OSM LS9 ....37 F1
n Ter OSM LS9 ....37 F1
ter MOR LS27 ....46 B1
rt Dr MOR LS27 ....46 B1
Pl LDS LS1 ....2 C4
w Gn WOR/ARM LS12 ..35 F3
w Gv WOR/ARM LS12 ..35 F3
w Vw WOR/ARM LS12 ..35 F3
ck Cft CHAL LS7 ....20 D4
Av MOR LS27 ....41 E3
Gv BEE/HOL LS11 ....36 A5
st BEE/HOL LS11 ....36 A5
er BEE/HOL LS11 ....36 A5
arm WOR/ARM LS12 ..33 H1
ld East MSTN/BAR LS15 ..38 C1
eld West MSTN/BAR LS15 ..38 C1
La RHAY LS8 ....29 F1
ls La OSM LS9 ....29 H3
ls Park Av OSM LS9 * ..29 H3
ls Park Ter OSM LS9 ..29 H3
ls Park Vw OSM LS9 ..29 H3
Pl RHAY LS8 ....29 F1
ls Rd RHAY LS8 ....29 F1
a PDSY/CALV LS28 ....32 D1
ark Mt WOR/ARM LS12 ..33 G1
RHAY LS8 ....29 F1

Hares Mt RHAY LS8 ....29 E1
Hares Rd RHAY LS8 ....29 E1
Hares Ter RHAY LS8 ....29 E1
Hares Vw RHAY LS8 ....29 E1
Harewood St LDSU LS2 ....3 H4
Harewood Wy BRAM LS13 ..23 H3
Hargreaves Cl MOR LS27 ....46 A4
Harker Ter PDSY/CALV LS28 ..24 B4
Harlech Av BEE/HOL LS11 ..42 B1
Harlech Crs BEE/HOL LS11 ..42 B1
Harlech Gv BEE/HOL LS11 ..42 B1
Harlech Mt BEE/HOL LS11 ..42 A1
Harlech Park Ct BEE/HOL LS11 ..42 B1
Harlech Rd BEE/HOL LS11 ..42 B1
Harlech St BEE/HOL LS11 ..42 B1
Harlech Ter BEE/HOL LS11 ..42 B1
Harley Cl BRAM LS13 ....25 E5
Harley Ct BRAM LS13 ....25 E5
Harley Dr BRAM LS13 ....25 E5
Harley Gdns PDSY/CALV LS28 ..25 E5
Harley Gn BRAM LS13 ....25 E5
Harley Ri BRAM LS13 ....25 E5
Harley Rd BRAM LS13 ....25 E5
Harley Ter BRAM LS13 ....25 E5
Harley Vw BRAM LS13 ....25 E5
Harley Wk BRAM LS13 ....25 E5
Harlington Ct MOR LS27 ....46 C4
Harlington Rd MOR LS27 ....46 C4
Harlow Ct RHAY LS8 ....22 A3
Harold Av HDGY LS6 ....27 G3
Harold Gdns MOR LS27 ....47 E1
Harold Mt HDGY LS6 ....27 G3
Harold Pl HDGY LS6 ....27 G3
Harold Rd HDGY LS6 ....27 G3
Harold Sq HDGY LS6 ....27 G3
Harold St HDGY LS6 ....27 G3
Harold Ter HDGY LS6 ....27 G3
Harold Wk HDGY LS6 ....27 G3
Harper La RHAY LS8 ....8 D1
Harper St LDSU LS2 ....3 J5
Harrier Wy MOR LS27 ....47 F2
Harriet St BRAM LS13 ....28 D2
Harrison Crs OSM LS9 ....30 B4
Harrisons Av PDSY/CALV LS28 ..24 D3
Harrison St LDS LS1 ....3 H3
Harrogate Rd AL/HA/HU LS17 ..13 H5
  CHAL LS7 * 20 C4
  YEA LS19 ....8 D5
Harrogate Vw AL/HA/HU LS17 ..15 E2
Harrop Av MOR LS27 ....46 D4
Harrop La MOR LS27 ....46 D4
Harrop Ter MOR LS27 ....46 D4
Harrowby Crs BHP/TINH LS16 ..18 D3
Harrowby Rd BHP/TINH LS16 ..18 D3
Hartley Av HDGY LS6 ....28 B1
Hartley Gdns HDGY LS6 ....28 B1
Hartley Gv HDGY LS6 ....28 A1
Hartley Hl LDSU LS2 ....3 H2
Hartley Pl MOR LS27 * 46 D2
Hartley St MOR LS27 ....46 D2
Hartwell Rd HDGY LS6 ....27 G3
Harwill Ap MOR LS27 ....41 E4
Harwill Av MOR LS27 ....41 E4
Harwill Cft MOR LS27 ....41 E4
Harwill Gv MOR LS27 ....41 E4
Harwill Ri MOR LS27 ....41 E4
Harwill Rd MOR LS27 ....41 E4
Haslewood Cl OSM LS9 ....29 E5
Haslewood Dene OSM LS9 ....29 F5
Haslewood Dr OSM LS9 ....29 F5
Haslewood Gdns OSM LS9 ..29 F5
Haslewood Gn OSM LS9 ....29 F5
Haslewood Ms OSM LS9 ....29 F5
Haslewood Pl OSM LS9 ....29 F5
Haslewood Sq OSM LS9 ....29 F5
Haslewood Vw OSM LS9 ....29 F5
Hastings Ct AL/HA/HU LS17 ..15 G3
Hathaway La SCFT LS14 ....23 F2
Hathaway Ms SCFT LS14 ....23 F1
Hauxwell Dr YEA LS19 ....8 D1
Haven Cha BHP/TINH LS16 ..11 F4
Haven Ct BHP/TINH LS16 ....11 F4
Haven Cft BHP/TINH LS16 ..11 F4
Haven Garth BHP/TINH LS16 ..11 F4
Haven Gn BHP/TINH LS16 ....11 F4
Haven Mt BHP/TINH LS16 ..11 E4
Haven Ri BHP/TINH LS16 ....11 F4
The Haven MSTN/BAR LS15 ..11 F4
Haven Vw BHP/TINH LS16 ..11 F4
Havercroft WOR/ARM LS12 ..34 A3
Haw Av YEA LS19 ....6 A4
Hawkhill Av GSLY LS20 ....4 D4
Hawkhill Dr MSTN/BAR LS15 ..31 F2
Hawkhill Gdns MSTN/BAR LS15 ..31 F2
Hawkhills CHAL LS7 ....20 C3
Hawkhurst Rd WOR/ARM LS12 ..35 E2
Hawkins Dr CHAL LS7 ....3 F1
Hawkshead Crs SCFT LS14 ..30 D2
Hawksley Ct MOR LS27 ....40 B4
Hawk's Nest Gdns East
  AL/HA/HU LS17 ....13 H3
Hawk's Nest Gdns South
  AL/HA/HU LS17 ....13 H3
Hawk's Nest Gdns West
  AL/HA/HU LS17 ....13 H3
Hawkstone Av GSLY LS20 ....4 C5
Hawkstone Vw GSLY LS20 ....4 C5
Hawkswood Av KSTL LS5 ....18 A3
Hawkswood Crs KSTL LS5 ..18 A3
Hawkswood Gv KSTL LS5 ..18 A4
Hawkswood Mt KSTL LS5 ..18 A3
Hawkswood Pl KSTL LS5 ..18 A4
Hawkswood St KSTL LS5 ..18 B4
Hawkswood Ter KSTL LS5 ..18 A4
Hawksworth Cl ILK LS29 ....4 A1

Hawksworth Dr ILK LS29 ....4 A1
Hawksworth Rd HORS LS18 ..17 H5
Haw La YEA LS19 ....6 A4
Hawley Cl MID LS10 ....48 A5
Hawley Wy MOR LS27 ....46 B4
Haworth La YEA LS19 ....5 H5
Hawthorn Av YEA LS19 ....5 H5
Hawthorn Ct EARD/LOFT WF3 ..50 A5
Hawthorn Crs CHAL LS7 * 20 D3
Hawthorn Dr BRAM LS13 ....16 B5
  YEA LS19 ....6 A4
Hawthorne Gdns
  BHP/TINH LS16 ....11 H2
Hawthorne Ri SCFT LS14 ....23 G2
Hawthorn Gv CHAL LS7 ....20 D3
Hawthorn Mt CHAL LS7 ....16 B5
  RTHW LS26 ....50 D2
Hawthorn La CHAL LS7 * 20 D3
Hawthorn Mt CHAL LS7 * ..20 D3
Hawthorn Rd CHAL LS7 * 20 D3
Hawthorn Vw CHAL LS7 * 20 D3
Haydn's Ter WOR/ARM LS12 ..35 E2
Hayfield Ter WOR/ARM LS12 ..35 E2
Hayleigh Av BRAM LS13 ....25 G2
Hayleigh Mt BRAM LS13 ....25 G2
Hayleigh St BRAM LS13 ....25 G2
Hazel Ct RTHW LS26 ....50 D2
Hazelhurst Ct PDSY/CALV LS28 ..32 D1
Headingley Av HDGY LS6 ....19 E5
Headingley Crs HDGY LS6 ..27 F1
Headingley La HDGY LS6 ....27 F1
Headingley Mt HDGY LS6 ....19 E5
Headingley Vw HDGY LS6 ..27 F1
The Headrow LDS LS1 ....3 F3
Heath Crs BEE/HOL LS11 ....35 G5
Heathcroft Bank BEE/HOL LS11 ..41 G1
Heathcroft Crs BEE/HOL LS11 ..41 G1
Heathcroft Dr BEE/HOL LS11 ..41 G1
Heathcroft Ri BEE/HOL LS11 ..41 G1
Heathcroft V BEE/HOL LS11 ..41 G1
Heathercroft CHAL LS7 ....21 E4
Heather Gdns BRAM LS13 ....26 A5
Heather Gv BRAM LS13 * 25 H5
Heathfield BHP/TINH LS16 ..11 H2
Heath Gv BEE/HOL LS11 ....35 F4
  PDSY/CALV LS28 ....32 A1
Heath Mt BEE/HOL LS11 ....35 G5
Heath Pl BEE/HOL LS11 ....35 G5
Heath Ri BEE/HOL LS11 ....35 G5
Heath Rd BEE/HOL LS11 ....35 G5
Heaton Av WOR/ARM LS12 ..2 E7
Hebden Ap SCFT LS14 ....23 F4
Hebden Cl SCFT LS14 * 23 F4
Hebden Gn SCFT LS14 ....23 F4
Heddon St HDGY LS6 ....19 G4
Hedley Cha WOR/ARM LS12 ..35 G1
Hedley Gdns WOR/ARM LS12 ..35 G1
Hedley Gn WOR/ARM LS12 ..35 G1
Heights Bank WOR/ARM LS12 ..34 B1
Heights Cl WOR/ARM LS12 ..26 A5
Heights Dr WOR/ARM LS12 ..34 A1
Heights Garth WOR/ARM LS12 ..34 A1
Heights La AL/HA/HU LS17 ..12 A5
Heights Pde WOR/ARM LS12 ..34 B1
Heights Wy WOR/ARM LS12 ..34 B1
Helmsley Ct MID LS10 ....48 C2
Helmsley Dr BHP/TINH LS16 ..18 D3
Helmsley Rd BHP/TINH LS16 ..18 D3
Helston Cl MID LS10 ....42 A5
Helston Garth MID LS10 ....48 A1
Helston Pl MID LS10 ....42 A5
Helston Rd MID LS10 ....42 A5
Helston Sq MID LS10 ....42 A5
Helston St MID LS10 ....41 H5
Helston Wk MID LS10 ....47 H1
Helston Wy MID LS10 ....42 A5
Hemingway Cl MID LS10 * ..37 G5
Hemingway Garth MID LS10 * ..37 G5
Hemingway Gn MID LS10 * ..37 G5
Henbury St LDSU LS2 ....3 K1
Henconner Av CHAL LS7 ....20 C4
Henconner Crs CHAL LS7 ....20 C4
Henconner Dr CHAL LS7 ....20 C4
Henconner Gdns CHAL LS7 ..20 C4
Henconner Gn CHAL LS7 ....20 C4
Henconner La BRAM LS13 ..25 H4
  CHAL LS7 ....20 C4
Henconner Rd CHAL LS7 ....20 C4
Henley Av BRAM LS13 ....9 F4
Henley Cl YEA LS19 ....9 F4
Henley Crs BRAM LS13 ....9 F4
Henley Dr YEA LS19 ....9 F4
Henley Gv BRAM LS13 ....9 E4
Henley Hl YEA LS19 ....9 F4
Henley Mt YEA LS19 ....9 F4
Henley Pl BRAM LS13 ....25 G3
Henley Rd BRAM LS13 ....25 G3
Henley St BRAM LS13 ....25 G3
Henley Ter BRAM LS13 ....25 G3
Henley Vw BRAM LS13 ....25 G3
Henry Av WOR/ARM LS12 ..34 D3
Henry St BRAM LS13 ....2 B1
Henshaw Av YEA LS19 ....8 D1
Henshaw Crs YEA LS19 ....8 D1
Henshaw La YEA LS19 ....8 D1
Henshaw Ov YEA LS19 ....8 D1
Hepton Ct OSM LS9 ....29 G4
Hepworth Av MOR LS27 ....40 D3
Hepworth Crs MOR LS27 ....40 D3
Herbalist St WOR/ARM LS12 ..35 G2
Hermon Av KSTL LS5 ....18 B4
Hermon St KSTL LS5 ....18 B4
Heron Cl AL/HA/HU LS17 ..14 B3
Heron Ct MOR LS27 ....46 C4
Heron Gv AL/HA/HU LS17 ..14 C3
Hertford Cha MSTN/BAR LS15 ..39 G2
Hertford Cl MSTN/BAR LS15 ..39 G2

Hertford Cft MSTN/BAR LS15 ..39 H2
Hertford Fold MSTN/BAR LS15 ..39 G2
Hertford Lawn MSTN/BAR LS15 ..39 G2
Hesketh Av KSTL LS5 ....26 C1
Hesketh Mt KSTL LS5 ....18 C5
Hesketh Pl KSTL LS5 ....18 C5
Hesketh Rd KSTL LS5 ....18 C5
Hesketh Ter KSTL LS5 ....26 C1
Hessle Av HDGY LS6 ....27 G2
Hessle Mt HDGY LS6 * 27 G2
Hessle Pl HDGY LS6 ....27 G2
Hessle Rd HDGY LS6 ....27 G2
Hessle Ter HDGY LS6 ....27 G2
Hessle Vw HDGY LS6 ....27 G2
Hessle Wk HDGY LS6 ....27 G2
Hetton Rd RHAY LS8 ....29 H1
High Ash Av AL/HA/HU LS17 ..14 A2
High Ash Crs AL/HA/HU LS17 ..14 A2
High Ash Dr AL/HA/HU LS17 ..14 A2
High Ash Mt AL/HA/HU LS17 ..14 A2
High Bank Ap MSTN/BAR LS15 ..39 H1
High Bank Cl MSTN/BAR LS15 ..31 H5
High Bank Ga MSTN/BAR LS15 ..39 H1
High Bank Pl MSTN/BAR LS15 ..39 H1
High Bank Vw MSTN/BAR LS15 ..39 H1
High Bank Wy MSTN/BAR LS15 ..39 H1
Highbury La HDGY LS6 ....19 G4
Highbury Pl BRAM LS13 ....19 G4
Highbury Rd HDGY LS6 ....19 G4
Highbury Ter HDGY LS6 ....19 G4
High Cliffe BULY LS4 ....27 E2
Highcliffe Rd MOR LS27 ....46 B2
High Cl GSLY LS20 ....4 B4
High Ct LDSU LS2 ....3 J5
High Court La LDSU LS2 ....3 J5
Highcroft Cl PDSY/CALV LS28 ..24 A5
Higher Grange Rd
  PDSY/CALV LS28 ....24 C5
Highfield EARD/LOFT WF3 ..47 F5
Highfield Cl WOR/ARM LS12 ..35 F3
Highfield Cr MOR LS27 ....40 D3
Highfield Crs PDSY/CALV LS28 ..24 B5
  RTHW LS26 ....45 G4
  WOR/ARM LS12 ....35 F2
Highfield Dr YEA LS19 ....9 E4
Highfield Gdns WOR/ARM LS12 ..35 F3
Highfield Garth WOR/ARM LS12 ..35 F3
Highfield Gn PDSY/CALV LS28 ..24 B5
Highfield La RTHW LS26 * 45 C5
Highfield Pl MOR LS27 ....40 D3
Highfield Rd BRAM LS13 ....25 H3
  PDSY/CALV LS28 ....24 A5
Highfield St BRAM LS13 * 25 H3
Highfield Ter PDSY/CALV LS28 ..24 A5
Highfield Vw MOR LS27 ....40 A4
Highfold YEA LS19 ....8 D3
Highlands Cl MID LS10 ....43 F4
Highlands Dr MID LS10 ....43 F4
Highlands Gv MID LS10 ....43 F4
Highlands Wk MID LS10 ....43 F4
Highlea Cl YEA LS19 ....8 B2
High Moor Av AL/HA/HU LS17 ..14 A5
High Moor Cl AL/HA/HU LS17 ..14 A5
High Moor Crs AL/HA/HU LS17 ..14 A5
High Moor Dr AL/HA/HU LS17 ..14 A5
High Ridge Av RTHW LS26 ..44 B4
High Ridge Ct RTHW LS26 ..44 B4
High Ridge Pk RTHW LS26 ..44 B4
High Royds Dr ILK LS29 ....4 A1
High St MOR LS27 ....46 D3
  PDSY/CALV LS28 ....24 B2
  YEA LS19 ....5 H5
Highthorne Ct AL/HA/HU LS17 ..14 B3
Highthorne Dr AL/HA/HU LS17 ..14 C3
Highthorne Gv
  WOR/ARM LS12 ....26 C5
Highthorne Mt AL/HA/HU LS17 ..14 B3
Highthorne St WOR/ARM LS12 ..26 C5
Highthorne Vw
  WOR/ARM LS12 * 26 C5
Highway GSLY LS20 ....4 B3
Highwood Av AL/HA/HU LS17 ..13 G5
Highwood Crs AL/HA/HU LS17 ..13 G5
Highwood Gv AL/HA/HU LS17 ..13 G5
Hillary Pl LDSU LS2 ....28 B5
Hillcourt Av BRAM LS13 ....25 G1
Hillcourt Cft BRAM LS13 ....25 G1
Hillcourt Dr BRAM LS13 ....25 G1
Hillcourt Gv BRAM LS13 ....25 G1
Hill Crs YEA LS19 ....9 E2
Hillcrest Av CHAL LS7 ....20 D3
Hillcrest Mt BHP/TINH LS16 ..11 E3
Hillcrest Pl CHAL LS7 ....29 E1
Hillcrest Ri BHP/TINH LS16 ..11 E3
Hill End Crs WOR/ARM LS12 ..26 B5
Hill End Rd WOR/ARM LS12 ..34 A4
Hill Gv South MID LS10 ....43 F4
Hillidge Rd MID LS10 ....36 D4
Hillidge Sq MID LS10 ....36 D4
Hillingdon Wy AL/HA/HU LS17 ..13 G2
Hill Mount Pleasant MID LS10 ..48 C1
Hill Rise Av BRAM LS13 ....25 G1
Hill Rise Gv BRAM LS13 ....25 G1
Hillside Av GSLY LS20 ....4 C5
Hill Side Buildings
  BEE/HOL LS11 ....36 A5
Hillside Ct CHAL LS7 ....21 E5
Hill Side Mt PDSY/CALV LS28 ..33 E1
Hillside Rd CHAL LS7 ....20 D2
Hillside Vw PDSY/CALV LS28 ..32 D1
Hill St BEE/HOL LS11 ....36 A5
  OSM LS9 ....29 E4
Hillthorpe Ct MID LS10 ....48 C3
Hillthorpe Ri PDSY/CALV LS28 ..32 C3

Hillthorpe Rd PDSY/CALV LS28 ..32 C3
Hillthorpe Sq PDSY/CALV LS28 ..32 B3
Hillthorpe St PDSY/CALV LS28 * ..32 C3
Hillthorpe Ter PDSY/CALV LS28 * ..32 C3
Hill Top PDSY/CALV LS28 ....32 C3
Hill Top Cl WOR/ARM LS12 ..29 F1
Hill Top Mt RHAY LS8 ....29 F1
Hill Top Pl HDGY LS6 ....27 H5
  RHAY LS8 ....29 F1
Hill Top Rd WOR/ARM LS12 ..26 B5
Hill View Mt CHAL LS7 * 20 D3
Hill View Pl CHAL LS7 * 20 D3
Hill View Ter CHAL LS7 * 20 D3
Hillway GSLY LS20 ....4 C5
Hilton Gra BHP/TINH LS16 ..7 F4
Hilton Gv RHAY LS8 ....21 F5
Hilton Ms BHP/TINH LS16 ..7 F1
Hilton Pl RHAY LS8 ....29 F1
Hilton Rd RHAY LS8 ....29 F1
Hilton St RHAY LS8 * 29 F1
Hilton Ter RHAY LS8 * 29 F1
Hindle Pl MOR LS27 * 40 D4
Hinsley Ct HDGY LS6 ....27 G1
Hird St BEE/HOL LS11 ....36 A5
Hobberley La AL/HA/HU LS17 ..15 H4
Hodgson Av AL/HA/HU LS17 ..14 C4
Hodgson Crs AL/HA/HU LS17 ..14 C4
Hodgson Pl MOR LS27 ....40 D4
Hodgson St MOR LS27 ....47 E5
Holbeck La BEE/HOL LS11 ....35 H3
Holbeck Moor Rd BEE/HOL LS11 ..36 A3
Holbeck Towers BEE/HOL LS11 ..36 A4
Holborn Ap HDGY LS6 ....28 A2
Holborn Ct HDGY LS6 ....28 A2
Holborn Gdns HDGY LS6 * ..28 A2
Holborn Gn HDGY LS6 ....28 A2
Holborn Gv HDGY LS6 ....28 A2
Holborn St HDGY LS6 ....28 A2
Holborn Ter HDGY LS6 ....28 A2
Holborn Vw HDGY LS6 ....28 A2
Holborn Wk HDGY LS6 ....28 A2
Holdforth Cl WOR/ARM LS12 ..35 G4
Holdforth Gdns WOR/ARM LS12 ..35 G4
Holdforth Gn WOR/ARM LS12 ..35 G4
Holdforth Pl WOR/ARM LS12 * ..35 G1
Hollin Ct BHP/TINH LS16 ..19 F3
Hollin Dr BHP/TINH LS16 ..19 E3
Hollin Gdns BHP/TINH LS16 ..19 E3
Hollin Hill Av RHAY LS8 ....22 A5
Hollin La BHP/TINH LS16 ..19 E3
Hollin Mt BHP/TINH LS16 ..19 F3
Hollin Park Av RHAY LS8 ....22 B5
Hollin Park Crs RHAY LS8 ....22 B5
Hollin Park Mt RHAY LS8 ....22 B5
Hollin Park Pl RHAY LS8 ....22 A5
Hollin Park Rd RHAY LS8 ....22 A5
Hollin Park Ter RHAY LS8 ....22 B5
Hollin Rd BHP/TINH LS16 ..19 F3
Hollis Pl BVRD LS3 ....2 A3
Holly Av BHP/TINH LS16 ..10 D4
Holly Bank HDGY LS6 ....19 F4
Holly Cl MID LS10 ....48 B2
Hollycroft Ct BHP/TINH LS16 ..10 D4
Holly Dr BHP/TINH LS16 ..10 D4
Holly Park Mills
  PDSY/CALV LS28 ....24 C1
Hollyshaw Crs MSTN/BAR LS15 ..31 G5
Hollyshaw Gv MSTN/BAR LS15 ..31 G5
Hollyshaw La MSTN/BAR LS15 ..31 G5
Hollyshaw Ter MSTN/BAR LS15 ..31 G5
Hollyshaw Wk MSTN/BAR LS15 ..31 G4
Hollywell Gv WOR/ARM LS12 ..26 D5
Hollywell La WOR/ARM LS12 ..26 D5
Holme Farm Ct WOR/ARM LS12 ..33 H5
Holmes St BEE/HOL LS11 ....36 C2
Holme Well Rd MID LS10 ....49 E1
Holmfield Dr RHAY LS8 ....22 A5
Holmsley Crest RTHW LS26 ..45 E4
Holmsley Field Ct RTHW LS26 ..45 F5
Holmsley Field La RTHW LS26 ..45 F5
Holmsley Garth RTHW LS26 ..45 F5
Holmsley La RTHW LS26 ....45 E4
Holmwood Av HDGY LS6 ....19 G2
Holmwood Cl HDGY LS6 ....19 G2
Holmwood Crs HDGY LS6 ..19 G2
Holmwood Dr HDGY LS6 ....19 G2
Holmwood Gv HDGY LS6 ..19 G2
Holmwood Mt HDGY LS6 ..19 H2
Holroyd St CHAL LS7 ....28 D3
Holt Av BHP/TINH LS16 ....12 A2
Holt Cl BHP/TINH LS16 ....12 A3
Holtdale Ap BHP/TINH LS16 ..11 F2
Holtdale Av BHP/TINH LS16 ..11 F2
Holtdale Cl BHP/TINH LS16 ..11 F2
Holtdale Cft BHP/TINH LS16 ..11 F2
Holtdale Dr BHP/TINH LS16 ..11 F2
Holtdale Fold BHP/TINH LS16 ..11 F2
Holtdale Garth BHP/TINH LS16 ..11 F2
Holtdale Gdns BHP/TINH LS16 ..11 F2
Holtdale Ga BHP/TINH LS16 ..12 A2
Holtdale Gn BHP/TINH LS16 ..11 F2
Holtdale Gv BHP/TINH LS16 ..11 F2
Holtdale Lawn BHP/TINH LS16 ..11 F2
Holtdale Pl BHP/TINH LS16 ..11 F2
Holtdale Rd BHP/TINH LS16 ..11 F2
Holtdale Vw BHP/TINH LS16 ..11 F2
Holtdale Wy BHP/TINH LS16 ..11 F2
Holt Farm Cl BHP/TINH LS16 ..11 F2
Holt Farm Ri BHP/TINH LS16 ..11 F2
Holt Gdns BHP/TINH LS16 ..12 A2
Holt Garth BHP/TINH LS16 ..12 A2
Holt Ga BHP/TINH LS16 ....11 F2
Holt La BHP/TINH LS16 ....12 A2
Holt Park Ap BHP/TINH LS16 ..11 F2
Holt Park Cl BHP/TINH LS16 ..11 F2
Holt Park Crs BHP/TINH LS16 ..11 F2
Holt Park Dr BHP/TINH LS16 ..11 F2
Holt Park Gdns BHP/TINH LS16 ..11 F2
Holt Park Ga BHP/TINH LS16 ..11 F2

Holt Park Gra *BHP/TINH* LS16 ......11 G2
Holt Park Gn *BHP/TINH* LS16 ......11 G2
Holt Park Gv *BHP/TINH* LS16 ......11 F2
Holt Park La *BHP/TINH* LS16 ......11 G2
Holt Park Ri *BHP/TINH* LS16 ......11 G2
Holt Park V *BHP/TINH* LS16 ......11 G2
Holt Park Vw *BHP/TINH* LS16 ......11 G2
Holt Ri *BHP/TINH* LS16 ......11 G2
Holt Rd *BHP/TINH* LS16 ......11 G2
Holt Vw *BHP/TINH* LS16 ......11 F2
Holt Wy *BHP/TINH* LS16 ......11 F2
Holywell La *AL/HA/HU* LS17 ......15 F2
Homefield Av *MOR* LS27 ......46 C4
Home Lea *RTHW* LS26 ......44 B4
Home Lea Dr *RTHW* LS26 ......44 B4
Hopefield Cha *EARD/LOFT* WF3 ...49 H2
Hopefield Ct *EARD/LOFT* WF3 .....49 H2
Hopefield Crs *RTHW* LS26 ......49 H2
Hopefield Dr *EARD/LOFT* WF3 ....49 H2
Hopefield Gdns
   EARD/LOFT WF3 ......49 H2
Hopefield Gn *RTHW* LS26 ......49 H2
Hopefield Gv *EARD/LOFT* WF3 * ...49 H2
Hopefield Ms *EARD/LOFT* WF3 ....49 H2
Hopefield Pl *RTHW* LS26 ......49 H2
Hopefield Vw *RTHW* LS26 ......49 H2
Hopefield Wk *RTHW* LS26 ......49 H2
Hopefield Wy *EARD/LOFT* WF3 ....49 H2
Hope Rd *LDSU* LS2 ......3 K3
Hopes Farm Mt *MID* LS10 * 43 F4
Hopes Farm Rd *MID* LS10 ......43 F4
Hopes Farm Vw *MID* LS10 ......43 F4
Hope St *MOR* LS27 ......46 C2
Hopewell Pl *HDGY* LS6 * 27 G3
Hopewell Vw *MID* LS10 ......48 D1
Hopton Ms *WOR/ARM* LS12 ......34 D1
Hopwood Bank *HORS* LS18 ......10 C5
Hopwood Cl *HORS* LS18 ......10 C5
Hopwood Rd *HORS* LS18 ......10 C5
Hornbeam Wy *SCFT* LS14 ......23 G2
Horsfall St *MOR* LS27 ......46 C2
Horsforth New Rd *BRAM* LS13 ...16 C4
Horton Cl *BRAM* LS13 ......24 D1
Horton Garth *BRAM* LS13 * 24 D1
Horton Ri *BRAM* LS13 ......24 D1
Hospital La *BHP/TINH* LS16 ......11 F5
Hough End Av *BRAM* LS13 ......25 H4
Hough End Cl *BRAM* LS13 * 25 H4
Hough End Ct *BRAM* LS13 ......25 H4
Hough End Gdns *BRAM* LS13 ......25 G4
Hough End Gdns *BRAM* LS13 .....25 G4
Hough End Garth *BRAM* LS13 ....25 G4
Hough End La *BRAM* LS13 ......25 G4
Hough La *BRAM* LS13 ......25 G3
Hough Side *BHP/TINH* LS16 .....25 H4
Houghley Cl *BRAM* LS13 ......26 A3
Houghley Crs *WOR/ARM* LS12 ...26 A3
Houghley La *BRAM* LS13 ......26 A3
Houghley Pl *WOR/ARM* LS12 ....26 B3
Houghley Sq *WOR/ARM* LS12 ....26 B3
Hough Side Cl *PDSY/CALV* LS28 ...33 F1
Hough Side La
   PDSY/CALV LS28 ......33 E1
Hough Side Rd
   PDSY/CALV LS28 ......33 E1
Hough Ter *BRAM* LS13 ......25 G3
Hough Top *BRAM* LS13 ......25 E5
Hough Tree Rd *BRAM* LS13 ......25 G3
Hovingham Av *RHAY* LS8 ......29 G1
Hovingham Gv *RHAY* LS8 ......29 G1
Hovingham Mt *RHAY* LS8 ......29 G1
Hovingham Ter *RHAY* LS8 ......29 G1
Howard Av *MSTN/BAR* LS15 ......38 D1
Howard Ct *MSTN/BAR* LS15 ......38 D1
Howarth Pl *CHAL* LS7 ......3 H1
Howden Gdns *HDGY* LS6 ......27 G3
Howden Pl *HDGY* LS6 ......27 G3
Howley Park Cl *MOR* LS27 ......46 B4
Howley Park Rd *MOR* LS27 ......46 B4
Howley Park Rd East
   MOR LS27 ......46 C5
Howson Cl *GSLY* LS20 ......5 F4
Hoxton Mt *BEE/HOL* LS11 ......35 H5
Hudson Av *OSM* LS9 ......29 G4
Hudson Dr *OSM* LS9 ......29 G4
Hudson Rd *OSM* LS9 ......29 G4
Hudson St *OSM* LS9 ......29 G4
   PDSY/CALV LS28 * 24 B4
Hudswell Rd *MID* LS10 ......41 H4
Hughenden Vw *MOR* LS27 * 40 C5
Hull St *MOR* LS27 ......46 D2
Hunger Hill *MOR* LS27 ......46 D3
Hunger Hills Av *HORS* LS18 ......17 E1
Hunger Hills Dr *HORS* LS18 ......17 E1
Hunslet Green Wy *MID* LS10 ......36 A5
Hunslet Hall Rd *BEE/HOL* LS11 ...36 A4
Hunslet La *MID* LS10 ......3 H7
Hunslet Rd *MID* LS10 ......3 H6
Husler Gv *CHAL* LS7 ......28 D2
Husler Pl *CHAL* LS7 ......28 D2
Hustlers Rw *HDGY* LS6 ......19 G2
Hutchinson's Pl *KSTL* LS5 ......26 C2
Hutton Ter *PDSY/CALV* LS28 ......32 C1
Hyde Park Cl *HDGY* LS6 ......27 H3
Hyde Park Cnr *HDGY* LS6 ......27 H3
Hyde Park Rd *HDGY* LS6 ......27 H3
Hyde Park Ter *HDGY* LS6 ......27 H2
Hyde Pl *LDSU* LS2 ......2 C2
Hyde St *LDSU* LS2 ......2 C2
Hyde Ter *LDSU* LS2 ......2 C2

I

Ibbetson Cl *MOR* LS27 ......40 C4
Ibbetson Ct *MOR* LS27 ......40 C4
Ibbetson Cft *MOR* LS27 ......40 C4
Ibbetson Dr *MOR* LS27 ......40 C4
Ibbetson Ov *MOR* LS27 ......40 C4

Ibbetson Ri *MOR* LS27 * 40 C4
Ibbetson Rd *MOR* LS27 ......40 C4
Ida St *MID* LS10 ......43 G1
Ilford St *MOR* LS27 ......46 D2
Illingworth Cl *YEA* LS19 ......9 E2
Industrial St *OSM* LS9 ......29 F4
Infirmary St *LDS* LS1 ......3 F4
Ingham St *MID* LS10 ......36 D3
Ingle Av *MOR* LS27 ......40 B5
Ingleborough Dr *MOR* LS27 ......47 E4
Ingleby Wy *MID* LS10 ......43 E4
Ingle Crs *MOR* LS27 ......40 B5
Ingle Crs *MOR* LS27 ......46 C1
Ingledew Crs *RHAY* LS8 ......14 D5
Ingledew Dr *RHAY* LS8 ......21 H1
Ingle Gv *MOR* LS27 ......46 C1
Ingle Rw *CHAL* LS7 ......20 C4
Ingleton Cl *BEE/HOL* LS11 ......36 B5
Ingleton Dr *MSTN/BAR* LS15 ......38 C1
Ingleton Gv *BEE/HOL* LS11 ......36 B5
Ingleton Pl *BEE/HOL* LS11 ......36 B5
Ingleton St *BEE/HOL* LS11 ......36 B5
Inglewood Dr *SCFT* LS14 ......31 F2
Inglewood Pl *SCFT* LS14 ......31 F2
Inglewood Ter *HDGY* LS6 ......28 A1
Ingram Cl *BEE/HOL* LS11 ......35 H3
Ingram Cr *BEE/HOL* LS11 ......35 H3
Ingram Ct *BEE/HOL* LS11 ......35 H4
Ingram Gdns *BEE/HOL* LS11 ......35 H3
Ingram Pde *RTHW* LS26 ......50 C1
Ingram Rw *BEE/HOL* LS11 ......36 B2
Ingram Sq *BEE/HOL* LS11 ......36 B2
Ingram Vw *BEE/HOL* LS11 ......35 H3
Ings Av *GSLY* LS20 ......4 D2
Ings Cl *GSLY* LS20 ......4 C2
Ings Crs *GSLY* LS20 ......4 C2
   OSM LS9 ......37 H1
Ings La *GSLY* LS20 ......4 C2
Ings Rd *OSM* LS9 ......37 H1
Inner Ring Rd *LDS* LS1 ......2 D4
   OSM LS9 ......29 E5
Intake La *BRAM* LS13 ......24 D2
   MID LS10 ......48 C3
   YEA LS19 ......9 F4
Intake Mt *MID* LS10 ......48 C2
Intake Rd *PDSY/CALV* LS28 ......24 B4
Intake Sq *MID* LS10 ......48 C3
Intake Vw *MID* LS10 ......48 C3
Intercity Wy *PDSY/CALV* LS28 ...25 E4
Intermezzo Dr *MID* LS10 ......43 H2
Invertrees Av *YEA* LS19 ......9 E3
Ireland Crs *BHP/TINH* LS16 ......11 F4
Ironwood Ap *SCFT* LS14 ......31 E2
Ironwood Crs *SCFT* LS14 ......31 E2
Ironwood Vw *SCFT* LS14 ......31 E1
Irwin Ap *MSTN/BAR* LS15 ......30 D1
Irwin St *PDSY/CALV* LS28 ......24 B5
Islay Cl *RTHW* LS26 ......51 E1
Ivegate *YEA* LS19 ......8 D1
Ivesen Garth *BHP/TINH* LS16 ....11 F5
Ivesen Ap *BHP/TINH* LS16 ......11 F5
Iveson Cr *BHP/TINH* LS16 ......11 F5
Iveson Crs *BHP/TINH* LS16 ......11 F5
Iveson Dr *BHP/TINH* LS16 ......11 F5
Iveson Gdns *BHP/TINH* LS16 ....11 F5
Iveson Gn *BHP/TINH* LS16 ......11 F5
Iveson Lawn *BHP/TINH* LS16 ....11 G5
Iveson Ri *BHP/TINH* LS16 ......11 F5
Iveson Rd *BHP/TINH* LS16 ......11 F5
Ivory St *BEE/HOL* LS11 ......36 C3
Ivy Av *OSM* LS9 ......29 H5
Ivy Cha *BRAM* LS13 ......33 F1
Ivy Crs *OSM* LS9 ......29 G5
Ivy Gdns *BRAM* LS13 ......33 F1
Ivy Garth *CHAL* LS7 ......20 D4
Ivy Gv *OSM* LS9 ......29 G5
Ivy Mt *OSM* LS9 ......29 G5
Ivy Pl *BRAM* LS13 ......25 H1
Ivy Rd *OSM* LS9 ......37 G1
Ivy St *OSM* LS9 ......29 G5
Ivy Vw *OSM* LS9 ......29 G5

J

Jackie Smart Ct *CHAL* LS7 ......29 E2
Jack La *BEE/HOL* LS11 ......36 B3
   MID LS10 ......36 D4
Jackman Dr *HORS* LS18 ......17 H3
Jackson Av *RHAY* LS8 ......21 H1
Jackson Rd *CHAL* LS7 ......28 C2
Jacob St *LDSU* LS2 ......3 H2
James Av *RHAY* LS8 ......21 F2
James St *YEA* LS19 ......8 D3
Jaques Cl *HDGY* LS6 ......26 D1
Jarvis Sq *EARD/LOFT* WF3 ......49 G3
Jarvis Wk *EARD/LOFT* WF3 ......49 G3
Jean Av *MSTN/BAR* LS15 ......39 E1
Jenkinson Cl *MID* LS10 * 36 A3
Jenkinson Lawn *BEE/HOL* LS11 ...36 A3
Jenkinsons Pl *MID* LS10 ......42 D3
John Charles Wy
   WOR/ARM LS12 ......35 H4
John O'Gaunts Wk *RTHW* LS26 ...44 D5
Johnson Ter *MOR* LS27 ......46 D2
Johnston St *HDGY* LS6 ......28 B2
John St *HDGY* LS6 ......27 H1
   YEA LS19 ......8 D5
Joseph St *MID* LS10 ......37 E4
Josephs Well *LDS* LS1 * 2 D3
Jubilee Ct *MOR* LS27 ......46 D2
Jubilee St *MOR* LS27 ......46 D2
Jubilee Ter *MOR* LS27 ......46 D2
Jumbles Ct *EARD/LOFT* WF3 ......50 A5
Jumbles La *EARD/LOFT* WF3 ......50 A5
Junction St *MID* LS10 ......36 C2
Juniper Av *RTHW* LS26 ......45 H4
Juniper Pl *OSM* LS9 ......29 H4

K

Karnac Rd *RHAY* LS8 ......29 F1
Kay Cl *MOR* LS27 ......40 B4
Kedleston Rd *RHAY* LS8 ......14 B4
Keelham Dr *YEA* LS19 ......9 E3
Keel Moorings *BRAM* LS13 ......16 D5
Keeper La *BOW* BD4 ......32 B5
Keeton St *OSM* LS9 ......29 G5
Keighley Pl *PDSY/CALV* LS28 ......24 C3
Kelcliffe Av *GSLY* LS20 ......5 E3
Kelcliffe La *GSLY* LS20 ......4 D2
Keldholme Cl *BRAM* LS13 ......16 D5
Keldholme Rd *BRAM* LS13 * 16 D5
Kellett Av *WOR/ARM* LS12 ......35 E4
Kellett Crs *WOR/ARM* LS12 ......35 E4
Kellett Dr *WOR/ARM* LS12 ......35 E4
Kellett Gv *WOR/ARM* LS12 ......35 E4
Kellett La *WOR/ARM* LS12 ......34 D3
Kellett Mt *WOR/ARM* LS12 ......35 E4
Kellett Pl *WOR/ARM* LS12 * 35 E4
Kellett Rd *WOR/ARM* LS12 ......35 E4
Kellett Ter *WOR/ARM* LS12 * 35 E4
Kellett Wk *WOR/ARM* LS12 ......35 E5
Kelmscott Av *MSTN/BAR* LS15 ...31 H2
Kelmscott Crs *MSTN/BAR* LS15 ...31 H2
Kelmscott Gdns *MSTN/BAR* LS15 ..31 H2
Kelmscott Gn *MSTN/BAR* LS15 ...31 H2
Kelmscott Gv *MSTN/BAR* LS15 ...31 H2
Kelmscott La *MSTN/BAR* LS15 ...31 H2
Kelsall Av *HDGY* LS6 ......27 G4
Kelsall Gv *HDGY* LS6 ......27 G4
Kelsall Pl *HDGY* LS6 ......27 G3
Kelsall Rd *HDGY* LS6 ......27 G3
Kelsall Ter *HDGY* LS6 ......27 G3
Kelso Gdns *LDSU* LS2 ......2 B1
Kelso Pl *LDSU* LS2 ......27 H3
Kelso Rd *LDSU* LS2 ......2 B1
Kelso St *LDSU* LS2 ......2 B2
Kendal Bank *BVRD* LS3 ......2 B2
Kendal Cl *BVRD* LS3 ......2 B2
Kendal Dr *MSTN/BAR* LS15 ......38 C2
Kendal La *BVRD* LS3 ......2 B2
Kendal Ri *BVRD* LS3 ......2 B3
Kendal Rd *BVRD* LS3 ......2 B2
Kendal Wk *BVRD* LS3 * 2 B2
Kendell St *MID* LS10 ......3 H6
Kenilworth Rd *WOR/ARM* LS12 ...34 D1
Kennerleigh Av *MSTN/BAR* LS15 ..31 H4
Kennerleigh Crs
   MSTN/BAR LS15 ......31 H4
Kennerleigh Dr *MSTN/BAR* LS15 ..31 G4
Kennerleigh Garth
   MSTN/BAR LS15 ......31 H4
Kennerleigh Gln
   MSTN/BAR LS15 ......31 G4
Kennerleigh Gv *MSTN/BAR* LS15 ..31 H4
Kennerleigh Ri *MSTN/BAR* LS15 ..31 H4
Kennerleigh Wk
   MSTN/BAR LS15 ......31 G4
Kenneth St *BEE/HOL* LS11 ......35 H3
Kensington Cl *MID* LS10 ......43 F3
Kensington Gdns *MID* LS10 ......43 F4
Kensington St *HDGY* LS6 ......27 G2
Kensington Wy *MID* LS10 ......43 F4
Kent Av *PDSY/CALV* LS28 ......33 E1
Kent Cl *PDSY/CALV* LS28 ......33 E1
Kent Crs *PDSY/CALV* LS28 ......33 E1
Kent Dr *PDSY/CALV* LS28 ......33 E1
Kentmere Ap *SCFT* LS14 ......22 D3
Kentmere Av *SCFT* LS14 ......22 D3
Kentmere Crs *SCFT* LS14 ......22 D4
Kentmere Gdns *SCFT* LS14 ......22 D4
Kentmere Gn *SCFT* LS14 ......22 D4
Kentmere Gv *SCFT* LS14 ......22 D3
Kentmere Ri *SCFT* LS14 ......23 E5
Kent Rd *PDSY/CALV* LS28 ......33 D1
Kenworthy Cl *BHP/TINH* LS16 ...11 G2
Kenworthy Gdns
   BHP/TINH LS16 ......11 G2
Kenworthy Garth
   BHP/TINH LS16 ......11 G2
Kenworthy Ga *BHP/TINH* LS16 ...11 G2
Kenworthy Ri *BHP/TINH* LS16 ...11 G2
Kenworthy V *BHP/TINH* LS16 ....11 G2
Kepler Gv *RHAY* LS8 ......29 E3
Kepler Mt *RHAY* LS8 ......29 E3
Kepler Ter *RHAY* LS8 ......29 E3
Kepstorn Cl *KSTL* LS5 ......18 C5
Kepstorn Ri *KSTL* LS5 ......18 D5
Kepstorn Rd *BHP/TINH* LS16 ....18 D5
Kerry Hi *HORS* LS18 ......17 F1
Kerry St *HORS* LS18 ......17 F1
Kestrel Cl *AL/HA/HU* LS17 ......14 B3
Kestrel Garth *MOR* LS27 ......46 B1
Kestrel Gv *AL/HA/HU* LS17 ......14 B3
Kidacre St *BEE/HOL* LS11 ......36 C5
Kilburn Rd *WOR/ARM* LS12 ......35 G4
Kildare Ter *WOR/ARM* LS12 ......35 G4
Killingbeck Br *OSM* LS9 ......30 B4
Killingbeck Dr *SCFT* LS14 ......30 C4
Kimberley Av *OSM* LS9 ......29 H5
Kimberley Rd *OSM* LS9 ......29 H5
Kimberley Vw *OSM* LS9 ......29 H5
King Alfred's Dr *HDGY* LS6 ......20 A1
King Alfred's Wy *HDGY* LS6 ......20 A1
King Charles St *LDS* LS1 * 3 G4
King Cl *AL/HA/HU* LS17 ......12 D5
King Dr *AL/HA/HU* LS17 ......12 D5
King Edward Crs *HORS* LS18 ......17 G1
King Edward St *LDS* LS1 ......3 H4
King Edwin's Ct *RHAY* LS8 ......21 G5
Kingfield *GSLY* LS20 ......5 F2
Kingfisher Cl *AL/HA/HU* LS17 ....14 B3
Kingfisher Ms *MOR* LS27 ......46 B1
Kingfisher Wy *AL/HA/HU* LS17 ...14 B3
King George Av *CHAL* LS7 ......20 D5
   HORS LS18 ......17 G1
   MOR LS27 ......40 D5
King George Cft *MOR* LS27 ......46 D1

King George Gdns *CHAL* LS7 * ...20 D3
King George Rd *HORS* LS18 ......17 G1
King La *AL/HA/HU* LS17 ......13 E5
Kings Ap *BRAM* LS13 ......26 A3
King's Av *HDGY* LS6 ......27 G2
Kings Cha *RTHW* LS26 ......45 F5
King's Croft Gdns
   AL/HA/HU LS17 ......20 D1
Kingsdale Ct *SCFT* LS14 ......22 D4
Kingsfield *RTHW* LS26 ......49 H1
Kingsley Av *BHP/TINH* LS16 ......11 H2
Kingsley Dr *BHP/TINH* LS16 ......11 H2
Kingsley Rd *BHP/TINH* LS16 ......11 H2
Kings Md *RTHW* LS26 ......45 E5
Kingsmead *SCFT* LS14 ......23 E2
Kingsmead Dr *SCFT* LS14 ......22 D1
Kingsmill Cl *MOR* LS27 ......46 B1
King's Mt *CHAL* LS7 ......20 C2
King's Rd *HDGY* LS6 ......27 G3
Kingston Gdns *MSTN/BAR* LS15 ...31 F2
Kingston Ter *LDSU* LS2 ......28 B3
King St *LDS* LS1 ......2 E5
   MOR LS27 ......46 C3
   PDSY/CALV LS28 ......24 B4
   YEA LS19 ......8 A5
   YEA LS19 ......6 A5
Kingsway *MSTN/BAR* LS15 ......31 G5
Kingswear Cl *MSTN/BAR* LS15 ...31 H4
Kingswear Cres *MSTN/BAR* LS15 ..31 H4
Kingswear Garth
   MSTN/BAR LS15 ......31 H4
Kingswear Gln *MSTN/BAR* LS15 ..31 H4
Kingswear Gv *MSTN/BAR* LS15 ..31 H4
Kingswear Pde *MSTN/BAR* LS15 ..31 H4
Kingswear Ri *MSTN/BAR* LS15 ...31 H4
Kingswear Vw *MSTN/BAR* LS15 ..31 H4
Kingswood Av *RHAY* LS8 ......14 C4
Kingswood Crs *RHAY* LS8 ......14 B4
Kingswood Dr *RHAY* LS8 ......14 B4
Kingswood Gdns *RHAY* LS8 ......14 B4
Kingswood Gv *RHAY* LS8 ......14 C4
Kingswood Rd *WOR/ARM* LS12 ..34 D2
Kippax Pl *OSM* LS9 ......37 F1
Kirk Beston Cl *BEE/HOL* LS11 ....41 G1
Kirkdale Av *WOR/ARM* LS12 ......34 C4
Kirkdale Crs *WOR/ARM* LS12 ....34 C4
Kirkdale Dr *WOR/ARM* LS12 ......34 D4
Kirkdale Gdns *WOR/ARM* LS12 ...34 C4
Kirkdale Gv *WOR/ARM* LS12 ......34 C4
Kirkdale Mt *WOR/ARM* LS12 ......34 D5
Kirkdale Ter *WOR/ARM* LS12 ....34 C4
Kirkdale Vw *WOR/ARM* LS12 ....34 D4
Kirkfield Dr *MSTN/BAR* LS15 ....39 G1
Kirkfield Gdns *MSTN/BAR* LS15 ..31 H4
Kirkfield Vw *MSTN/BAR* LS15 ...39 H1
Kirkham St *BRAM* LS13 ......16 D5
Kirk ings Yd *LDSU* LS2 * 5 C5
Kirklands Cl *YEA* LS19 ......5 G5
Kirk La *YEA* LS19 ......5 G5
Kirklees Cl *PDSY/CALV* LS28 ......24 B1
Kirklees Cft *PDSY/CALV* LS28 ....24 B1
Kirklees Dr *PDSY/CALV* LS28 ....24 B1
Kirklees Garth *PDSY/CALV* LS28 ..24 B1
Kirkstall Av *KSTL* LS5 ......26 D3
Kirkstall Hi *BULY* LS4 ......26 D3
Kirkstall La *KSTL* LS5 ......26 D3
Kirkstall Mt *KSTL* LS5 ......26 C3
Kirkstall Rd *BULY* LS4 ......26 D2
   BVRD LS3 ......2 A3
Kirkwall Av *OSM* LS9 ......37 H1
Kirkwood Av *BHP/TINH* LS16 ...10 D2
Kirkwood Cl *BHP/TINH* LS16 ....10 D2
Kirkwood Crs *BHP/TINH* LS16 ..11 E2
Kirkwood Dr *BHP/TINH* LS16 ...10 D2
Kirkwood Gdns *BHP/TINH* LS16 ..11 E2
Kirkwood Gv *BHP/TINH* LS16 ...11 E2
Kirkwood Ri *BHP/TINH* LS16 ....11 E2
Kirkwood Vw *BHP/TINH* LS16 ...11 E2
Kitchener Av *OSM* LS9 ......29 H4
Kitchener Gv *OSM* LS9 ......29 H3
Kitchener Mt *OSM* LS9 ......29 H4
Kitchener Pl *OSM* LS9 ......29 H4
Kitchener St *OSM* LS9 ......29 H4
   RTHW LS26 ......44 D5
Kitson Cl *WOR/ARM* LS12 ......35 G2
Kitson Gdns *WOR/ARM* LS12 ....35 G2
Kitson St *EARD/LOFT* WF3 ......47 F5
   OSM LS9 ......37 F1
Knavesmire *RTHW* LS26 ......50 D1
Knightsclose *MSTN/BAR* LS15 ...31 G5
Knightscroft Av *RTHW* LS26 ......44 C5
Knightscroft Dr *RTHW* LS26 ......44 C5
Knightshill *MSTN/BAR* LS15 ......31 G5
Knightsway *EARD/LOFT* WF3 ....49 H5
   MSTN/BAR LS15 ......31 G5
Knoll Wood Pk *HORS* LS18 ......17 G1
Knott La *YEA* LS19 ......16 C1
Knowle Av *BULY* LS4 ......27 F2
Knowle Gv *BULY* LS4 ......27 F2
Knowle Mt *BULY* LS4 ......27 F2
Knowle Pl *BULY* LS4 ......27 F2
Knowle Rd *BULY* LS4 * 27 F2
Knowle Ter *BULY* LS4 ......27 F2
Knowsthorpe Crs *OSM* LS9 ......37 F2
Knowsthorpe Ga *OSM* LS9 ......37 H4
Knowsthorpe La *OSM* LS9 ......37 G4
Knowsthorpe Rd *OSM* LS9 ......38 A4
Knowsthorpe Wy *OSM* LS9 ......37 H4
Knox St *BRAM* LS13 ......16 B5
Kyffin Av *MSTN/BAR* LS15 ......38 C1

L

Laburnum St *PDSY/CALV* LS28 ...24 B4
Lady Beck Cl *LDSU* LS2 ......3 J3

Lady La *LDSU* LS2 ......3 H4
Lady Park Ct *AL/HA/HU* LS17 ....12 G1
Lady Pit La *BEE/HOL* LS11 ......36 A4
Ladywood Gra *RHAY* LS8 * 22 C1
Ladywood Md *RHAY* LS8 ......22 C1
Laith Cl *BHP/TINH* LS16 ......10 D4
Laith Gdns *BHP/TINH* LS16 ......11 E4
Laith Garth *BHP/TINH* LS16 ......11 E4
Laith Gn *BHP/TINH* LS16 ......11 E4
Lakeland Crs *AL/HA/HU* LS17 ...13 F5
Lakeland Dr *AL/HA/HU* LS17 ....13 F5
Lakeside Cha *YEA* LS19 ......9 E2
Lakeside Gdns *YEA* LS19 ......9 E2
Lakeside Rd *WOR/ARM* LS12 ....34 D4
Lakeside Ter *YEA* LS19 ......9 E2
Lakeside Vw *YEA* LS19 ......9 E2
Lake St *MID* LS10 ......42 C1
Lake View Ct *RHAY* LS8 ......22 C1
Lambert Av *RHAY* LS8 ......14 A5
Lambert Dr *RHAY* LS8 ......14 A5
Lambrigg Crs *SCFT* LS14 ......23 E5
Lambton Gv *RHAY* LS8 * 29 F1
Lambton Pl *RHAY* LS8 * 29 F1
Lambton St *RHAY* LS8 * 29 F1
Lambton Ter *RHAY* LS8 * 29 F1
Lanark Dr *HORS* LS18 ......10 C4
Lancaster Crs *KSTL* LS5 ......26 C3
Lancet Ri *EARD/LOFT* WF3 ......49 H5
Landmark Ct *BEE/HOL* LS11 ......36 A4
Landseer Av *BRAM* LS13 ......25 G2
Landseer Cl *BRAM* LS13 ......25 H2
Landseer Crs *BRAM* LS13 ......25 H2
Landseer Dr *BRAM* LS13 ......25 H2
Landseer Gdns *BRAM* LS13 ......25 H2
Landseer Gv *BRAM* LS13 ......25 H2
Landseer Mt *BRAM* LS13 ......25 H2
Landseer Ri *BRAM* LS13 ......25 G2
Landseer Rd *BRAM* LS13 ......25 G2
Landseer Ter *BRAM* LS13 ......25 H2
Landseer Vw *BRAM* LS13 ......25 H2
Lands La *GSLY* LS20 ......5 F4
   LDS LS1 ......3 F4
Lane End *PDSY/CALV* LS28 ......24 C4
Lane End Ct *AL/HA/HU* LS17 ....13 G5
Lane End Cft *AL/HA/HU* LS17 ...13 G5
Lane End Fold *PDSY/CALV* LS28 ..24 C4
Lane End Pl *BEE/HOL* LS11 ......36 A4
Lane End Pl *PDSY/CALV* LS28 ...11 E4
Laneside *MSTN/BAR* LS15 ......39 E1
Laneside Cl *MOR* LS27 ......46 C2
Laneside Fold *MOR* LS27 ......46 C2
Laneside Gdns *MOR* LS27 ......46 C2
The Lanes *PDSY/CALV* LS28 ......24 C4
The Lane *AL/HA/HU* LS17 ......21 E4
   LDSU LS2 ......3 J5
Langbar Ap *SCFT* LS14 ......23 G1
Langbar Cl *SCFT* LS14 ......23 G1
Langbar Garth *SCFT* LS14 ......23 G1
Langbar Gn *SCFT* LS14 ......23 G1
Langbar Gv *SCFT* LS14 ......23 G1
Langbar Rd *SCFT* LS14 ......23 G1
Langdale Av *HDGY* LS6 ......27 F1
Langdale Gdns *HDGY* LS6 ......27 F1
Langdale Rd *RTHW* LS26 ......51 E1
Langdale Ter *HDGY* LS6 ......27 F1
Langley Av *BRAM* LS13 ......25 G1
Langley Cl *BRAM* LS13 ......25 G1
Langley Crs *BRAM* LS13 ......25 F1
Langley Garth *BRAM* LS13 ......25 G1
Langley Mt *BRAM* LS13 ......25 G1
Langley Pl *BRAM* LS13 ......25 G1
Langley Rd *BRAM* LS13 ......25 G1
Langthorne Ct *MOR* LS27 * 46 B5
Langton Gn *WOR/ARM* LS12 ....35 G3
Langtons Whf *LDS* LS1 ......3 G5
Lansdowne St *WOR/ARM* LS12 ..35 G3
Lanshaw Cl *MID* LS10 ......48 B1
Lanshaw Crs *MID* LS10 ......48 B1
Lanshaw Pl *MID* LS10 ......48 B1
Lanshaw Rd *MID* LS10 ......48 B1
Lanshaw Ter *MID* LS10 ......48 B1
Lanshaw Vw *MID* LS10 ......48 B1
Lanshaw Wk *MID* LS10 ......48 B1
Larchfield Rd *MID* LS10 ......37 E4
Larkfield Av *YEA* LS19 ......9 F1
Larkfield Crs *YEA* LS19 ......9 F1
Larkfield Dr *YEA* LS19 ......9 F1
Larkfield Mt *YEA* LS19 ......9 F1
Larkfield Rd *PDSY/CALV* LS28 ...24 A5
   YEA LS19 ......9 F1
Larkhill Cl *RHAY* LS8 ......14 D5
Larkhill Gn *AL/HA/HU* LS17 ....14 D5
Larkhill Rd *AL/HA/HU* LS17 .....14 D5
Larkhill Vw *RHAY* LS8 ......14 D5
Larkhill Wk *AL/HA/HU* LS17 ....14 D5
Larkhill Wy *AL/HA/HU* LS17 ....14 D5
Lascelles Mt *RHAY* LS8 * 29 F1
Lascelles Pl *RHAY* LS8 * 29 F1
Lascelles Rd East *RHAY* LS8 * ...29 F1
Lascelles Rd West *RHAY* LS8 * ...29 F1
Lascelles Ter *RHAY* LS8 * 29 F1
Lascelles Vw *RHAY* LS8 * 29 F1
Lastingham Rd *BRAM* LS13 ......15 H5
Latchmere Av *BHP/TINH* LS16 ...18 C1
Latchmere Cl *BHP/TINH* LS16 ...18 C1
Latchmere Crest
   BHP/TINH LS16 ......18 C1
Latchmere Cross
   BHP/TINH LS16 ......18 C1
Latchmere Dr *BHP/TINH* LS16 ...18 C1
Latchmere Rd *BHP/TINH* LS16 ...18 C1
Latchmere Vw *BHP/TINH* LS16 ...18 C1
Latchmere Wk *BHP/TINH* LS16 ...18 C1
Laura St *WOR/ARM* LS12 ......35 F3
Laurel Bank Ct *BULY* LS4 ......27 E2
Laurel Fold *WOR/ARM* LS12 ......37 H1
Laurel Gv *WOR/ARM* LS12 ......37 H1

Av MSTN/BAR LS15 ......39 H1
ft MSTN/BAR LS15 ...39 H1
dns
AR LS15 ....39 H1
v MSTN/BAR LS15 ......39 H1
Wy MSTN/BAR LS15 .....39 H1
AL LS7 * 20 D5
LV LS28 ....24 C5
ID LS10 ....48 B3
M LS12 ....35 E1
RHAY LS8 ....21 F4
OR/ARM LS12 ....35 E1
PDSY/CALV LS28 ....24 C5
t RTHW LS26 ....45 H4
Wk OSM LS9 ....37 F1
WOR/ARM LS12 ....44 A5
WOR/ARM LS12 ....33 H5
WOR/ARM LS12 ....33 H5
WOR/ARM LS12 ....33 H5
WOR/ARM LS12 ....33 H5
e WOR/ARM LS12 ....33 H5
WOR/ARM LS12 ....33 H5
WOR/ARM LS12 ....33 H5
Cl BHP/TINH LS16 .....11 H4
WOR/ARM LS12 ....33 H5
WOR/ARM LS12 ....33 H5
d Gdns
AV LS16 ....11 H5
x RHAY LS8 ....30 A1
rs RHAY LS8 ....30 A1
Gdns RHAY LS8 ....22 A5
d RHAY LS8 ....30 A1
Wk RHAY LS8 ....30 A1
WOR/ARM LS12 * 34 C1
ood Dr RHAY LS6 ......19 H1
CHAL LS7 ....2 D5
t RTHW LS26 * 50 C1
Gdns RTHW LS26 ....50 C2
Met RTHW LS26 ....50 C2
Pl RTHW LS26 ....50 C2
g RTHW LS26 ....50 C2
YEA LS19 ....9 G4
YEA LS19 ....9 F4
YEA LS19 ....9 F4
YEA LS19 ....9 F4
rk Av YEA LS19 ....9 C5
rk Cl YEA LS19 ....9 G5
rk Cft YEA LS19 ......9 G5
k Dr YEA LS19 ....9 F4
HORS LS18 ....9 H4
rk Av YEA LS19 ....9 C5
EARD/LOFT WF3 ....50 B2
S26 ....50 B2
Crs KSTL LS5 ....18 B4
LS26 ....18 A4
t KSTL LS5 ....18 A3
Mt KSTL LS5 ....18 A3
Rd KSTL LS5 ....18 B3
Wk KSTL LS5 ....18 B3
AL/HA/HU LS17 ....13 F5
AL/HA/HU LS17 ....13 F5
ALV LS28 ....32 C3
ark Cl YEA LS19 ......35 H2
rk Dr YEA LS19 ....5 G5
t MID LS10 ....43 F4
f MID LS10 ....43 F4
dns MID LS10 ....43 F4
arth MID LS10 * 43 F4
MID LS10 ....43 F4
Cl MID LS10 ....43 E1
Gdns MID LS10 ....43 E1
Garth MID LS10 ....43 E1
MID LS10 ....43 E1
v ILK LS29 ....4 B1
st MID LS10 ....36 C3
t MID LS10 ....36 C3
MID LS10 ....49 E2
MID LS10 ....49 F2
I MID LS10 ....49 F2
v MID LS10 ....49 E2
MID LS10 * 49 E2
Wy WOR/ARM LS12 .....50 A5
EARD/LOFT WF3 ....50 A5
adford Rd
ALV LS28 ....32 C3
ntry Wy HORS LS18....10 A2
BHP/TINH LS16 ....7 H1
OFT WF3 ....49 H4
20 ....5 E4
S26 ....44 A3
g
rs LS18 ....10 B5
st HORS LS18 ....10 B5
SY/CALV LS28 ....24 B1
Cl CHAL LS7 ....28 C3
PI LDS LS1 ....2 C3
st LDS LS1 ....2 C3
I MOR LS27 ....28 C2
dns MSTN/BAR LS15 ...28 ..
g BULY LS4 ....27 ..
Av WOR/ARM LS12 .....26 C2
BEE/HOL LS11 ....42 C1
RTHW LS26 ....43 H3
v CHAL LS7 ....28 D2
CHAL LS7 ....28 D2

Leslie Av YEA LS19 ......5 H4
Leslie Ter HDGY LS6 .....28 A2
Levens Bank MSTN/BAR LS15 ..38 B2
Levens Cl MSTN/BAR LS15 ....38 C2
Levens Garth MSTN/BAR LS15 .38 C2
Levens Pl MSTN/BAR LS15 ....38 C2
Leventhorpe Ct RTHW LS26 ...51 G1
Leventhorpe Wy RTHW LS26 ...51 G1
Levita Pl MSTN/BAR LS15 ....50 C5
Lewisham Gv MOR LS27 ....46 D2
Lewisham St MOR LS27 ....46 A3
Leylands Rd LDSU LS2 ....3 K2
Ley La WOR/ARM LS12 ....27 F5
Leysholme Crs WOR/ARM LS12 .34 D2
Leysholme Dr WOR/ARM LS12 ..34 D2
Leysholme Ter WOR/ARM LS12 .34 C2
Leysholme Vw WOR/ARM LS12 ..34 C2
Leywell Ter WOR/ARM LS12 ...26 C5
Lickless Av HORS LS18 ......17 H1
Lickless Dr HORS LS18 ......17 H1
Lickless Gdns HORS LS18 ....17 H1
Lickless Ter HORS LS18 .....17 H1
Lidget HI PDSY/CALV LS28 ...24 C5
Lidgett Av RHAY LS8 ....21 F3
Lidgett Ct RHAY LS8 ....21 F2
Lidgett Gv RHAY LS8 ....21 F2
Lidgett HI RHAY LS8 ....21 F2
Lidgett La AL/HA/HU LS17 ...21 E1
Lidgett Mt RHAY LS8 ....21 F2
Lidgett Park Av RHAY LS8 ...21 F1
Lidgett Park Ct RHAY LS8 ...21 F2
Lidgett Park Gv RHAY LS8 ...21 F2
Lidgett Park Ms RHAY LS8 ...21 F2
Lidgett Park Rd RHAY LS8 ...21 F1
Lidgett Park Vw RHAY LS8 ...21 F1
Lidgett Pl RHAY LS8 ....21 F2
Lidgett Wk RHAY LS8 ....21 F1
Litton Pl ILD LS12 ....28 A3
The Lilacs GSLY LS20 ....5 E3
Lime Gv YEA LS19 ....8 C3
Lime Tree Cl RTHW LS26 .....45 H4
Limewood Ap SCFT LS14 ......23 E3
Limewood Rd SCFT LS14 ......23 E3
Lincoln Green Ct OSM LS9 ...29 E4
Lincoln Green Rd OSM LS9 ...29 E4
Lincoln Rd OSM LS9 ....29 E4
Lincombe Bank RHAY LS8 .....21 E2
Lincombe Dr RHAY LS8 ....21 E1
Lincombe Mt RHAY LS8 ....21 E2
Lincombe Ri RHAY LS8 ....21 E2
Lincroft Crs BRAM LS13 .....25 H2
Lindale Cl MID LS10 ....42 D4
Linden Cl BHP/TINH LS16 ....19 F3
Linden Gdns BEE/HOL LS11 ...36 C5
Linden Gv BEE/HOL LS11 .....36 C5
Linden Mt BEE/HOL LS11 .....36 B5
Linden Pl BEE/HOL LS11 .....36 C5
Linden Rd BEE/HOL LS11 .....36 C5
Lindsey Ct OSM LS9 ....29 E4
Lindsey Gdns OSM LS9 * 29 E4
Lindsey Mt OSM LS9 ....29 E4
Lindsey Rd OSM LS9 ....29 E4
Lingfield Ap AL/HA/HU LS17 .13 F4
Lingfield Bank AL/HA/HU LS17 13 F4
Lingfield Cl AL/HA/HU LS17 .13 G4
Lingfield Crs AL/HA/HU LS17 13 G4
Lingfield Dr AL/HA/HU LS17 .13 G4
Lingfield Gdns AL/HA/HU LS17 13 F4
Lingfield Ga AL/HA/HU LS17 .13 F4
Lingfield Gv AL/HA/HU LS17 .13 G4
Lingfield Mt AL/HA/HU LS17 .13 G4
Lingfield Rd AL/HA/HU LS17 .13 F4
Lingfield Vw AL/HA/HU LS17 .13 F4
Lingfield Wk AL/HA/HU LS17 .13 F4
Lingwell Ap MID LS10 ....48 C2
Lingwell Av MID LS10 ....48 C2
Lingwell Ct MID LS10 ....48 C2
Lingwell Crs MID LS10 ......48 C2
Lingwell Gdns MID LS10 .....48 C2
Lingwell Gate La
  EARD/LOFT WF3 ....49 F5
Lingwell Gn MID LS10 ....48 C2
Lingwell Gv MID LS10 ....48 C2
Lingwell Mt MID LS10 * 48 C2
Lingwell Rd MID LS10 ....48 C1
Lingwell Vw MID LS10 * 48 C2
Lingwell Wk MID LS10 ....48 C2
The Links BEE/HOL LS11 .....42 A4
Linnet Ct MOR LS27 ....47 F3
Linton Av AL/HA/HU LS17 ....14 B3
Linton Cl AL/HA/HU LS17 ....14 A3
Linton Crs AL/HA/HU LS17 ...14 A3
Linton Dr AL/HA/HU LS17 ....14 A3
Linton Ri AL/HA/HU LS17 ....14 A3
Linton Vw AL/HA/HU LS17 ....14 A2
Lisbon Sq LDS LS1 ....2 C4
Lisbon St LDS LS1 ....2 C4
Lismore Cl RTHW LS26 ....50 D1
Lister HI HORS LS18 ....10 C5
Lister Wk MOR LS27 ....40 B5
Little Cross St LDS LS1 ....3 G4
Little Fountain St MOR LS27 .46 C2
Little King St LDS LS1 .....3 F5
Little La EARD/LOFT WF3 .....50 C3
  MOR LS27 ....41 E3
Little Lane Ct MOR LS27 ....41 E3
Littlemoor Ct PDSY/CALV LS28 32 D2
Littlemoor Crs
  PDSY/CALV LS28 ....32 C3
Littlemoor Crs South
  PDSY/CALV LS28 ....32 C3
Littlemoor Gdns
  PDSY/CALV LS28 ....32 C3
Little Moor Pl WOR/ARM LS12 .28 A3
Littlemoor Rd PDSY/CALV LS28 32 C2
Littlemoor Vw PDSY/CALV LS28 32 D3
Little Neville St LDS LS1 ..3 F6
Little Queen St LDS LS1 ....2 D5
Little Woodhouse St LDSU LS2 2 D2
Litton Wy SCFT LS14 ....23 F2

Livinia Gv CHAL LS7 ....28 B3
Lockwood Cl BEE/HOL LS11 ...42 B2
Lockwood Wy BEE/HOL LS11 ...42 C2
Lodge Hill Cl WOR/ARM LS12 .13 H5
Lodge La BEE/HOL LS11 ......36 B5
Lodge Rd PDSY/CALV LS28 ....24 B5
Lodge St LDS LS1 ....3 F2
  LDSU LS2 ....2 E1
Lodge Ter BEE/HOL LS11 * ...42 B1
Lofthouse Pl LDSU LS2 ......28 B3
Lofthouse Ter CHAL LS7 .....28 C3
Lolner Ct CHAL LS7 ....38 A3
Lombard St MSTN/BAR LS15 ...38 D1
  OSM LS9 ....8 C3
Lomond Av HORS LS18 ....10 B3
Londesboro Gv OSM LS9 ......37 G1
Londesboro Ter OSM LS9 .....37 G1
London La YEA LS19 ....8 C3
London St YEA LS19 ....8 C3
Long Causeway BHP/TINH LS16 12 B2
  OSM LS9 ....37 F3
Long Close La OSM LS9 ......37 F1
Longfield Av PDSY/CALV LS28 32 D1
Longfield Ct PDSY/CALV LS28 32 D1
Longfield Dr BRAM LS13 .....24 D1
  MSTN/BAR LS15 ....31 E5
Longfield Garth BRAM LS13 ..16 D5
Longfield Gv PDSY/CALV LS28 32 D1
Longfield Mt PDSY/CALV LS28 32 D1
Longfield Rd PDSY/CALV LS28 32 D1
Longfield Ter PDSY/CALV LS28 32 C1
Longford Ter RTHW LS26 .....37 G1
Longroyd Crs BEE/HOL LS11 ..36 C5
Longroyd Crs North
  BEE/HOL LS11 ....36 C5
Longroyd Gv BEE/HOL LS11 ...36 C5
Longroyd Pl BEE/HOL LS11 ...36 C5
Longroyd St BEE/HOL LS11 ...36 C5
Longroyd St North
  BEE/HOL LS11 ....36 C5
Longroyd Ter MID LS10 ......36 C5
Longroyd Vw BEE/HOL LS11 ...36 C5
Long Thorpe La
  EARD/LOFT WF3 ....49 G5
Longwood Cl AL/HA/HU LS17 ..14 D2
Longwood Crs AL/HA/HU LS17 .14 D2
Longwood Wy AL/HA/HU LS17 ..14 D2
Lonsdale Cl MID LS10 ....42 D2
Lord St WOR/ARM LS12 ....34 D5
Lord Ter WOR/ARM LS12 ......2 A7
Lorry Bank CHAL LS7 ....28 C1
Louis Ct CHAL LS7 ....28 D2
Louis Gv CHAL LS7 ....28 D2
Louis Le Prince Ct RHAY LS8 29 F2
Louis St CHAL LS7 ....28 D2
Love La RTHW LS26 ....50 C1
Lovell Park Cl CHAL LS7 ....3 J1
Lovell Park Ga CHAL LS7 ....3 H1
Lovell Park Gra CHAL LS7 ...3 J1
Lovell Park Hts CHAL LS7 ...3 H1
Lovell Park Hl CHAL LS7 ....3 J1
Lovell Park Ms CHAL LS7 ....3 J1
Lovell Park Rd CHAL LS7 ....3 H1
Lovell Park Vw CHAL LS7 ....3 J1
Low Bank St PDSY/CALV LS28 .24 A2
Low Close St LDSU LS2 * 28 A2
Lowell Gv BRAM LS13 ....25 E5
Lowell Pl BRAM LS13 ....25 E5
Lower Bankhouse
  PDSY/CALV LS28 ....32 B4
Lower Basinghall St LDS LS1 3 F4
Lower Brunswick St LDSU LS2 3 J2
Lower Tofts Rd
  PDSY/CALV LS28 ....32 C1
Lower Town St BRAM LS13 ....25 H3
Lower Wortley Rd
  WOR/ARM LS12 ....34 D5
Low Fields Av BEE/HOL LS11 .35 G4
Low Fields Rd BEE/HOL LS11 .35 G5
Low Gipton Crs OSM LS9 .....30 B2
Low Grange Crs MID LS10 ....43 E2
Low Grange Vw MID LS10 .....43 E3
Low Gn YEA LS19 ....9 E4
Low Hall Pl BEE/HOL LS11 ...36 H2
Low Hall Rd YEA LS19 ....10 B2
Low La HORS LS18 ....17 H1
Low Mills GSLY LS20 * 5 E4
Low Mills Rd WOR/ARM LS12 ..34 C4
Low Moor Side WOR/ARM LS12 .33 H5
Low Moorside Cl
  WOR/ARM LS12 * 34 A5
Low Shops La RTHW LS26 .....37 E4
Low St EARD/LOFT WF3 ....47 G5
Lowther St RHAY LS8 ....29 F1
Lowtown PDSY/CALV LS28 .....24 D5
Lucas Ct CHAL LS7 ....28 C3
Lucas Pl HDGY LS6 ....28 A1
Lucas St HDGY LS6 ....28 A1
Lucy Av MSTN/BAR LS15 .....31 G3
Ludolf Dr AL/HA/HU LS17 ...15 G3
Lulworth Av MSTN/BAR LS15 ..31 H5
Lulworth Cl MSTN/BAR LS15 ..31 H4
Lulworth Crs MSTN/BAR LS15 .31 H4
Lulworth Garth MSTN/BAR LS15 31 H5
Lulworth Wk MSTN/BAR LS15 ..31 H5
Lumby Cl PDSY/CALV LS28 ....32 D3
Lumley Av BULY LS4 ....27 F2
Lumley Gv BULY LS4 ....27 F2
Lumley Mt BULY LS4 ....27 F2
Lumley Pl BULY LS4 ....27 F2
Lumley Rd BULY LS4 ....27 F2
Lumley St BULY LS4 ....27 F2
Lumley Ter BULY LS4 ....27 F2
Lumley Vw BULY LS4 ....27 F2
Lumley Wk BULY LS4 ....27 F2
Lunan Pl RHAY LS8 ....29 F1
Lunan Ter RHAY LS8 ....29 F1
Lupton Av OSM LS9 ....37 G5
Lupton St MID LS10 ....37 E5
Luttrell Cl BHP/TINH LS16 ..11 G5

Luttrell Crs BHP/TINH LS16 .11 C5
Luttrell Gdns BHP/TINH LS16 11 G5
Luttrell Pl BHP/TINH LS16 ..11 G5
Luttrell Rd BHP/TINH LS16 ..11 G5
Luxor Av RHAY LS8 ....29 F1
Luxor Rd RHAY LS8 ....29 F1
Luxor St RHAY LS8 ....29 F1
Luxor Vw RHAY LS8 ....29 F1
Lyddon Ter LDSU LS2 ....29 F4
Lydgate OSM LS9 ....29 F4
Lydia St LDSU LS2 ....3 H3
Lyme Cha SCFT LS14 ....30 D3
Lynwood Gdns
  PDSY/CALV LS28 ....8 B2
Lynton Av EARD/LOFT WF3 ....49 E4
Lynwood Crs RTHW LS26 ......35 E4
  WOR/ARM LS12 ....35 E4
Lynwood Garth WOR/ARM LS12 .35 E2
Lynwood Gv WOR/ARM LS12 ....35 E2
Lynwood Mt WOR/ARM LS12 ....35 E3
Lynwood Vw WOR/ARM LS12 ....35 E3
Lytham Gv WOR/ARM LS12 .....34 C4
Lytham Pl WOR/ARM LS12 .....34 C4
Lytton St MID LS10 ....36 D5

M

Mabgate OSM LS9 ....3 K2
Mabgate Gn OSM LS9 ....3 K3
Macaulay St OSM LS9 ....29 E5
Mafeking Av BEE/HOL LS11 ...42 A2
Mafeking Gv BEE/HOL LS11 ...42 A2
Mafeking Mt BEE/HOL LS11 ...42 A2
Magdalene Cl BHP/TINH LS16 .11 G4
Magdalin Dr PDSY/CALV LS28 .11 G4
Magpie La MOR LS27 ....46 D5
Main St AL/HA/HU LS17 .....15 F3
  EARD/LOFT WF3 ....50 B5
Malden Rd HDGY LS6 ....19 F3
Malham Cl SCFT LS14 ....31 E1
Mallard Cl MOR LS27 ....47 F2
Mallard Wy MOR LS27 ....47 F2
Malmesbury Cl WOR/ARM LS12 .35 E2
Malmesbury Gv WOR/ARM LS12 .35 E2
Malmesbury Pl WOR/ARM LS12 .35 E2
Malmesbury St WOR/ARM LS12 .35 E2
Malmesbury Ter
  WOR/ARM LS12 ....35 E2
Maltby Ct MSTN/BAR LS15 * ..39 H1
Malting Cl EARD/LOFT WF3 ...49 F3
Malting Ri EARD/LOFT WF3 ...49 F3
Maltings Cl BEE/HOL LS11 * .36 C4
Maltings Rd BEE/HOL LS11 ...36 C4
The Maltings EARD/LOFT WF3 .49 F5
  HDGY LS6 ....27 G3
Malvern Gv BEE/HOL LS11 ....36 A5
Malvern Ri BEE/HOL LS11 ....36 A4
Malvern Rd BEE/HOL LS11 ....36 A4
Malvern St BEE/HOL LS11 ....36 A5
Malvern Vw BEE/HOL LS11 ....36 A5
Mandarin Wy MID LS10 ......43 F4
Manitoba Pl CHAL LS7 ......20 C3
Manor Av HDGY LS6 ....27 G2
Manor Cl BHP/TINH LS16 ....7 H1
  RTHW LS26 ....50 C5
  YEA LS19 ....5 H5
Manor Crs RTHW LS26 ....50 C5
Manor Dr HDGY LS6 ....27 G2
Manor Farm Cl MID LS10 ....42 D5
Manor Farm Dr MID LS10 ....42 D5
  MOR LS27 ....41 E5
Manor Farm Gdns MID LS10 ..42 D5
Manor Farm Gn MID LS10 ....42 D5
Manor Farm Gv MID LS10 ....42 D5
Manor Farm Ri MID LS10 ....42 D5
Manor Farm Rd MID LS10 ....42 C5
Manor Farm Wk MID LS10 ....42 D5
Manor Farm Wy MID LS10 ....48 C1
Manor Garth MSTN/BAR LS15 .39 H1
Manor Gv CHAL LS7 ....20 D4
Manor House Cft
  BHP/TINH LS16 ....12 B4
Manor House La BHP/TINH LS17 11 G2
Manor Mill La BEE/HOL LS11 .41 C2
Manor Rd BEE/HOL LS11 .....36 C4
  HORS LS18 ....10 D4
  MOR LS27 ....41 E3
Manor Sq YEA LS19 ....5 H5
Manor St CHAL LS7 ....28 D3
Manor Ter HDGY LS6 ....27 G2
Manor Vw HDGY LS6 ....27 G2
  PDSY/CALV LS28 ....32 C3
Mansion Ga CHAL LS7 ....20 D4
Mansion Gate Dr CHAL LS7 ..21 E4
Mansion Gate Sq CHAL LS7 ..21 E4
Mansion La RHAY LS8 ....21 E4
Manston Av MSTN/BAR LS15 ..31 H1
Manston Crs MSTN/BAR LS15 .31 H4
Manston Dr MSTN/BAR LS15 ..31 G1
Manston Gdns MSTN/BAR LS15 31 H1
Manston Gv MSTN/BAR LS15 ..31 G1
Manston Ri MSTN/BAR LS15 ..31 G1
Manston Ter MSTN/BAR LS15 .31 H1
Manston Wy MSTN/BAR LS15 ..31 G1
Maple Cft AL/HA/HU LS17 ...14 A4
Maple Dr WOR/ARM LS12 .....33 H5
Maple Fold WOR/ARM LS12 ...33 H5
Maple Gv WOR/ARM LS12 .....33 H5
Maple Ri RTHW LS26 * 50 D1
Maple Wy SCFT LS14 ....23 F2
Mardale Crs SCFT LS14 .....31 E2
Margaret Cl MOR LS27 ......46 D3
Margate RTHW LS26 * 45 G5
Marian Gv BEE/HOL LS11 * ..36 B5

Marian Rd HDGY LS6 ....28 B2
Marian Ter HDGY LS6 ....28 B2
Marina Crs MOR LS27 ....46 B5
Market Pl PDSY/CALV LS28 ..32 C1
Market Street Ar LDS 3 G5
Markham Av RHAY LS8 ....29 F1
  YEA LS19 ....9 F2
Markham Crs YEA LS19 ......9 F2
Markham Cft YEA LS19 ......9 F2
Markington Ms MID LS10 ....48 C3
Markington Pl MID LS10 ....48 C3
Marlborough Gdns LDSU LS2 * 28 B3
Marlborough Gra LDS LS1 ...2 C5
Marlborough Gv LDSU LS2 * ..28 B3
Marlborough St LDS LS1 ....2 C4
Marley Gv BEE/HOL LS11 ....35 H5
Marley Pl BEE/HOL LS11 ....35 H5
Marley St BEE/HOL LS11 ....35 H5
Marley Ter BEE/HOL LS11 ...35 H5
Marley Vw BEE/HOL LS11 ....35 H5
Marlowe Cl PDSY/CALV LS28 .32 D3
Marsden Av BEE/HOL LS11 ...42 A1
Marsden Gv BEE/HOL LS11 ...42 A1
Marsden Mt BEE/HOL LS11 ...42 A1
Marsden Pl BEE/HOL LS11 ...42 A1
Marsden Vw BEE/HOL LS11 ...42 A1
Marsett Wy SCFT LS14 ......23 F2
Marsh PDSY/CALV LS28 ......32 A1
Marsh Ct MSTN/BAR LS15 ....31 C3
  MSTN/BAR LS15 ....31 H5
Marsh La OSM LS9 ....3 K5
Marsh St HDGY LS6 ....28 A2
  RTHW LS26 ....28 A2
Marsh Ter PDSY/CALV LS28 ..32 A1
Marsh V HDGY LS6 ....28 A2
Marston Av MOR LS27 ....46 C3
Marston Mt OSM LS9 ....29 E4
Martin Cl MOR LS27 ....47 E2
Martin Ct MSTN/BAR LS15 ...31 H5
Martindale Dr BRAM LS13 ...26 A4
Martingale Dr MID LS10 ....48 C3
Martin Ter BULY LS4 ....27 E3
Marwood Rd WOR/ARM LS12 ...33 H1
Maryfield Av MSTN/BAR LS15 31 E5
Maryfield Cl MSTN/BAR LS15 31 E5
Maryfield Ct MSTN/BAR LS15 31 E5
Maryfield Gdns MSTN/BAR LS15 31 E5
Maryfield Gn MSTN/BAR LS15 31 E5
Maryfield Ms MSTN/BAR LS15 31 E5
Maryfield Vw MSTN/BAR LS15 31 E5
Mary St PDSY/CALV LS28 ....24 C1
Masefield St GSLY LS20 ....5 F4
Masham Gv WOR/ARM LS12 ....35 F1
Masham St WOR/ARM LS12 ....35 F1
Matrix Ct BEE/HOL LS11 ....42 B2
Maud Av BEE/HOL LS11 .....42 A1
Maude St LDSU LS2 ....3 H5
Maud Pl BEE/HOL LS11 .....36 B5
Mavis Av RHAY LS8 ....11 E1
Mavis Gv BHP/TINH LS16 ....11 E1
Mavis La BHP/TINH LS16 ....11 E1
Mawcroft Cl YEA LS19 ......8 C2
Mawcroft Grange Dr YEA LS19 8 C2
Maxwell St MOR LS27 ....46 B3
Mayo Cl RHAY LS8 ....22 B4
May Ter OSM LS9 ....37 F2
Mayville Av HDGY LS6 ......27 G2
Mayville Pl HDGY LS6 ......27 G2
Mayville Rd HDGY LS6 ......27 G2
Mayville St HDGY LS6 ......27 G2
Mayville Ter HDGY LS6 .....27 G2
McLaren Flds BRAM LS13 ....25 H3
Meadow Cft BEE/HOL LS11 ...36 B3
Meadowcroft Ms OSM LS9 * ..37 F1
Meadowgate Cft
  EARD/LOFT WF3 ....49 H4
Meadowgate Dr
  EARD/LOFT WF3 ....49 H5
Meadowgate V
  EARD/LOFT WF3 ....49 H5
Meadowhurst Gdns
  PDSY/CALV LS28 ....32 B1
Meadow La EARD/LOFT WF3 ...3 G7
Meadow Rd BEE/HOL LS11 ....36 B3
The Meadows RTHW LS26 .....12 A4
Meadow Va AL/HA/HU LS17 ...13 C2
Meadow Vw HDGY LS6 ....27 G2
Meadow Wy AL/HA/HU LS17 ...13 C2
Meanwood Cl BHP/TINH LS16 .28 B1
Meanwood Gv HDGY LS6 ......19 G1
Meanwood Rd CHAL LS7 ......20 A5
Meanwood St CHAL LS7 ......28 C3
Meanwood Valley Dr CHAL LS7 19 H4
Meanwood Valley Gn CHAL LS7 19 H4
Meanwood Valley Gv CHAL LS7 19 H4
Meanwood Valley Mt CHAL LS7 19 H4
Medeway PDSY/CALV LS28 ....24 A3
Melbourne Gv BRAM LS13 ....25 G3
Melbourne St LDSU LS2 .....3 J2
  MOR LS27 ....46 D2
  PDSY/CALV LS28 ....24 B3
Melrose Gv HORS LS18 ......18 A2
Melrose Pl HORS LS18 ......17 H2
  PDSY/CALV LS28 ....32 B2
Melrose Wk HORS LS18 * 17 H2
Melton Av MID LS10 ....49 F2
Melton Cl MID LS10 ....49 F1
Melton Garth MID LS10 .....49 F2
Melville Cl HDGY LS6 ......28 B2
Melville Gdns HDGY LS6 ....28 B2
Melville Pl HDGY LS6 ......28 B2
Melville Rd HDGY LS6 ......28 B2
Memorial Dr HDGY LS6 ......19 H5
Menston Dr ILK LS29 ......4 A1
Merchants Quay OSM LS9 * ..3 K6
Merlin Cl MOR LS27 ....47 E3
Merlyn-Rees Av MOR LS27 ...46 C2
Merrion Pl LDS LS1 ....3 H3
Merrion St LDSU LS2 ......3 G3

Merrion Wy LDSU LS2 ....3 G2
Merton Av PDSY/CALV LS28 ....24 B3
Merton Dr PDSY/CALV LS28 ....24 A3
Merton Gdns PDSY/CALV LS28 ....24 A3
Methley Dr CHAL LS7 ....20 D4
Methley Gv CHAL LS7 ....20 C4
Methley La CHAL LS7 ....20 C4
Methley Mt CHAL LS7 ....20 C4
Methley Pl CHAL LS7 ....20 C4
Methley Ter CHAL LS7 ....20 C4
Methley Vw CHAL LS7 ....20 C4
Mexborough Av CHAL LS7 ....28 D1
Mexborough Dr CHAL LS7 ....28 D1
Mexborough Gv CHAL LS7 ....28 D1
Mexborough Pl CHAL LS7 ....28 D2
Mexborough Rd CHAL LS7 ....28 D2
Mexborough St CHAL LS7 ....28 D1
Meynell Ap BEE/HOL LS11 ....36 A5
Meynell Av RTHW LS26 ....50 C1
Meynell Ct MSTN/BAR LS15 ....39 F1
Meynell Hts BEE/HOL LS11 ....36 A3
Meynell La MSTN/BAR LS15 ....39 H2
Meynell Mt RTHW LS26 ....50 C1
Meynell Rd MSTN/BAR LS15 ....39 H2
Meynell Sq BEE/HOL LS11 ....36 A5
Meynell Wk BEE/HOL LS11 ....36 A5
Micklefield Ct YEA LS19 ....8 C3
Micklefield La YEA LS19 ....8 C3
Micklefield Ms YEA LS19 * 8 C3
Micklefield Rd YEA LS19 ....8 C3
Mickley St WOR/ARM LS12 ....35 E1
Middleham Moor
  EARD/LOFT WF3 ....49 G3
  MID LS10 ....42 D5
Middlemoor SCFT LS14 ....23 F2
Middlethorne Cl AL/HA/HU LS17 .....13 D3
Middlethorne Ct
  AL/HA/HU LS17 ....14 C2
Middlethorne Ms
  AL/HA/HU LS17 ....14 D2
Middlethorne Ri AL/HA/HU LS17 .....14 C3
Middleton Av OSM LS9 ....29 F4
  RTHW LS26 ....49 G1
Middleton Cl MOR LS27 ....46 D2
Middleton Gv BEE/HOL LS11 ....42 C2
  MOR LS27 * 46 D2
Middleton La MID LS10 ....49 D4
  MID LS10 ....49 F1
Middleton Park Av MID LS10 ....48 B2
Middleton Park Crs MID LS10 ....48 B2
Middleton Park Gn MID LS10 ....48 B2
Middleton Park Gv MID LS10 ....48 B2
Middleton Park Mt MID LS10 ....48 B2
Middleton Park Rd MID LS10 ....48 C1
Middleton Park Ter MID LS10 ....48 C1
Middleton Rd MID LS10 ....43 E2
  MOR LS27 ....47 E2
Middleton Ter MOR LS27 ....47 E2
Midgley Pl HDGY LS6 ....28 B2
Midgley Rd HDGY LS6 ....28 B2
Midland Cl OSM LS10 ....37 F5
Midland Garth MID LS10 ....37 F5
Midland Pas HDGY LS6 ....27 H2
Midland Rd HDGY LS6 ....27 H2
  MID LS10 ....37 F5
Midland St RTHW LS26 ....45 G5
Milan Rd RHAY LS8 ....29 F2
Milan St RHAY LS8 ....29 G2
Miles Hill Av CHAL LS7 ....20 B4
Miles Hill Crs CHAL LS7 ....20 B4
Miles Hill Gv CHAL LS7 ....20 B4
Miles Hill Mt CHAL LS7 ....20 A4
Miles Hill Pl CHAL LS7 ....20 B4
Miles Hill Rd CHAL LS7 ....20 B4
Miles Hill St CHAL LS7 ....20 B4
Miles Hill Ter CHAL LS7 ....20 B4
Miles Hill Vw CHAL LS7 ....20 B4
Milford Pl BULY LS4 ....27 F4
Millbank PDSY/CALV LS28 ....32 D2
Millbank Ct PDSY/CALV LS28 ....32 D3
Millbeck Ap MOR LS27 ....40 B5
Millenium Ct PDSY/CALV LS28 * 24 D5
Millennium Sq LDS LS1 ....3 F2
Millennium Wy BEE/HOL LS11 ....42 A2
Millers Dl MOR LS27 ....40 B5
Millgarth St LDSU LS2 ....3 J4
Mill Gn BEE/HOL LS11 ....14 B1
Mill Green Cl SCFT LS14 ....23 G5
Mill Green Dr SCFT LS14 ....23 G5
Mill Green Garth SCFT LS14 * 23 G5
Mill Green Rd SCFT LS14 ....23 G5
Mill Green Vw SCFT LS14 ....23 F5
Mill Hill LDS LS1 ....3 G5
  PDSY/CALV LS28 ....32 C3
  RTHW LS26 ....50 C1
Mill Hill Gn RTHW LS26 * 50 C1
Mill Hill Sq RTHW LS26 ....50 C1
Mill La BOW BD4 ....55 E2
  BRAM LS13 ....25 E2
Mill Pit La RTHW LS26 ....50 B4
Mill Pond Cl HDGY LS6 ....19 G4
Mill Pond Gv HDGY LS6 ....19 G4
Mill Pond La HDGY LS6 ....19 G4
Mill Pond Sq HDGY LS6 ....19 G3
Mill Rd PDSY/CALV LS28 ....32 D2
Millshaw BEE/HOL LS11 ....41 G2
Millshaw Mt BEE/HOL LS11 ....41 G4
Millshaw Park Av BEE/HOL LS11 .....41 F3
Millshaw Park Cl BEE/HOL LS11 ......41 F3
Millshaw Park La BEE/HOL LS11 ......41 F3
Millshaw Park Wy
  BEE/HOL LS11 ....41 F2
Millshaw Rd BEE/HOL LS11 ....41 G4
Millside Wk MOR LS27 ....46 C4
Mill St MOR LS27 ....46 C3
Millwright St LDSU LS2 ....3 K2
Milne Ct MSTN/BAR LS15 ....39 H2
Milner Gdns OSM LS9 * 36 C1
Milner La EARD/LOFT WF3 ....49 G3
Milner's Rd YEA LS19 ....8 B1
Milnes St WOR/ARM LS12 ....35 G2

Milton Ter KSTL LS5 ....26 C1
Miry La YEA LS19 ....5 H5
Mistress La WOR/ARM LS12 ....27 E5
Mitford Pl WOR/ARM LS12 ....35 F1
Mitford Rd WOR/ARM LS12 ....35 F1
Mitford Ter WOR/ARM LS12 ....35 F1
Mitford Vw WOR/ARM LS12 ....35 F1
Modder Av WOR/ARM LS12 ....34 D1
Modder Pl WOR/ARM LS12 ....34 D1
Model Av WOR/ARM LS12 ....35 F1
Model Rd WOR/ARM LS12 ....35 F1
Model Ter WOR/ARM LS12 ....35 F1
Monk Bridge Av HDGY LS6 ....19 H4
Monk Bridge Dr HDGY LS6 ....19 H4
Monk Bridge Pl HDGY LS6 ....19 G4
Monk Bridge Rd HDGY LS6 ....19 H4
Monk Bridge Ter HDGY LS6 ....19 H4
Monkswood Av SCFT LS14 ....22 D2
Monkswood Bank SCFT LS14 ....22 D2
Monkswood Cl SCFT LS14 ....22 D2
Monkswood Dr SCFT LS14 ....22 D2
Monkswood Gn SCFT LS14 * 23 E2
Monkswood Hl SCFT LS14 ....22 D2
Monkswood Ri SCFT LS14 ....22 D2
Monkswood Wk SCFT LS14 ....23 E2
Montagu Av RHAY LS8 ....22 A5
Montagu Ct RHAY LS8 ....21 H4
Montagu Cres RHAY LS8 ....22 A5
Montagu Dr RHAY LS8 ....22 A5
Montagu Gdns RHAY LS8 ....21 H5
Montagu Gv RHAY LS8 ....22 A5
Montagu Pl RHAY LS8 ....21 H5
Montagu Ri RHAY LS8 ....30 A1
Montagu Vw RHAY LS8 ....21 H5
Montcalm Crs MID LS10 ....43 E1
Montfort Cl HORS LS18 ....10 B4
Montgomery Av
  BHP/TINH LS16 ....19 E3
Montpelier Ter HDGY LS6 ....27 H1
Montreal Av CHAL LS7 ....20 D4
Montreal Ter BRAM LS13 ....25 E5
Moor Allerton Av
  AL/HA/HU LS17 ....14 A5
Moor Allerton Crs
  AL/HA/HU LS17 ....14 A5
Moor Allerton Dr
  AL/HA/HU LS17 ....14 B5
Moor Allerton Gdns
  AL/HA/HU LS17 ....13 H5
Moor Av MSTN/BAR LS15 ....38 D1
Moor Cl MID LS10 ....42 D1
Moor Crs BEE/HOL LS11 ....36 C4
Moor Crescent Cha
  BEE/HOL LS11 ....36 C4
Moor Cft BHP/TINH LS16 ....18 B3
Moor Dr HDGY LS6 ....19 G4
  PDSY/CALV LS28 ....32 D3
Moorehouse Gv OSM LS9 ....29 E4
Moor Farm Gdns CHAL LS7 ....20 C5
Moorfield Av WOR/ARM LS12 ....26 C5
Moorfield Cl YEA LS19 ....9 F1
Moorfield Ct YEA LS19 ....9 F1
Moorfield Crs PDSY/CALV LS28 ....32 B2
  WOR/ARM LS12 ....26 C5
  YEA LS19 ....9 F1
Moorfield Cft YEA LS19 ....9 F1
Moorfield Dr YEA LS19 ....9 F1
Moorfield Gdns
  PDSY/CALV LS28 ....32 A2
Moorfield Gv PDSY/CALV LS28 ....32 A2
  WOR/ARM LS12 ....26 C5
  YEA LS19 ....9 F1
Moorfields AL/HA/HU LS17 * 13 H5
  BRAM LS13 ....25 C2
Moor Flatts Av MID LS10 ....48 C1
Moor Flatts Rd MID LS10 ....48 C1
Moor Grange Ri BHP/TINH LS16 ......18 D2
Moor Grange Vw
  BHP/TINH LS16 ....18 C2
Moor Gv PDSY/CALV LS28 ....32 D3
  PDSY/CALV LS28 ....32 C3
Moorhouse Av BEE/HOL LS11 ....41 H2
The Moorings AL/HA/HU LS17 ....14 A2
  MID LS10 ....42 D5
Moor Knoll La EARD/LOFT WF3 ......48 D5
Moorland Av GSLY LS20 ....5 H5
  HDGY LS6 ....27 H5
Moorland Crs GSLY LS20 ....5 H5
  HDGY LS6 ....27 H5
Moorland Dr AL/HA/HU LS17 ....20 C1
  GSLY LS20 ....5 H5
Moorland Gdns AL/HA/HU LS17 ....13 H5
Moorland Garth AL/HA/HU LS17 ......20 C1
Moorland Ings AL/HA/HU LS17 ....20 C1
Moorland Rd BHP/TINH LS16 ....19 G2
  HDGY LS6 ....27 H5
Moorlands Av YEA LS19 ....9 F1
Moorlands Dr YEA LS19 ....9 F1
The Moorlands AL/HA/HU LS17 ......14 A3
Moorland Vw AL/HA/HU LS17 ....13 G5
Moorland Wk AL/HA/HU LS17 ....13 G5
Moor La GSLY LS20 ....6 A5
Moor Park Av HDGY LS6 ....19 F4
Moor Park Dr HDGY LS6 ....19 F4
Moor Park Mt HDGY LS6 ....19 F4
Moor Park Vw HDGY LS6 ....19 F4
Moor Rd BEE/HOL LS11 ....36 D4
  BHP/TINH LS16 ....7 H2
  HDGY LS6 ....19 F4
  MID LS10 ....42 D1
Moorside Dr BRAM LS13 ....25 C2
Moorside Maltings
  BEE/HOL LS11 ....36 C5
Moorside St BRAM LS13 ....25 C1
Moorside Ter BRAM LS13 ....25 C1
Moor Vw BEE/HOL LS11 ....36 A3
Moorville Av BEE/HOL LS11 ....36 B4
Moorville Cl BEE/HOL LS11 ....36 A4
Moorville Gv BEE/HOL LS11 ....36 A4
Moorville Rd BEE/HOL LS11 ....36 B4

Moorway GSLY LS20 ....4 B5
Moresdale La SCFT LS14 ....30 D2
Morpeth Pl OSM LS9 ....37 E4
Morphet Ter CHAL LS7 * 3 H1
Morris Av KSTL LS5 ....18 C5
Morris Gv KSTL LS5 ....26 C1
Morris La KSTL LS5 ....18 C5
Morris Mt KSTL LS5 ....26 C1
Morris Pl MOR LS27 ....46 B1
Morris Vw KSTL LS5 ....26 C1
Morritt Av MSTN/BAR LS15 ....31 F4
Morritt Gv MSTN/BAR LS15 ....30 D5
Mortuary La WOR/ARM LS12 ....26 A5
Moseley Pl RHAY LS8 ....28 B2
Moseley Wood Ap
  BHP/TINH LS16 ....10 D3
Moseley Wood Av
  BHP/TINH LS16 ....10 D3
Moseley Wood Bank
  BHP/TINH LS16 ....10 D2
Moseley Wood Cl
  BHP/TINH LS16 ....10 D2
Moseley Wood Crs
  BHP/TINH LS16 ....10 D2
Moseley Wood Cft HORS LS18 ....10 D3
Moseley Wood Dr
  BHP/TINH LS16 ....10 D2
Moseley Wood Gdns
  BHP/TINH LS16 ....10 D2
Moseley Wood Gn
  BHP/TINH LS16 ....10 D2
Moseley Wood La
  BHP/TINH LS16 ....11 E1
Moseley Wood Ri
  BHP/TINH LS16 ....10 D2
Moseley Wood Vw
  BHP/TINH LS16 ....11 E1
Moseley Wood Wk
  BHP/TINH LS16 ....10 D2
Moseley Wood Wy
  BHP/TINH LS16 ....10 D1
Moss Av BRAM LS13 ....16 D5
Moss Gdns AL/HA/HU LS17 ....13 E2
Moss Ri AL/HA/HU LS17 ....13 E2
Moss Va AL/HA/HU LS17 ....13 E2
Motley La GSLY LS20 ....5 E2
Mountcliffe Vw MOR LS27 ....40 D4
Mount Ct PDSY/CALV LS28 ....24 C5
Mount Dr AL/HA/HU LS17 ....13 F1
Mount Gdns AL/HA/HU LS17 ....13 F1
Mount Pleasant BRAM LS13 ....25 F1
  GSLY LS20 ....5 E2
Mount Pleasant Av RHAY LS8 ....21 F5
Mount Pleasant Gdns
  RHAY LS8 * 21 F5
Mount Pleasant Rd
  PDSY/CALV LS28 ....24 C5
Mount Preston LDSU LS2 ....2 C1
Mount Preston St LDSU LS2 ....2 C1
Mount Ri AL/HA/HU LS17 ....13 F1
Mount Tabor St
  PDSY/CALV LS28 ....32 A1
The Mount AL/HA/HU LS17 ....13 F1
  MSTN/BAR LS15 ....31 F4
  YEA LS19 * 9 E1
Mount Vernon Rd YEA LS19 ....9 E3
Mowbray Cha RTHW LS26 ....45 E4
Mowbray Ct SCFT LS14 ....31 E2
Mowbray Crs SCFT LS14 ....31 E2
Moynihan Cl RHAY LS8 ....29 H1
Muir Ct HDGY LS6 ....27 E1
Mulberry Av BHP/TINH LS16 ....12 B4
Mulberry Garth BHP/TINH LS16 ......12 B3
Mulberry Ri BHP/TINH LS16 ....12 B3
Mulberry St MID LS10 ....36 D5
  PDSY/CALV LS28 ....32 C1
Mulberry Vw BHP/TINH LS16 ....12 B4
Mullins Ct OSM LS9 ....37 F2
Murton Cl SCFT LS14 ....31 E1
Museum St OSM LS9 ....29 F4
Musgrave Bank BRAM LS13 ....26 A3
Musgrave Buildings
  MID LS10 * 24 D5
Musgrave Mt BRAM LS13 ....26 A3
Musgrave Ri BRAM LS13 ....26 A3
Musgrave Vw BRAM LS13 ....26 A3
Mushroom St CHAL LS7 ....3 K1

N

Naburn Ap SCFT LS14 ....23 F1
Naburn Cha SCFT LS14 ....23 G3
Naburn Cl SCFT LS14 ....23 F1
Naburn Dr SCFT LS14 ....23 F2
Naburn Gdns SCFT LS14 ....23 F2
Naburn Gn OSM LS14 ....23 F2
Naburn Pl SCFT LS14 ....23 F1
Naburn Rd SCFT LS14 ....23 G2
Naburn Vw SCFT LS14 ....23 G2
Naburn Wk SCFT LS14 ....23 G1
Nancroft Crs WOR/ARM LS12 ....35 E1
Nancroft Ter WOR/ARM LS12 ....35 E1
Nansen Av BRAM LS13 ....25 F3
Nansen Gv BRAM LS13 ....25 F3
Nansen Mt BRAM LS13 ....25 F3
Nansen Pl BRAM LS13 ....25 F3
Nansen St BRAM LS13 ....25 F3
Nansen Ter BRAM LS13 ....25 F3
Nansen Vw BRAM LS13 ....25 F3
Narrowboat Whf BRAM LS13 ....16 D5
Naseby Gdns OSM LS9 ....29 E5
Naseby Garth OSM LS9 ....29 E4
Naseby Gra OSM LS9 ....29 E4
Naseby Pl OSM LS9 ....29 E5
Naseby Ter OSM LS9 ....29 E5
Naseby Vw OSM LS9 ....29 E5
Naseby Wk OSM LS9 ....29 E5
Nassau Pl CHAL LS7 ....29 E2

Nateby Ri EARD/LOFT WF3 ....50 A3
National Rd MID LS10 ....37 E4
Navigation Wk MID LS10 ....3 H6
Naylors Garth HDGY LS6 ....19 H5
Neath Gdns OSM LS9 ....30 B2
Needles Inn La RTHW LS26 ....45 G4
Nelson Ct MOR LS27 ....46 B4
Nelson Pl MOR LS27 ....46 B4
Nepshaw La MOR LS27 ....46 B1
Nepshaw La North MOR LS27 ....46 A1
Neptune St OSM LS9 ....3 K6
Nesfield Cl MID LS10 ....43 F5
Nesfield Crs MID LS10 ....43 F5
Nesfield Gdns MID LS10 ....43 E5
Nesfield Garth MID LS10 ....43 E5
Nesfield Rd MID LS10 ....43 E5
Nesfield Vw MID LS10 ....43 E5
Nesfield Wk MID LS10 ....43 E5
Nethercliffe Rd GSLY LS20 ....5 H5
Netherfield Cl YEA LS19 ....9 H3
Netherfield Dr GSLY LS20 ....4 D2
Netherfield Rd GSLY LS20 ....4 D2
Nether St PDSY/CALV LS28 ....24 A4
Nettleton Ct MSTN/BAR LS15 ....31 H5
Neville Ap OSM LS9 ....38 A2
Neville Av OSM LS9 ....38 A2
Neville Cl OSM LS9 ....38 A2
Neville Crs OSM LS9 ....30 B5
Neville Garth OSM LS9 ....38 A2
Neville Gv OSM LS9 ....38 A2
Neville Mt OSM LS9 ....38 A2
Neville Pde OSM LS9 ....38 A2
Neville Pl OSM LS9 ....38 B1
Neville Rd MSTN/BAR LS15 ....38 C1
  OSM LS9 ....38 A2
Neville Rw OSM LS9 ....38 A2
Neville Sq OSM LS9 ....38 A1
Neville St LDS LS1 ....3 F6
Neville Ter OSM LS9 ....38 A2
Neville Vw OSM LS9 ....38 A2
Neville Wk OSM LS9 ....38 A2
New Adel Av BHP/TINH LS16 ....11 G4
New Adel Gdns BHP/TINH LS16 ......11 G4
New Adel La BHP/TINH LS16 ....11 G4
Newark V EARD/LOFT WF3 ....49 G3
New Bank St MOR LS27 ....46 D1
New Briggate LDSU LS2 ....3 H3
Newby Garth AL/HA/HU LS17 ....14 A2
New Craven Ga BEE/HOL LS11 ....36 C5
New Crs HORS LS18 ....17 F2
New Cft HORS LS18 ....17 F2
New Farmers Hl RTHW LS26 ....45 H4
Newhall Bank MID LS10 ....42 D5
Newhall Cha MID LS10 ....42 D5
Newhall Cl MID LS10 ....42 D5
Newhall Crs MID LS10 ....42 D5
Newhall Gdns MID LS10 ....42 D5
Newhall Garth MID LS10 ....48 D1
Newhall Gn MID LS10 ....42 D5
Newhall Mt MID LS10 ....42 D5
Newhall Rd MID LS10 ....42 D5
New Inn St WOR/ARM LS12 ....34 C1
Newlaithes Gdns HORS LS18 ....17 F3
Newlaithes Garth HORS LS18 ....17 E4
Newlaithes Rd HORS LS18 ....17 F4
Newlands PDSY/CALV LS28 ....24 B3
Newlands Av YEA LS19 ....5 G5
Newlands Crs MOR LS27 ....47 F2
Newlands Dr MOR LS27 ....47 F2
Newlands Ri YEA LS19 ....5 G5
New La BEE/HOL LS11 ....36 B5
  MID LS10 ....48 B1
Newlay Gv HORS LS18 ....17 F4
Newlay La BRAM LS13 ....25 G1
  HORS LS18 ....17 F3
Newlay Lane Pl BRAM LS13 ....25 G1
Newlay Wood Av HORS LS18 ....17 G3
Newlay Wood Cl HORS LS18 ....17 G3
Newlay Wood Dr HORS LS18 ....17 G3
Newlay Wood Gdns
  HORS LS18 ....17 G3
Newlay Wood Ri HORS LS18 ....17 F3
Newlay Wood Rd HORS LS18 ....17 F3
Newley Mt HORS LS18 ....17 F4
Newmarket Ap OSM LS9 ....37 H3
Newmarket La OSM LS9 ....37 H3
New Market St LDS LS1 ....3 H5
New Occupation La
  PDSY/CALV LS28 ....32 A2
New Park Av PDSY/CALV LS28 ....24 C2
New Park Cft PDSY/CALV LS28 ....24 C2
New Park Cft PDSY/CALV LS28 ....24 C2
New Park Pl PDSY/CALV LS28 ....24 C2
New Park Rd MOR LS27 ....46 B3
New Park V PDSY/CALV LS28 ....24 C2
New Park Vw PDSY/CALV LS28 ....24 B3
New Park Wk PDSY/CALV LS28 * 24 B2
New Park Wy PDSY/CALV LS28 ....24 C2
Newport Av BRAM LS13 ....25 E3
Newport Crs HDGY LS6 ....27 F2
Newport Gdns HDGY LS6 ....27 F2
Newport Mt HDGY LS6 ....27 F2
Newport Rd HDGY LS6 ....27 F2
Newport Vw HDGY LS6 * 27 F2
New Princess St BEE/HOL LS11 ....36 B3
New Pudsey Sq
  PDSY/CALV LS28 ....24 A3
New Rd EARD/LOFT WF3 ....50 B5
New Road Side HORS LS18 ....17 E3
  YEA LS19 ....16 D2
Newsam Ct MSTN/BAR LS15 * 39 E1
Newsam Dr MSTN/BAR LS15 ....39 E1
Newsam Green Rd
  MSTN/BAR LS15 ....45 H1
New Station St LDS LS1 ....3 F5
New St HORS LS18 ....17 E3
  PDSY/CALV LS28 ....24 B4
  PDSY/CALV LS28 ....32 C2
New Street Gdns
  PDSY/CALV LS28 ....32 C2

New Street Gv PDSY/CALV LS
New Temple Ga
  MSTN/BAR LS15 ....
Newton Cl RTHW LS26 ....
Newton Ct RHAY LS8 ....
Newton Garth CHAL LS7 ....
Newton Hill Rd CHAL LS7 ....
Newton Lodge Cl CHAL LS7 ....
Newton Lodge Dr CHAL LS7 ....
Newton Pde CHAL LS7 ....
Newton Park Ct CHAL LS7 * ....
Newton Park Dr CHAL LS7 ....
Newton Park Vw CHAL LS7 ....
Newton Rd CHAL LS7 ....
Newton Vw CHAL LS7 ....
Newton Vls CHAL LS7 * ....
Newton Wk CHAL LS7 ....
New Wy GSLY LS20 ....
New Windsor Dr RTHW LS26 ......
New York La YEA LS19 ....
New York Rd LDSU LS2 ....
New York St LDSU LS2 ....
Nice Av RHAY LS8 ....
Nice St RHAY LS8 ....
Nice Vw RHAY LS8 ....
Nicholson Ct RHAY LS8 * ....
Nickleby Rd OSM LS9 ....
Nijinsky Wy MID LS10 ....
Nile St LDSU LS2 ....
Nineveh Gdns BEE/HOL LS11 .....
Nineveh Pde BEE/HOL LS11 ....
Nineveh Rd BEE/HOL LS11 ....
Nippet La OSM LS9 ....
Nixon Av OSM LS9 ....
The Nook AL/HA/HU LS17 ....
Nora Pl BRAM LS13 ....
Nora Rd BRAM LS13 ....
Nora Ter BRAM LS13 ....
Norfolk Cl CHAL LS7 ....
  RTHW LS26 ....
Norfolk Dr RTHW LS26 ....
Norfolk Gdns CHAL LS7 ....
Norfolk Mt CHAL LS7 ....
Norfolk Pl CHAL LS7 ....
Norfolk Ter CHAL LS7 ....
Norfolk Vw CHAL LS7 ....
Norfolk Wk CHAL LS7 ....
Norman Gv KSTL LS5 ....
Norman Mt KSTL LS5 ....
Normanton Pl BEE/HOL LS11 ....
Norman Pl RHAY LS8 ....
Norman Rw KSTL LS5 ....
Norman St KSTL LS5 ....
Norman Ter RHAY LS8 ....
Normanton Gr BEE/HOL LS11 ...
Normanton St BEE/HOL LS11 ....
Norman Vw KSTL LS5 ....
Nortech Cl CHAL LS7 ....
North Broadgate La HORS LS ...
Northbrook Cft CHAL LS7 * ....
Northbrook Pl CHAL LS7 ....
Northbrook St CHAL LS7 ....
North Cl RHAY LS8 ....
Northcote Crs BEE/HOL LS11 ....
Northcote Dr BEE/HOL LS11 .....
Northcote St PDSY/CALV LS26 ...
North Ct LDSU LS2 ....
Northern St LDS LS1 ....
North Farm Rd RHAY LS8 ....
Northfield Av RTHW LS26 ....
Northfield Pl RTHW LS26 ....
Northgate RTHW LS26 ....
North Grange Ms HDGY LS6 ......
North Grange Mt HDGY LS6 ......
North Grange Rd HDGY LS6 ......
North Grove Cl RHAY LS8 ....
North Grove Dr RHAY LS8 ....
North Grove Mt RHAY LS8 ....
North Hill Cl RHAY LS8 ....
North Hill Rd HDGY LS6 ....
North La RHAY LS8 ....
  RTHW LS26 ....
North Lingwell Rd MID LS10 ......
Northolme Av BHP/TINH LS16 ...
Northolme Crs BHP/TINH LS16 ..
North Pde BHP/TINH LS16 ....
North Park Av RHAY LS8 ....
North Park Gv RHAY LS8 ....
North Park Rd RHAY LS8 ....
North Park St MOR LS27 ....
North Rd HORS LS18 ....
  MSTN/BAR LS15 ....
North St CHAL LS7 ....
  LDSU LS2 ....
  PDSY/CALV LS28 ....
North Ter MSTN/BAR LS15 * .....
  YEA LS19 ....
North View Sl PDSY/CALV LS2 ...
North View Ter
  PDSY/CALV LS28 ....
North W RHAY LS8 ....
North West Rd LDSU LS2 ....
Northwood Cl PDSY/CALV LS2 ...
  RTHW LS26 ....
Northwood Falls RTHW LS26 .....
Northwood Mt PDSY/CALV LS ...
Northwood Pk RTHW LS26 ....
Northwood Vw
  PDSY/CALV LS28 ....
Norton Rd RHAY LS8 ....
Norton Wy MOR LS27 ....
Norville Ter HDGY LS6 ....
Norwood Av MID LS10 ....
Norwood Cr PDSY/CALV LS28 ....
Norwood Gv HDGY LS6 ....
Norwood Mt HDGY LS6 ....
Norwood Pl HDGY LS6 ....
Norwood Rd HDGY LS6 ....
Norwood Rd PDSY/CALV LS28 ....
Norwood St PDSY/CALV LS28 ....
Norwood Ter HDGY LS6 ....
Norwood Vw HDGY LS6 ....
Noster Gv BEE/HOL LS11 ....

EE/HOL LS11 .....35 H5
EE/HOL LS11 .....35 H5
EE/HOL LS11 .....35 H5
BEE/HOL LS11 .....35 H5
n Cl
OFT WF3 * 49 C3
OSM LS9 .....29 H4
OSM LS9 .....29 H4
OSM LS9 .....29 H4
OSM LS9 .....29 H4
l Rw OSM LS9 .....29 H4
OSM LS9 .....29 H4
OSM LS9 .....29 H4
OSM LS9 .....29 H4
OSM LS9 .....29 H4
OSM LS9 .....29 H4
Av WOR/ARM LS12 ..27 E5
St WOR/ARM LS12 ..27 E5
Ter WOR/ARM LS12...27 E5
Vw WOR/ARM LS12...27 E5
GSLY LS20 .....5 F4
OSM LS9
RM LS12 .....34 A3

O

R LS27 .....46 D3
STN/BAR LS15 .....38 D1
arth SCFT LS14 .....23 F1
eadow SCFT LS14 ...23 F1
l PDSY/CALV LS28 ...32 D3
ct AL/HA/HU LS17 ...14 C3
r AL/HA/HU LS17 .....14 C3
dns AL/HA/HU LS17..14 C3
Wy AL/HA/HU LS17 ..14 C3
v RTHW LS26 * 19 C5
DGY LS6 .....19 G5
R LS27 .....46 D3
on Ct RHAY LS8 .....22 A4
y OSM LS9 .....37 H1
Av BEE/HOL LS11 ....41 H2
Gv BEE/HOL LS11 ....41 H2
Rd BEE/HOL LS11 ....41 H2
St BEE/HOL LS11 .....42 A2
Av BHP/TINH LS16 ...12 B4
ll D BHP/TINH LS16 ..12 B4
ld BHP/TINH LS16 ...12 B4
old MOR LS27 * 50 C2
er MOR LS27 * 41 E3
ALV LS28 .....40 A5
M LS27 .....40 D4
ALV LS28 .....30 A2
OSM LS9 .....30 A2
Crs OSM LS9 .....30 A2
Dr RHAY LS8 .....30 A2
Mt OSM LS9 .....30 A2
M OSM LS9 .....30 A2
Wk OSM LS9 .....30 A2
v RHAY LS8 .....21 G4
t BRAM LS13 .....21 C4
dns RHAY LS8 .....21 G4
v BRAM LS13 .....25 F2
t RHAY LS8 .....21 G4
/CALV LS28 * 24 D2
Av RHAY LS8 .....21 G4
Boundary Rd
.....21 H4
Ct RHAY LS8 .....22 A4
Dr RHAY LS8 .....44 D4
Gdns
CALV LS28 .....32 C2
Garth RHAY LS8 .....22 A4
Gra RHAY LS8 .....22 A4
Grange La RHAY LS8..22 A4
Gn RHAY LS8 .....22 A4
Gv RHAY LS8 .....22 A4
La RHAY LS8 .....30 B2

RHAY LS8 .....21 H4
Oakwood Mt RHAY LS8 ....21 H4
Oakwood Nook RHAY LS8 ..21 H4
Oakwood Pk RHAY LS8 .....22 A5
Oakwood Pl RHAY LS8 .....22 A4
Oakwood Ri RHAY LS8 .....22 A4
Oakwood Ter PDSY/CALV LS28 ..32 C2
Oakwood Vw RHAY LS8 * ..22 A4
Oakwood Wk RHAY LS8 ....22 A4
Oast House Cft EARD/LOFT WF3 ..49 H5
Oatland Cl CHAL LS7 .....28 C3
Oatland Dr CHAL LS7 .....28 C3
Oatland Gdns CHAL LS7 ...28 C3
Oatland Hts CHAL LS7 .....28 C3
Oatland La CHAL LS7 .....28 C3
Oatland Pl CHAL LS7 .....28 C2
Oatland Rd CHAL LS7 .....28 C2
Oatland Ter CHAL LS7 .....28 C2
Oban Cl EARD/LOFT WF3 ..47 F5
Oban Pl WOR/ARM LS12 ...26 D5
Oban St WOR/ARM LS12 ...26 D5
Oban Ter WOR/ARM LS12..26 D5
Occupation La BHP/TINH LS16 ...7 F1
PDSY/CALV LS28 .....32 A2
Oddfellow St MOR LS27 ...46 C2
Oddy's Fold HDGY LS6 .....20 C2
Ogilby Ct RTHW LS26 .....45 F4
Ogilby Ms RTHW LS26 .....45 F4
O'Grady Sq OSM LS9 .....37 F1
Old Barn Cl AL/HA/HU LS17 ..13 G2
Old Brandon La AL/HA/HU LS17 ..20 D1
Old Cl BEE/HOL LS11 .....41 F5
Oldfarm Ap BHP/TINH LS16 ..18 B2
Oldfarm Cl BHP/TINH LS16 ...18 B2
Oldfarm Cross BHP/TINH LS16 ..18 C2
Oldfarm Dr BHP/TINH LS16 ...18 B2
Oldfarm Garth BHP/TINH LS16..18 C2
Oldfarm Pde BHP/TINH LS16 ..18 C2
Oldfarm Wk BHP/TINH LS16 ..18 B2
Old Farnley La YEA LS19 * ..8 B1
Oldfield Ct CHAL LS7 .....21 E5
Oldfield La WOR/ARM LS12 ..35 F2
Oldfield St WOR/ARM LS12 ..35 E2
Old Forge Ms BHP/TINH LS16 ..9 H1
Old Haworth La YEA LS19 ..5 H5
Old La BEE/HOL LS11 .....41 H1
BHP/TINH LS16 .....7 E1
Old Marsh PDSY/CALV LS28 ..32 A1
Old Mill La MID LS10 .....37 E4
Old Oak Cl BHP/TINH LS16 ..18 B3
Old Oak Dr BHP/TINH LS16 ..18 B3
Old Oak Garth BHP/TINH LS16..18 B3
Old Oak Lawn BHP/TINH LS16..18 B3
Old Park Rd AL/HA/HU LS17 ..21 G3
Old Run Rd MID LS10 .....42 D1
Old Run Vw MID LS10 .....43 E5
Old School Ms MOR LS27 ..41 E3
Old Whack House La YEA LS19 ..8 B1
Oliver Hi HORS LS18 .....17 G3
Ontario Pl CHAL LS7 .....20 D4
Orchard Mt MSTN/BAR LS15 ..31 G3
Orchard Rd MSTN/BAR LS15..31 F3
Orchard Sq MSTN/BAR LS15..31 F3
The Orchards MSTN/BAR LS15..15 G3
Orchard Wy RTHW LS26 ....50 D1
Orchid Ct EARD/LOFT WF3 ..49 H4
Oriental St WOR/ARM LS12..35 E1
Orion Crs MID LS10 .....43 E4
Orion Dr MID LS10 .....43 E4
Orion Gdns MID LS10 .....43 E4
Orion Vw MID LS10 .....43 F4
Orion Wk MID LS10 .....43 F5
Orville Gdns HDGY LS6 .....27 G1
Osbourne Ct BRAM LS13 ..25 H4
Osmondthorpe La OSM LS9 ..38 A1
Osmondthorpe Ter OSM LS9..29 H5
Osprey Cl AL/HA/HU LS17 ..14 B3
Osprey Gv AL/HA/HU LS17..14 B3
Osprey Meadow MOR LS27..47 F2
Oswald Cl GSLY LS20 .....5 H5
Otley La YEA LS19 .....5 H5
Otley Old Rd BHP/TINH LS16 ..11 F3
HORS LS18 .....7 E3
Otterburn Gdns
.....11 H4
Oulton Dr RTHW LS26 .....51 G5
Oulton La RTHW LS26 .....51 E1
Out Gang BRAM LS13 .....26 A2
Outgang La BRAM LS13 ....26 A2
Outwood Av HORS LS18 ...17 H3
Outwood Cha HORS LS18...17 H2
Outwood La HORS LS18 ...17 G3
Ouzlewell Grn EARD/LOFT WF3..50 B4
The Oval GSLY LS20 .....5 F4
MID LS10 .....37 G4
RTHW LS26 .....50 D2
SCFT LS14 .....30 D3
Overdale Av AL/HA/HU LS17 ..14 C2
Overdale Ter MSTN/BAR LS15..39 G4
Over La YEA LS19 .....9 E4
Owlcotes Dr PDSY/CALV LS28 ..24 A5
Owlcotes Gdns
PDSY/CALV LS28 .....24 A5
Owlcotes La PDSY/CALV LS28 ..24 A5
Owlcotes Ter PDSY/CALV LS28..24 A5
Owlett Md EARD/LOFT WF3 ..49 H5
Owlett Mead Cl
EARD/LOFT WF5 .....49 H5
Owl Rdg MOR LS27 .....47 E3
Oxford Av GSLY LS20 .....4 D3
Oxford Pl LDS LS1 .....2 E4
CHAL LS7 .....28 C2
GSLY LS20 .....4 D3
Oxford Rd CHAL LS7 .....28 C2
Oxford Rw LDS LS1 .....2 E4
Oxley Cl GSLY LS20 .....5 E5
Oxley St OSM LS9 .....29 H5
Oxton Mt OSM LS9 .....29 H5
Oxton Wy OSM LS9 .....29 H5
Oyster Cl MOR LS27 .....47 E3

P

The Paddock HDGY LS6 .....19 H3
RTHW LS26 .....50 C1
Padstow Gdns MID LS10...48 A1
Paisley Gv WOR/ARM LS12*..26 D5
Paisley Pl WOR/ARM LS12 *..26 D5
Paisley Rd WOR/ARM LS12..26 D5
Paisley St WOR/ARM LS12..26 D5
Paisley Ter WOR/ARM LS12 *..26 D5
The Parade BRAM LS13 * ..25 G3
HDGY LS6 .....19 F5
OSM LS9 .....37 F1
YEA LS19 * 8 B1
Paradise St PDSY/CALV LS28 ..24 B2
Park Av MOR LS27 .....46 B3
MSTN/BAR LS15 .....31 H5
RHAY LS8 .....21 H5
WOR/ARM LS12 .....26 D5
YEA LS19 .....5 G5
Park Cl BRAM LS13 .....25 C2
Park Copse HORS LS18 ....17 E1
GSLY LS20 .....4 C4
RHAY LS8 .....21 H1
RTHW LS26 .....50 C1
WOR/ARM LS12 .....26 D5
Parkcroft PDSY/CALV LS28..24 B3
Park Cross St LDS LS1 .....2 E4
Park Dr HORS LS18 .....16 D2
Park Edge Cl RHAY LS8 ....22 A3
Parkfield Av BEE/HOL LS11..36 A5
Parkfield Cl PDSY/CALV LS28..32 A1
Parkfield Ct SCFT LS14 * ..30 C2
Parkfield Dr BEE/HOL LS11..36 A5
Parkfield Mt BEE/HOL LS11..35 H5
PDSY/CALV LS28 .....32 C1
Parkfield Pl BEE/HOL LS11..36 A5
Parkfield Rd BEE/HOL LS11 *..36 A5
Parkfield Rw BEE/HOL LS11..36 A5
Parkfield St BEE/HOL LS11..36 A5
Parkfield Ter PDSY/CALV LS28..24 C4
Parkfield Vw BEE/HOL LS11..36 A5
Parkfield Wy SCFT LS14 ...30 C2
Park Gate Cl HORS LS18...19 F4
Park Gv HDGY LS6 .....19 F4
HORS LS18 .....16 D2
YEA LS19 .....5 G5
Park Holme CHAL LS7 .....29 E1
Parkland Av MOR LS27 ....46 A3
Parkland Crs RHAY LS8 ....20 A1
Parkland Dr AL/HA/HU LS17..14 A5
Parkland Gdns HDGY LS6 ..20 A1
Parklands BHP/TINH LS16 ...7 H1
Parkland Ter HDGY LS6 ....20 A1
Parkland Vw YEA LS19 .....8 D1
Park La BVRD LS3 .....2 A3
GSLY LS20 .....4 C5
RHAY LS8 .....21 G1
RTHW LS26 .....50 D1
Park Lane Ms AL/HA/HU LS17..14 D3
Park Lea MID LS10 * 48 C1
Parklee HDGY LS6 .....19 F5
WOR/ARM LS12 .....26 C5
Park Pde MOR LS27 * 46 B3
OSM LS9 .....37 G2
Park Pl LDS LS1 .....2 D4
Park Ri BRAM LS13 .....25 G1
Park Rd BRAM LS13 .....25 G1
GSLY LS20 .....4 D5
MSTN/BAR LS15 .....39 H3
WOR/ARM LS12 .....26 C5
YEA LS19 .....5 G5
Park Rw LDS LS1 .....3 F4
Park Side HORS LS18 .....17 E2
Parkside Av HDGY LS6 ....19 H5
Parkside Cl HDGY LS6 .....19 H2
Parkside Crs HDGY LS6 ....19 H2
Parkside Gdns HDGY LS6..19 H5
Parkside Gn HDGY LS6 ....19 H5
Parkside La BEE/HOL LS11..42 C1
Parkside Lawns HDGY LS6..19 H5
Parkside Mt BEE/HOL LS11..42 A2
Parkside Pde HDGY LS6 ...19 H2
Parkside Pl HDGY LS6 .....19 H2
Parkside Rd HDGY LS6 ....19 H2
PDSY/CALV LS28 .....24 B3
Parkside Rw BEE/HOL LS11..42 A2
Parkside Vw HDGY LS6 ....19 H5
Park Spring Gdns BRAM LS13 ..24 C5
Park Spring Ri BRAM LS13..25 F5
Park Sq East LDS LS1 .....2 E4
Park Sq North LDS LS1 ....2 E4
Park Sq South LDS LS1 ....2 E4
Park Sq West LDS LS1 .....2 E4
Parkstone Av BHP/TINH LS16..18 C1
Parkstone Gn BHP/TINH LS16..18 C1
Parkstone Gv BHP/TINH LS16..18 C1
Parkstone Mt BHP/TINH LS16..18 C1
Parkstone Pl BHP/TINH LS16 *..18 C1
Park St LDS LS1 .....2 E3
MOR LS27 .....41 E3
MSTN/BAR LS15 .....31 H5
WOR/ARM LS12 .....27 E5
YEA LS19 .....5 G5
Park Ter HDGY LS6 .....19 F4
Park Top PDSY/CALV LS28..24 C3
Park Vw BEE/HOL LS11 ....41 F5
PDSY/CALV LS28 .....32 C1
Park View Av HDGY LS6 ...27 F1
Parkview Ct RHAY LS8 .....22 D1
Park View Crs RHAY LS8 ...21 H1
Park View Gv BULY LS4 ....27 F2
Park View Ter YEA LS19 ....8 D3
Park Vis RHAY LS8 .....21 G1
Parkville Pl BRAM LS13 ....25 G1
Parkway Cl SCFT LS14 .....30 C1

Parkways RTHW LS26 .....45 F5
Parkways Cl RTHW LS26....51 F1
Parkways Cl RTHW LS26....45 F5
Parkways Ct RTHW LS26 ...45 F5
Parkways Dr RTHW LS26 ...45 F5
Parkways Garth RTHW LS26 *..51 F1
Parkways Gv RTHW LS26...45 F5
Parkway V SCFT LS14 .....30 C2
Park West RTHW LS26 .....50 D1
Park Wood Av BEE/HOL LS11..41 H4
Parkwood Av RHAY LS8 ....21 G2
Parkwood Cl BEE/HOL LS11..41 H4
Parkwood Ct RHAY LS8 ....21 G2
Park Wood Dr BEE/HOL LS11..41 H4
Parkwood Gdns RHAY LS8..21 G2
Parkwood Rd BEE/HOL LS11..41 H4
Parkwood Vw RHAY LS8 ...21 G2
Parkwood Wy RHAY LS8 ...21 G2
Parliament Pl WOR/ARM LS12..27 F5
Parliament Rd WOR/ARM LS12..35 F1
Parnaby Av MID LS10 .....43 F2
Parnaby Rd MID LS10 .....43 F2
Parnaby St MID LS10 .....43 F2
Parnaby Ter MID LS10 .....43 F2
Partridge Cl MOR LS27 ....47 F2
Pasture Av CHAL LS7 .....20 D3
Pasture Crs CHAL LS7 .....20 D3
Pasture La CHAL LS7 .....20 D3
Pasture Mt WOR/ARM LS12..26 D5
Pasture Pde CHAL LS7 ....20 D3
Pasture Pl CHAL LS7 .....20 D3
Pasture Rd RHAY LS8 .....29 E1
Pasture St CHAL LS7 * 20 D3
Pasture Ter CHAL LS7 .....20 D3
Pasture Vw WOR/ARM LS12..26 D5
Pasture View Rd RTHW LS26..50 B1
Pavilion Gdns RTHW LS26..45 E5
Pavilion Ms BULY LS4 .....27 F2
Pavilion Wy PDSY/CALV LS28..32 D1
Pawson St EARD/LOFT WF3..49 H4
MOR LS27 .....46 A3
Peacock Ct CHAL LS7 .....29 E2
Peacock Gn MOR LS27 ....47 E3
Pearson Av HDGY LS6 .....27 G2
Pearson Gv HDGY LS6 .....27 G2
Pearson St MID LS10 .....36 D5
Pearson Ter HDGY LS6 ....27 G2
Peasehill Cl YEA LS19 .....9 G5
Peasehill Pk YEA LS19 .....9 G5
Peel St MOR LS27 .....46 C3
Pelham Ct MID LS10 * 48 D3
Pelham Pl CHAL LS7 .....20 D3
Pembroke Cl MOR LS27....46 B1
Pembroke Rd PDSY/CALV LS28..32 A1
Penarth Rd MSTN/BAR LS15..31 H3
Penda's Dr MSTN/BAR LS15..31 H1
Penda's Gv MSTN/BAR LS15..31 H1
Penda's Wk MSTN/BAR LS15..31 H1
Pendil Cl MSTN/BAR LS15..32 A4
Penlands Crs MSTN/BAR LS15..39 H1
Penlands Lawn MSTN/BAR LS15..39 H1
Penlands Wk MSTN/BAR LS15..39 H1
Pennington Ct HDGY LS6 ...28 A2
Pennington La RTHW LS26..51 F4
Pennington Pl HDGY LS6 ...28 A2
Pennington St HDGY LS6...28 A2
Pennington Ter HDGY LS6..28 A2
Pennwell Garth SCFT LS14..23 H5
Pennwell Gn SCFT LS14 ...23 H5
Pennwell Lawn SCFT LS14..23 H5
Pennyfield Cl HDGY LS6 ....19 G4
Penny Lane Wy MID LS10..36 D4
Pennythorne Ct YEA LS19...8 C2
Pennythorne Dr YEA LS19...8 C2
Penraevon St CHAL LS7 ...28 C2
Penrith Gv WOR/ARM LS12..35 E2
Pentland Wy MOR LS27 ....47 F2
Pepper Gdns BRAM LS13...26 A1
Pepper La BRAM LS13 .....26 A1
MID LS10 .....37 F5
Pepper Rd MID LS10 .....43 F1
Percival St LDSU LS2 .....3 F2
Percy St WOR/ARM LS12...35 E2
Peregrine Av MOR LS27 ....47 F2
Perseverance St
PDSY/CALV LS28 .....32 A1
Perseverance Ter RTHW LS26..50 D1
Perth Mt HORS LS18 .....17 E1
Peter La MOR LS27 .....47 E4
Petersfield Av MID LS10 ...43 E4
Petrie Crs BRAM LS13 .....16 B5
Petrie St BRAM LS13 .....26 A1
Philippa Wy WOR/ARM LS12..35 E5
Phil May Ct WOR/ARM LS12..35 E2
Pickard Bank HDGY LS6 ...19 H5
Pickard Ct MSTN/BAR LS15..32 A4
Pickering Mt WOR/ARM LS12..27 F5
Pickering St WOR/ARM LS12..27 F5
Piece Wood Rd BHP/TINH LS16..10 D4
Pigeon Cote Cl SCFT LS14..22 D4
Pigeon Cote Rd SCFT LS14..22 D4
Pilgrim Wy PDSY/CALV LS28..24 A2
Pilot St OSM LS9 .....29 G5
Pinder Av WOR/ARM LS12..34 B2
Pinder Gv WOR/ARM LS12..34 B2
Pinder St WOR/ARM LS12..34 B2
Pine Ct LDSU LS2 .....3 F1
Pinfold Ct MSTN/BAR LS15 *..31 F5
Pinfold Gv MSTN/BAR LS15..31 F5
Pinfold Hi MSTN/BAR LS15..31 F5
Pinfold La MSTN/BAR LS15..31 F5
MSTN/BAR LS15 .....11 E1
WOR/ARM LS12 .....34 C2
Pinfold Mt MSTN/BAR LS15..39 F1
Pinfold Sq MSTN/BAR LS15..31 F5
Pinfold Rd MSTN/BAR LS15..31 F5
Pipe And Nook La
.....34 B1
Pipit Meadow MOR LS27...47 E3
Pitchstone Ct WOR/ARM LS12..33 H1
Pitfall St LDS LS1 .....3 H6

Pit Field Rd EARD/LOFT WF3..50 C3
Pitt Rw LDS LS1 .....3 G6
Place's Rd OSM LS9 .....37 F3
Plaid Rw OSM LS9 * 29 E5
Plane Tree Av AL/HA/HU LS17..14 B3
Plane Tree Cl AL/HA/HU LS17..14 B3
Plane Tree Cft AL/HA/HU LS17..14 B3
Plane Tree Gdns AL/HA/HU LS17..14 B3
Plane Tree Gv YEA LS19....9 F1
Plane Tree Ri AL/HA/HU LS17 *..14 B3
Plane Tree Vw AL/HA/HU LS17..14 B3
Plantation Av AL/HA/HU LS17..14 C2
MSTN/BAR LS15 .....38 D1
Plantation Gdns AL/HA/HU LS17..14 D2
Playfair Rd MID LS10 .....42 D1
Playground WOR/ARM LS12 *..33 H5
Playhouse Sq OSM LS9 ....3 H4
Pleasant Ct HDGY LS6 * ...28 A2
Pleasant Mt BEE/HOL LS11..36 A3
Pleasant Pl BEE/HOL LS11..36 A3
Pleasant St BEE/HOL LS11..35 H3
Pleasant Ter BEE/HOL LS11..36 A3
Plevna St MID LS10 .....43 G1
Plover Wy MID LS10 .....48 A1
Poet's Pl HORS LS18 .....10 C3
Pollard La BRAM LS13 .....17 G4
Ponderosa Cl RHAY LS8 ...29 F2
Pontefract Av OSM LS9 ....37 F1
Pontefract La OSM LS9 ....37 F1
MID LS10 .....43 G1
Pontefract Lane Cl OSM LS9 ..37 F1
Pontefract Rd MID LS10 ...43 G1
Pontefract St OSM LS9 ....37 F1
Poole Crs MSTN/BAR LS15..31 F3
Poole Mt MSTN/BAR LS15..31 F4
Poole Rd MSTN/BAR LS15..31 F4
Poole Sq MSTN/BAR LS15..31 F3
Poplar Av MSTN/BAR LS15..31 H5
Poplar Cl BRAM LS13 .....26 B5
Poplar Crs EARD/LOFT WF3..47 E5
Poplar Ct BRAM LS13 .....26 A5
Poplar Dr HORS LS18 .....16 D1
Poplar Gdns BRAM LS13...26 A5
Poplar Garth BRAM LS13...26 A5
Poplar Ga WOR/ARM LS12..26 A4
Poplar Ri BRAM LS13 .....26 A4
Poplar Sq PDSY/CALV LS28..24 B5
The Poplars GSLY LS20 ....5 G2
CHAL LS7 .....27 G2
Poplar Vw AL/HA/HU LS17 *..15 H4
BRAM LS13 .....26 A5
Poplar Wy BRAM LS13 ....26 A5
Poppleton Ct EARD/LOFT WF3..47 G5
Poppleton Dr EARD/LOFT WF3..47 G5
Poppleton Rd EARD/LOFT WF3..47 G5
Portage Av MSTN/BAR LS15..38 D1
Portage Crs MSTN/BAR LS15..38 D1
Portland Ga LDSU LS2 .....3 F2
Portland Rd WOR/ARM LS12..35 E2
Portland St LDS LS1 .....2 E4
PDSY/CALV LS28 .....33 E1
Post Hill Ct WOR/ARM LS12..33 H1
Potternewton Av CHAL LS7..20 B4
Potternewton Ct CHAL LS7..20 C4
Potternewton Crs CHAL LS7..20 C4
Potternewton Gdns CHAL LS7..20 C4
Potternewton Hts CHAL LS7..20 A4
Potternewton La CHAL LS7..20 A4
Potternewton Mt CHAL LS7..20 B4
Potternewton Vw CHAL LS7 *..20 B4
Pottery La RTHW LS26 .....45 H4
Pottery Rd MID LS10 .....36 C4
Poulton Pl BEE/HOL LS11..42 A1
Preston Pde BEE/HOL LS11..42 A1
Priesthorpe Av PDSY/CALV LS28..24 A1
Priesthorpe Rd PDSY/CALV LS28..24 A1
Priestley Ct PDSY/CALV LS28..24 D5
Priestley Ct PDSY/CALV LS28..24 D5
Priestley Dr PDSY/CALV LS28..24 D5
Priestley Gdns PDSY/CALV LS28..24 D5
Priestley Vw PDSY/CALV LS28..24 D5
Priestley Wk PDSY/CALV LS28..24 D5
Primitive St EARD/LOFT WF3..50 B5
Primley Gdns AL/HA/HU LS17..13 G2
Primley Park Av AL/HA/HU LS17..13 G2
Primley Park Cl AL/HA/HU LS17..13 G2
Primley Park Crs
AL/HA/HU LS17 .....13 G2
Primley Park Dr AL/HA/HU LS17..13 G3
Primley Park Garth
AL/HA/HU LS17 .....13 H2
Primley Park Gn AL/HA/HU LS17..13 H3
Primley Park La AL/HA/HU LS17..13 G2
Primley Park Mt AL/HA/HU LS17..13 H3
Primley Park Ri AL/HA/HU LS17..13 H3
Primley Park Vw
AL/HA/HU LS17 .....13 G2
Primley Park Wk
AL/HA/HU LS17 .....13 H3
Primley Park Wy
.....13 G2
Primrose Av MSTN/BAR LS15..31 G4
Primrose Cl MSTN/BAR LS15..31 G4
Primrose Crs AL/HA/HU LS17 *..13 H2
Primrose Dr MSTN/BAR LS15..31 G3
Primrose Gdns MSTN/BAR LS15..31 G4
Primrose Hl PDSY/CALV LS28..24 A5
Primrose La MSTN/BAR LS15..36 C5
Primrose Rd MSTN/BAR LS15..38 D1
Primrose Rd MSTN/BAR LS15..31 G4
Primrose Wk MOR LS27....41 E3
Prince Edward Gv
WOR/ARM LS12 .....34 C4
Prince Edward Rd
.....34 C4
Prince's Av RHAY LS8 .....21 H1
Princes Ct AL/HA/HU LS17..20 C1
Princes Gv HDGY LS6 .....19 F5
Princess Ct AL/HA/HU LS17..13 H4

d OSM LS9 .... 37 F2
WOR/ARM LS12 .... 26 C5
WOR/ARM LS12 .... 26 C5
p SCFT LS14 .... 31 E1
v HORS LS18 .... 17 G1
WOR/ARM LS12 .... 26 A5
r HORS LS18 .... 17 H1
s WOR/ARM LS12 .... 26 B5
Ct RHAY LS8 .... 29 E3
Ms WOR/ARM LS12 .... 26 B5
er HORS LS18 .... 17 H1
Vk HORS LS18 .... 17 H1
v HDGY LS6 .... 27 H3
ALV LS28 .... 24 B3
'l HDGY LS6 .... 27 H3
t YEA LS19 .... 8 C1
r YEA LS19 .... 8 C1
v HDGY LS6 .... 27 H3
d BVRD LS3 .... 2 B1
9 .... 8 C1
t RTHW LS26 .... 51 G1
er HDGY LS6 .... 27 H3
Vy YEA LS19 .... 8 C1
ce Cl
ALV LS28 .... 32 B1
ce Md
ALV LS28 .... 32 B2
e St CHAL LS7 * 20 D4
ce Ter
ALV LS28 .... 32 C2
rs BEE/HOL LS11 .... 36 A4
n BEE/HOL LS11 .... 36 A4
d BEE/HOL LS11 .... 36 A4
t BEE/HOL LS11 .... 36 A4
w BEE/HOL LS11 * 36 A4
et's Av HORS LS18 .... 17 F1
8 .... 21 G4
et's Cl HORS LS18 .... 10 B5
et's Dr HORS LS18 .... 10 B5
8 .... 21 G4
et's Gv RHAY LS8 .... 21 G4
et's Rd HORS LS18 .... 10 B5
et's Vw RHAY LS8 .... 21 G4
Av LDSU LS2 .... 28 A3
Rd LDSU LS2 .... 28 B3
St LDSU LS2 .... 28 A3
s Av CHAL LS7 .... 20 C5
Ct EARD/LOFT WF3 .... 49 H4
s Crs CHAL LS7 .... 20 D5
s Dr CHAL LS7 * 20 D4
Fold EARD/LOFT WF3 .... 49 H4
s Gdns CHAL LS7 .... 20 C5
s Gv CHAL LS7 .... 20 D5
s Rd CHAL LS7 .... 20 D5
s Ter CHAL LS7 * 20 D5
s Vw CHAL LS7 .... 20 D5
Cl CHAL LS7 .... 20 D5
RM LS12 .... 35 F2
Ct CHAL LS7 .... 20 D5
La OSM LS9 .... 29 E5
Park Ap
RM LS12 .... 26 B5
Park Ct
RM LS12 * 26 B5
Park Crs
RM LS12 .... 26 B5
Park Gn
RM LS12 * 26 B5
Rd CHAL LS7 .... 20 D5
Sq MOR LS27 * 46 C2
St OSM LS9 .... 3 K3
w's St BEE/HOL LS11 .... 36 A3
w's Wk CHAL LS7 .... 20 C2
s Ct BULY LS4 .... 27 F3
s' St BULY LS4 .... 27 F3
s Ter BULY LS4 .... 27 F3
's Crs HDGY LS6 .... 27 F1
's Gv HDGY LS6 .... 27 F1
's La HDGY LS6 .... 27 F1
's Rd HDGY LS6 .... 27 F1
's Ter HDGY LS6 .... 27 F1
s Vls HDGY LS6 .... 27 F1
s Garth GSLY LS20 .... 5 E3
Pl LDS LS1 * 2 E4
St LDS LS1 .... 2 D4
27 * 46 C3
Av RTHW LS26 .... 50 D1
Ct BEE/HOL LS11 .... 36 C4
LS13 .... 25 H2
Crs MOR LS27 .... 40 C5
Gdns BRAM LS13 .... 25 G2
Mt BRAM LS13 .... 25 G3
Sq OSM LS9 .... 3 K4
St LDSU LS2 .... 3 J4
Av MID LS10 .... 48 B1
Cl MID LS10 .... 48 C1
n's Ct OSM LS9 * 29 F5
n's Rd OSM LS9 .... 29 F5
s Rw LDSU LS2 .... 3 J2
t Rd PDSY/CALV LS28 .... 32 C2
's Av RHAY LS8 .... 29 H2
's Circ RHAY LS8 .... 29 H2
's Crs RHAY LS8 .... 29 H1
's Dr RHAY LS8 .... 29 G1
's Garth RHAY LS8 .... 29 H2
's Gv RHAY LS8 .... 29 H1
MID LS10 .... 3 H7
Av WOR/ARM LS12 .... 27 E5
Gv WOR/ARM LS12 .... 27 E5
Ms HORS LS18 .... 17 H1
Rd WOR/ARM LS12 .... 27 E5
St YEA LS19 .... 8 D3
Ter WOR/ARM LS12 .... 27 E5
Vw WOR/ARM LS12 .... 27 E5
rs HORS LS18 .... 17 G1
Ct MSTN/BAR LS15 .... 31 H2
La MSTN/BAR LS15 .... 31 H2
g Garth MID LS10 .... 48 D1
g Wy MID LS10 .... 48 D1
n La RTHW LS26 .... 51 E4
Av HDGY LS6 .... 19 G4
Garth HDGY LS6 .... 19 G4
Vw HDGY LS6 .... 19 G4
Pl KSTL LS5 .... 26 C1
Rd KSTL LS5 .... 26 D2

Sandhill Crs AL/HA/HU LS17 .... 14 A3
Sandhill Dr AL/HA/HU LS17 .... 14 A3
Sandhill Gv AL/HA/HU LS17 .... 14 A2
Sand Hill La AL/HA/HU LS17 .... 13 H4
Sand Hill Lawns AL/HA/HU LS17 .. 13 H4
Sandhill Mt AL/HA/HU LS17 .... 13 H2
Sandhill Ov AL/HA/HU LS17 .... 14 A2
Sandhurst Av RHAY LS8 .... 29 G1
Sandhurst Gv RHAY LS8 .... 29 G2
Sandhurst Pl RHAY LS8 .... 29 G2
Sandhurst Rd RHAY LS8 .... 29 G2
Sandhurst Ter RHAY LS8 .... 29 G1
Sandiford Cl MSTN/BAR LS15 .... 31 H2
Sandiford Ter MSTN/BAR LS15 .... 31 H2
Sandlewood Cl BEE/HOL LS11 .... 36 A3
Sandlewood Ct HDGY LS6 .... 19 H1
Sandlewood Crs HDGY LS6 .... 19 H1
Sandlewood Gn BEE/HOL LS11 .... 36 A3
Sandmead Cl MOR LS27 .... 40 C5
Sandmead Cft MOR LS27 .... 40 C5
Sandmead Wy MOR LS27 .... 40 C5
Sandmoor Av AL/HA/HU LS17 .... 13 H1
Sandmoor Cha AL/HA/HU LS17 .... 13 H2
Sandmoor Cl AL/HA/HU LS17 .... 13 H2
Sandmoor Dr AL/HA/HU LS17 .... 13 H1
Sandmoor Gn AL/HA/HU LS17 .... 13 G1
Sandmoor La AL/HA/HU LS17 .... 13 H1
Sandmoor Ms AL/HA/HU LS17 .... 13 H2
Sandon Gv MID LS10 * 43 E1
Sandon Mt MID LS10 .... 43 E1
Sandpiper Ap MOR LS27 .... 47 E3
Sandringham Ap
AL/HA/HU LS17 .... 14 A4
Sandringham Cl MOR LS27 .... 47 E1
Sandringham Crs
AL/HA/HU LS17 .... 13 H4
PDSY/CALV LS28 .... 32 C2
Sandringham Dr
AL/HA/HU LS17 .... 13 H4
Sandringham Gdns
AL/HA/HU LS17 .... 13 H4
Sandringham Gn
L/HA/HU LS17 * 14 A4
Sandringham Mt
AL/HA/HU LS17 .... 14 A3
Sandringham Wy
AL/HA/HU LS17 .... 13 H4
Sandstone Dr WOR/ARM LS12 .... 33 G1
Sandway MSTN/BAR LS15 .... 31 F3
Sandway Gdns
MSTN/BAR LS15 .... 31 F3
Sandway Gv MSTN/BAR LS15 .... 31 F3
Sandyacres RTHW LS26 .... 44 D5
Sandyacres Crs RTHW LS26 .... 44 D5
Sandyacres Dr RTHW LS26 .... 44 D5
Sandy Bank Av RTHW LS26 .... 44 D5
Sandy Gv RTHW LS26 .... 44 D5
Sandy Wy YEA LS19 .... 5 H5
Savile Av CHAL LS7 * 28 D2
Savile Dr CHAL LS7 .... 28 D2
Savile Mt CHAL LS7 .... 28 D2
Savile Pl CHAL LS7 .... 28 D2
Savile Rd CHAL LS7 .... 28 D2
Saville Cl EARD/LOFT WF3 .... 50 A5
Savins Mill Wy KSTL LS5 .... 26 C1
Saw Mill St BEE/HOL LS11 .... 2 E7
Saxon Ga AL/HA/HU LS17 .... 13 F5
Saxon Gn AL/HA/HU LS17 .... 13 E5
Saxon Gv AL/HA/HU LS17 .... 13 E5
Saxon Mt AL/HA/HU LS17 .... 13 F4
Saxon Rd AL/HA/HU LS17 .... 13 E5
Saxstead Ri WOR/ARM LS12 .... 35 E2
Saxton Gdns OSM LS9 * 3 K6
Saxton La OSM LS9 .... 3 K5
Sayers Cl KSTL LS5 .... 26 D1
Sayner La MID LS10 .... 36 D2
Sayner Rd MID LS10 .... 36 D2
Scarborough St
EARD/LOFT WF3 .... 47 F5
Scarbro' Jct BRAM LS13 .... 25 H4
Scargill Cl OSM LS9 .... 29 F4
Scargill Gra OSM LS9 .... 29 F5
Scarth Av OSM LS9 .... 29 G3
Scatcherd Gv MOR LS27 .... 46 B2
Scatcherd La MOR LS27 .... 46 B3
Scatcherd Park Av MOR LS27 .... 46 C1
Schofield Ct MOR LS27 * 46 C2
Scholebrook La BOW BD4 .... 32 A5
School Cl WOR/ARM LS12 .... 33 H5
School Cft RTHW LS26 .... 44 C5
School La CHAL LS7 .... 20 C3
HDGY LS6 .... 19 G4
MSTN/BAR LS15 .... 31 E5
School Ms WOR/ARM LS12 .... 35 E1
School St MOR LS27 .... 41 E3
MOR LS27 .... 46 D2
PDSY/CALV LS28 .... 24 B2
PDSY/CALV LS28 .... 32 B2
School Vw HDGY LS6 .... 27 G2
Scotchman Cl MOR LS27 .... 46 B4
Scotland Cl HORS LS18 .... 10 B4
Scotland La HORS LS18 .... 7 E5
Scotland Mill La BHP/TINH LS16 .. 12 D5
HDGY LS6 .... 19 H1
Scotland Wy HORS LS18 .... 10 A3
Scotland Wood Rd
AL/HA/HU LS17 .... 12 D5
Scott Hall Av CHAL LS7 .... 28 C1
Scott Hall Dr CHAL LS7 .... 28 C1
Scott Hall Gn CHAL LS7 .... 20 C5
Scott Hall Gv CHAL LS7 .... 20 C5
Scott Hall Pl CHAL LS7 .... 20 C5
Scott Hall Rd CHAL LS7 .... 20 C5
Scott Hall Rw CHAL LS7 .... 28 D1
Scott Hall Sq CHAL LS7 .... 20 C5
Scott Hall St CHAL LS7 .... 28 C1
Scott Hall Ter CHAL LS7 .... 20 C5
Scott Hall Wk CHAL LS7 .... 28 C1
Scott Hall Wy CHAL LS7 .... 20 C4
Scott La MOR LS27 .... 46 A3
Scott St PDSY/CALV LS28 .... 32 D2
Scott Wood La CHAL LS7 .... 20 B5
Seacroft Av SCFT LS14 .... 23 F5
Seacroft Cl SCFT LS14 .... 23 F5
Seacroft Crs SCFT LS14 .... 23 F5

Seacroft Ga SCFT LS14 * 23 F5
Seaforth Av OSM LS9 .... 29 G2
Seaforth Gv OSM LS9 .... 29 G2
Seaforth Mt OSM LS9 .... 29 G2
Seaforth Pl RHAY LS8 .... 29 G2
Seaforth Rd OSM LS9 .... 29 G2
Seaforth Ter RHAY LS8 .... 29 G2
Second Av RTHW LS26 .... 44 D4
WOR/ARM LS12 .... 35 G1
YEA LS19 .... 9 E2
Sedbergh Cl MSTN/BAR LS15 .... 38 B1
Sefton Av BEE/HOL LS11 .... 36 A5
Sefton Ct HDGY LS6 .... 19 F4
Sefton St BEE/HOL LS11 .... 36 B5
Sefton Ter BEE/HOL LS11 .... 36 A5
Selby Av OSM LS9 .... 30 C5
Selby Rd MSTN/BAR LS15 .... 31 F5
Seminary St LDSU LS2 .... 2 D1
Servia Dr CHAL LS7 .... 28 B2
Servia Hl CHAL LS7 .... 28 B2
Servia Rd CHAL LS7 .... 28 B2
Seventh Av RTHW LS26 .... 45 E5
Severn Wy MID LS10 .... 37 F4
Shadwell La AL/HA/HU LS17 .... 13 H5
Shadwell Park Av
AL/HA/HU LS17 .... 15 E2
Shadwell Park Cl
AL/HA/HU LS17 .... 15 E2
Shadwell Park Ct
AL/HA/HU LS17 .... 15 E3
Shadwell Park Dr
AL/HA/HU LS17 .... 15 E3
Shadwell Park Gdns
AL/HA/HU LS17 .... 15 E2
Shadwell Park Gv
AL/HA/HU LS17 .... 15 E3
Shadwell Wk AL/HA/HU LS17 .... 14 A4
Shaftesbury Av RHAY LS8 .... 21 G1
Shaftesbury Pde OSM LS9 * 30 A4
Shaftesbury Rd RHAY LS8 .... 14 C5
Shafton La BEE/HOL LS11 .... 35 H3
Shafton Pl BEE/HOL LS11 .... 35 H3
Shafton St BEE/HOL LS11 .... 35 H3
Shafton Vw BEE/HOL LS11 .... 35 H3
Shakespeare Ap OSM LS9 .... 29 F4
Shakespeare Av OSM LS9 .... 29 F4
Shakespeare Cl OSM LS9 .... 29 F4
Shakespeare Ct OSM LS9 .... 29 F4
Shakespeare Gdns OSM LS9 .... 29 F4
Shakespeare Gra OSM LS9 .... 29 F4
Shakespeare Lawn OSM LS9 .... 29 F4
Shakespeare Rd GSLY LS20 .... 5 E4
Shakespeare St OSM LS9 .... 29 F3
Shakespeare Towers OSM LS9 .... 29 F3
Shancara Ct EARD/LOFT WF3 .... 47 G5
Shannon Rd OSM LS9 .... 29 E5
Shannon St OSM LS9 .... 29 E5
Sharp House Rd MID LS10 .... 49 E2
Sharp La MID LS10 .... 49 F2
Sharp Ms HDGY LS6 .... 19 H5
Sharp Rw PDSY/CALV LS28 .... 32 D2
Shaw La GSLY LS20 .... 5 F3
HDGY LS6 .... 19 F4
Shaw Lane Gdns GSLY LS20 .... 5 F3
Shaw Leys YEA LS19 .... 5 G4
Shaw Royd YEA LS19 .... 5 G4
Shay Ct LDSU LS2 .... 28 B2
Shayfield La EARD/LOFT WF3 .... 50 B3
Shay St LDSU LS2 .... 28 B2
Sheaf St MID LS10 .... 3 J7
Sheepscar Ct CHAL LS7 * 28 D3
Sheepscar Gv CHAL LS7 .... 3 J1
Sheepscar St North CHAL LS7 .... 28 C2
Shelldrake Dr MID LS10 .... 48 D1
Shelley Cl RTHW LS26 .... 51 G3
Shelley Crs RTHW LS26 .... 51 G3
Shepcote Cl BHP/TINH LS16 .... 11 F4
Shepcote Crs BHP/TINH LS16 .... 11 F4
Shepherd's Gv RHAY LS8 .... 29 E1
Shepherd's La CHAL LS7 .... 29 E1
Shepherd's Pl RHAY LS8 * 29 F1
Sherbourne Dr HDGY LS6 .... 19 G1
Sherbrooke Av MSTN/BAR LS15 .... 38 D1
Sherburn Ap SCFT LS14 .... 23 G4
Sherburn Ct SCFT LS14 .... 23 G4
Sherburn Pl SCFT LS14 .... 23 G4
Sherburn Rd SCFT LS14 .... 23 G4
Sherburn Rd North SCFT LS14 .... 23 F2
Sheridan Cl PDSY/CALV LS28 .... 32 D2
Sheridan Ct PDSY/CALV LS28 * 32 D2
Sheridan Wy PDSY/CALV LS28 .... 32 C2
Sherwood Gdns
EARD/LOFT WF3 * 49 H4
Sherwood Gn EARD/LOFT WF3 .... 49 G3
Shipton Ms MOR LS27 .... 46 D3
Shire Gv MOR LS27 .... 46 C5
Shire Oak Rd HDGY LS6 .... 19 G5
Shire Oak St HDGY LS6 .... 19 F5
Shire Rd MOR LS27 .... 46 D5
Shirley Dr BRAM LS13 .... 25 G1
Sholebroke Av CHAL LS7 .... 28 D1
Sholebroke Mt CHAL LS7 .... 28 C1
Sholebroke Pl CHAL LS7 .... 28 D1
Sholebroke St CHAL LS7 .... 28 C1
Sholebroke Ter CHAL LS7 .... 20 D5
Sholebroke Vw CHAL LS7 .... 28 D1
Shone Ct MOR LS27 .... 46 D4
Shoreham Rd WOR/ARM LS12 .... 35 E2
Short La CHAL LS7 * 20 C3
Siddall St BEE/HOL LS11 .... 36 B2
The Sidings GSLY LS20 .... 4 D3
Sidney St LDS LS1 .... 3 H4
Siegen Cl MOR LS27 .... 46 C2
Silk Mill Ap BHP/TINH LS16 .... 11 E5
Silk Mill Av BHP/TINH LS16 .... 10 D4
Silk Mill Bank BHP/TINH LS16 .... 10 D5
Silk Mill Cl BHP/TINH LS16 .... 10 D4
Silk Mill Dr BHP/TINH LS16 .... 10 D5
Silk Mill Gdns BHP/TINH LS16 .... 10 D5
Silk Mill Gn BHP/TINH LS16 .... 10 D5
Silk Mill Ms BHP/TINH LS16 .... 11 F5
Silk Mill Rd BHP/TINH LS16 .... 10 D5
Silk Mill Wy BHP/TINH LS16 .... 11 E5
Silkstone Ct MSTN/BAR LS15 .... 31 G4
Silkstone Wy MSTN/BAR LS15 .... 31 G4

Silverdale Av AL/HA/HU LS17 .... 14 D2
GSLY LS20 .... 5 E4
Silverdale Cl GSLY LS20 .... 5 E5
Silverdale Dr GSLY LS20 .... 5 E5
Silverdale Gra GSLY LS20 .... 5 E5
Silverdale Gv GSLY LS20 .... 4 D5
Silverdale Mt GSLY LS20 .... 5 E5
Silverdale Rd GSLY LS20 .... 4 D5
Silver La YEA LS19 .... 5 H5
Silver Royd Av WOR/ARM LS12 .... 34 B2
Silver Royd Cl WOR/ARM LS12 .... 34 B2
Silver Royd Garth
WOR/ARM LS12 .... 34 B2
Silver Royd Gv WOR/ARM LS12 .... 34 B2
Silver Royd Hl WOR/ARM LS12 .... 34 B2
Silver Royd Pl WOR/ARM LS12 .... 34 B2
Silver Royd Rd WOR/ARM LS12 .... 34 B2
Silver Royd St WOR/ARM LS12 .... 34 B2
Silver Royd Ter WOR/ARM LS12 .... 34 B2
Silver St BEE/HOL LS11 .... 2 D7
Simmons Ct OSM LS9 .... 37 F2
Simmons Wy RHAY LS8 .... 29 H1
Simpson Gv WOR/ARM LS12 .... 35 F1
Sir George Martin Dr
BHP/TINH LS16 .... 12 B2
Sir Karl Cohen Sq
WOR/ARM LS12 .... 34 D1
Siskin Ct MOR LS27 .... 46 D3
Sissons Av MID LS10 .... 48 B2
Sissons Crs MID LS10 .... 48 B3
Sissons Dr MID LS10 .... 48 B2
Sissons Gn MID LS10 .... 48 B2
Sissons Gv MID LS10 .... 48 B2
Sissons La MID LS10 .... 48 B2
Sissons Mt MID LS10 .... 48 A3
Sissons Pl MID LS10 .... 48 B2
Sissons Rd MID LS10 .... 48 A3
Sissons Rw MID LS10 .... 48 B2
Sissons St MID LS10 .... 48 B2
Sissons Ter MID LS10 .... 48 B2
Sissons Vw MID LS10 .... 48 A3
Sixth Av RTHW LS26 .... 45 E4
Sizers Ct YEA LS19 .... 8 C2
Skelton Av OSM LS9 .... 29 H5
Skelton Crs OSM LS9 .... 29 H5
Skelton Grange Rd MID LS10 .... 43 H1
Skelton Mt OSM LS9 .... 29 H5
Skelton Pl OSM LS9 .... 29 H5
Skelton Rd OSM LS9 .... 29 H5
Skeltons La SCFT LS14 .... 23 F1
Skelton St OSM LS9 .... 29 H5
Skelton Ter OSM LS9 .... 29 H5
Skelwith Ap SCFT LS14 .... 31 E3
Skinner La LDSU LS2 .... 3 K1
Skinner St LDS LS1 .... 2 C4
Skye Vw RTHW LS26 .... 50 D1
Slaters Rd PDSY/CALV LS28 .... 24 C4
Sledmere Cft SCFT LS14 .... 23 G4
Sledmere Garth SCFT LS14 .... 23 G4
Sledmere La SCFT LS14 .... 23 G4
Sledmere Pl SCFT LS14 .... 23 G4
Sledmere Sq SCFT LS14 .... 23 G4
Smalewell Cl PDSY/CALV LS28 .... 32 B2
Smalewell Dr PDSY/CALV LS28 .... 32 A2
Smalewell Gdns
PDSY/CALV LS28 .... 32 A2
Smalewell Gn PDSY/CALV LS28 .... 32 B2
Smithson St RTHW LS26 .... 50 D2
Smithy La BHP/TINH LS16 .... 11 E1
Smithy Mills La BHP/TINH LS16 .... 12 B5
Snaith Wood Dr YEA LS19 .... 16 A1
Snaith Wood Ms YEA LS19 .... 16 A1
Snowden Ap BRAM LS13 .... 26 A2
Snowden Cl BRAM LS13 .... 25 H3
Snowden Crs BRAM LS13 .... 25 H3
Snowden Fold BRAM LS13 .... 25 H3
Snowden Gv BRAM LS13 .... 25 H3
Snowden Lawn BRAM LS13 .... 25 H3
Snowden Royd BRAM LS13 .... 25 H3
Snowden V BRAM LS13 .... 25 H3
Somerdale Cl BRAM LS13 .... 25 H4
Somerdale Gdns BRAM LS13 .... 25 H4
Somerdale Gv BRAM LS13 .... 25 H4
Somerdale Wk BRAM LS13 .... 25 H4
Somerset Rd PDSY/CALV LS28 .... 24 C5
Somers Pl LDS LS1 * 2 D4
Somers St LDS LS1 .... 2 D4
Somerville Av SCFT LS14 .... 30 D3
Somerville Dr SCFT LS14 .... 30 D3
Somerville Gn SCFT LS14 .... 30 D3
Somerville Gv SCFT LS14 .... 30 D2
Somerville Mt SCFT LS14 .... 30 D3
Somerville Vw SCFT LS14 .... 30 D3
South Accommodation Rd
MID LS10 .... 36 D3
South Cl GSLY LS20 .... 4 B4
Southcote St PDSY/CALV LS28 .... 24 B3
South Dr GSLY LS20 .... 4 B4
PDSY/CALV LS28 .... 24 B2
South End Av BRAM LS13 .... 25 H4
South End Gv BRAM LS13 .... 25 H4
South End Mt BRAM LS13 .... 25 H4
South End Ter BRAM LS13 .... 26 A4
South Farm Crs OSM LS9 .... 30 A3
South Farm Rd OSM LS9 .... 30 A3
Southfield Av AL/HA/HU LS17 .... 14 A5
Southfield Dr AL/HA/HU LS17 .... 14 A5
Southfield Mt WOR/ARM LS12 .... 35 E1
Southfield St WOR/ARM LS12 .... 35 E1
Southgate GSLY LS20 .... 4 B5
RTHW LS26 .... 45 G5
South Hill Cl MID LS10 .... 43 F4
South Hill Cft MID LS10 * 43 F4
South Hill Gdns MID LS10 .... 43 F4
South Hill Ri MID LS10 .... 43 F4
South Hill Wy MID LS10 .... 43 F4
Southlands Av AL/HA/HU LS17 .... 20 C2
YEA LS19 .... 9 F5
Southlands Crs AL/HA/HU LS17 .... 20 C2
Southlands Dr AL/HA/HU LS17 .... 20 C2
South Lea EARD/LOFT WF3 * 47 H5
South Lee HORS LS18 .... 17 F1
Southleigh Av BEE/HOL LS11 .... 42 A3
Southleigh Crs BEE/HOL LS11 .... 42 A3
Southleigh Cft BEE/HOL LS11 .... 42 B3

Southleigh Dr BEE/HOL LS11 .... 42 A3
Southleigh Gdns BEE/HOL LS11 .. 42 A3
Southleigh Gra BEE/HOL LS11 .... 42 B3
Southleigh Gv BEE/HOL LS11 .... 42 A3
Southleigh Rd BEE/HOL LS11 .... 42 A3
Southleigh Vw BEE/HOL LS11 .... 42 A3
South Nelson St MOR LS27 .... 46 D1
Southolme Cl KSTL LS5 .... 18 B5
South Pde HDGY LS6 .... 19 F5
LDS LS1 .... 3 F4
MOR LS27 .... 46 D2
PDSY/CALV LS28 .... 32 C2
South Parade Cl
PDSY/CALV LS28 .... 32 B2
South Pkwy SCFT LS14 .... 30 D2
South Parkway Ap OSM LS9 .... 30 C2
South Point MID LS10 * 37 E3
South Queen St MOR LS27 .... 46 D3
South Rd OSM LS9 .... 38 A5
Southroyd Ri PDSY/CALV LS28 .... 32 C3
South St MOR LS27 .... 46 D2
South Vw ILK LS29 .... 4 A1
PDSY/CALV LS28 .... 24 A4
PDSY/CALV LS28 .... 32 D1
RTHW LS26 .... 44 B5
YEA LS19 .... 5 F5
South View Cl YEA LS19 .... 5 E5
South View Rd MID LS10 .... 43 E2
YEA LS19 .... 5 H5
South View Ter YEA LS19 .... 9 E1
Southwaite La SCFT LS14 .... 30 D1
Southwaite Pl SCFT LS14 .... 30 D1
Southway GSLY LS20 .... 4 B4
HORS LS18 .... 10 A4
Southwood Cl SCFT LS14 .... 31 G1
Southwood Crs SCFT LS14 .... 31 G1
Southwood Ga MSTN/BAR LS15 .. 31 G1
Southwood Rd SCFT LS14 .... 31 G1
Sovereign Ct AL/HA/HU LS17 .... 14 A1
Sovereign Quay LDS LS1 * 3 H6
Sovereign St LDS LS1 .... 3 F6
Sowden's Yd HDGY LS6 * 19 F4
Sowood St BULY LS4 .... 27 E3
Speedwell Mt HDGY LS6 .... 28 B2
Spen Ap BHP/TINH LS16 .... 18 B3
Spen Bank BHP/TINH LS16 .... 18 B3
Spence La WOR/ARM LS12 .... 2 A7
Spenceley St LDSU LS2 * 28 A2
Spencer Av MOR LS27 .... 46 C4
Spencer Mt RHAY LS8 .... 29 E2
Spencer Pl RHAY LS8 .... 29 E2
Spencer Rd GSLY LS20 .... 5 F4
Spen Crs BHP/TINH LS16 .... 18 B3
Spen Dr BHP/TINH LS16 .... 18 C2
Spen Gdns BHP/TINH LS16 .... 18 D2
Spen Gn BHP/TINH LS16 .... 18 B3
Spen La HDGY LS6 .... 18 C4
Spen Ms BHP/TINH LS16 .... 18 C3
Spennithorne Av
BHP/TINH LS16 .... 18 C1
Spennithorne Dr
BHP/TINH LS16 .... 18 C1
Spen Rd BHP/TINH LS16 .... 18 D2
Spenser Ri GSLY LS20 .... 5 F4
Spenser Rd GSLY LS20 .... 5 F4
Spenslea Gv MOR LS27 .... 46 C4
Spen Wk BHP/TINH LS16 .... 18 B3
Spibey Crs RTHW LS26 .... 44 B4
Spibey La RTHW LS26 .... 44 B4
The Spindles MID LS10 .... 42 D3
Spinks Gdns SCFT LS14 .... 31 F1
Spink Well La EARD/LOFT WF3 .... 47 H5
Spinners Cha PDSY/CALV LS28 .... 32 C1
Spinneyfield Ct OSM LS9 * 37 E1
The Spinney AL/HA/HU LS17 .... 14 A5
IDLE BD10 .... 8 C5
OSM LS9 * 37 E1
Springbank YEA LS19 .... 8 C3
Springbank Av PDSY/CALV LS28 .. 24 C1
Springbank Cl PDSY/CALV LS28 .... 24 C2
Spring Bank Crs HDGY LS6 .... 27 G1
Springbank Dr
PDSY/CALV LS28 .... 24 C2
Springbank Gv PDSY/CALV LS28 .. 24 C2
Springbank Ri PDSY/CALV LS28 .... 24 C2
Springbank Rd PDSY/CALV LS28 .. 24 B2
Spring Cl MOR LS27 .... 40 C4
Spring Close Av OSM LS9 .... 37 E2
Spring Close Gdns OSM LS9 .... 37 F2
Spring Close St OSM LS9 .... 37 E2
Spring Close Wk OSM LS9 .... 37 F2
Springfield Av MOR LS27 .... 40 C5
Springfield Cl HORS LS18 .... 17 H1
Springfield Crs MOR LS27 .... 40 C5
Springfield Gdns HORS LS18 .... 17 H1
Springfield Gn MID LS10 * 43 E1
Springfield La MOR LS27 .... 40 C5
Springfield Mt HORS LS18 .... 17 H1
LDSU LS2 .... 2 C1
WOR/ARM LS12 * 34 C1
Springfield Pl MID LS10 .... 43 E1
Springfield Ri HORS LS18 .... 17 H1
RTHW LS26 .... 50 D2
Springfield Rd GSLY LS20 .... 5 E4
MOR LS27 .... 40 C5
Springfield St RTHW LS26 .... 50 D2
Springfield Ter GSLY LS20 .... 5 E3
PDSY/CALV LS28 .... 24 B4
Spring Gdns MOR LS27 .... 41 E4
Spring Grove Vw HDGY LS6 .... 27 G3
Spring Grove Wk HDGY LS6 * 27 G3
Springhead Rd RTHW LS26 .... 45 E5
Spring Hl BHP/TINH LS16 .... 12 C3
Spring Hill Ter HDGY LS6 .... 19 G4
Spring Rd HDGY LS6 .... 27 F1
Springs Rd BAIL BD17 .... 8 A2
Spring Va PDSY/CALV LS28 .... 24 C4
Spring Valley Av BRAM LS13 .... 25 G4
Spring Valley Cl BRAM LS13 .... 25 G4
Spring Valley Crs BRAM LS13 .... 25 G4
Spring Valley Cft BRAM LS13 .... 25 G4
Spring Valley Dr BRAM LS13 .... 25 G4
Spring Valley Vw BRAM LS13 .... 25 G4
Spring Valley Wk BRAM LS13 .... 25 G4
Springwell Cl YEA LS19 .... 9 E1

Springwell Ct BEE/HOL LS11 2 B7
EARD/LOFT WF3 47 G5
Springwell Rd WOR/ARM LS12 2 B7
Springwell St BEE/HOL LS11 2 B7
Springwell Vw BEE/HOL LS11 36 A2
Springwood Gdns RHAY LS8 21 H4
Springwood Gv RHAY LS8 22 A4
Springwood Rd RHAY LS8 21 H4
YEA LS19 8 C4
Squirrel Wy AL/HA/HU LS17 14 B3
Stadium Wy BEE/HOL LS11 35 G5
Stafford St MID LS10 37 E4
Stainbeck Av CHAL LS7 19 H4
Stainbeck Cnr CHAL LS7 20 C3
Stainbeck Gdns CHAL LS7 20 B4
Stainbeck La CHAL LS7 20 A3
Stainbeck Rd CHAL LS7 20 A4
Stainbeck Wk CHAL LS7 20 B4
Stainburn Av AL/HA/HU LS17 21 E1
Stainburn Crs AL/HA/HU LS17 20 D1
Stainburn Dr AL/HA/HU LS17 20 D1
Stainburn Gdns AL/HA/HU LS17 21 E1
Stainburn Mt AL/HA/HU LS17 21 E2
Stainburn Rd AL/HA/HU LS17 20 D2
Stainburn Ter AL/HA/HU LS17 20 D2
Stainburn Vw AL/HA/HU LS17 21 E1
Stainmore Cl SCFT LS14 31 E2
Stainmore Pl SCFT LS14 31 E2
Stainton La EARD/LOFT WF3 50 B2
Stairfoot Cl BHP/TINH LS16 12 B2
Stair Foot La BHP/TINH LS16 12 B2
Stairfoot Vw BHP/TINH LS16 12 B2
Staithe Av MID LS10 48 D1
Staithe Cl MID LS10 48 D1
Staithe Gdns MID LS10 48 D1
Standale Av PDSY/CALV LS28 24 B5
Standale Crs PDSY/CALV LS28 24 B5
Standale Ri PDSY/CALV LS28 24 B5
Stanhall Av PDSY/CALV LS28 24 B4
Stanhope Av HORS LS18 10 C5
Stanhope Cl HORS LS18 10 C5
Stanhope Dr HORS LS18 17 G2
Stanhope Gdns EARD/LOFT WF3 49 E5
Stanhope Gv EARD/LOFT WF3 49 E5
Stanks Ap SCFT LS14 31 H1
Stanks Av SCFT LS14 31 H1
Stanks Cross SCFT LS14 31 H1
Stanks Dr SCFT LS14 23 G4
Stanks Gdns SCFT LS14 23 H5
Stanks Garth MSTN/BAR LS15 31 H1
Stanks Gv SCFT LS14 31 H1
Stanks La North SCFT LS14 23 G4
Stanks La South SCFT LS14 31 H1
Stanks Pde SCFT LS14 31 H1
Stanks Rd SCFT LS14 31 H1
Stanks Wy SCFT LS14 31 H1
Stanley Av RHAY LS8 29 F3
Stanley Dr [illegible]
Stanley Pl OSM LS9 29 G3
Stanley Rd RHAY LS8 29 F3
Stanley Ter OSM LS9 29 G3
WOR/ARM LS12 34 D1
Stanley Vw WOR/ARM LS12 35 E1
Stanmore Av BULY LS4 27 E2
Stanmore Crs BULY LS4 27 E2
Stanmore Gv BULY LS4 27 E2
Stanmore Hl BULY LS4 27 F2
Stanmore Mt BULY LS4 27 E2
Stanmore Pl BULY LS4 27 E2
Stanmore Rd BULY LS4 27 E2
Stanmore St BULY LS4 27 E2
Stanmore Ter BULY LS4 27 E2
Stanmore Vw BULY LS4 27 E2
Stanningley Field Cl BRAM LS13 25 E4
Stanningley By-Pass
BRAM LS13 25 H5
PDSY/CALV LS28 24 A4
Stanningley Rd BRAM LS13 25 E3
PDSY/CALV LS28 24 D3
WOR/ARM LS12 26 B4
Station Av BRAM LS13 25 F3
Station Ct GSLY LS20 * 4 D3
Station Crs WOR/ARM LS12 34 D1
Station La EARD/LOFT WF3 47 G5
EARD/LOFT WF3 48 D5
RTHW LS26 45 H4
Station Mt BRAM LS13 25 G3
Station Pde KSTL LS5 26 C1
Station Pl BRAM LS13 25 G3
Station Rd GSLY LS20 4 D3
HORS LS18 10 C5
MOR LS27 46 C1
MSTN/BAR LS15 31 G3
WOR/ARM LS12 34 D1
Station St PDSY/CALV LS28 32 B2
Station Ter BRAM LS13 25 G3
Station Vw MSTN/BAR LS15 31 G4
Station Wy WOR/ARM LS12 34 D1
Stead's Yd HORS LS18 10 C5
Steander OSM LS9 3 K6
Stephenson Dr WOR/ARM LS12 33 H5
Stephenson Wy WOR/ARM LS12 33 H5
Sterling Ct EARD/LOFT WF3 47 G4
Sterling Wy EARD/LOFT WF3 47 F4
Stewart Cl MSTN/BAR LS15 39 G1
Stewart Pl BEE/HOL LS11 36 A5
Stirling Crs HORS LS18 10 A3
Stocks Ap SCFT LS14 31 F1
Stocks Hl BEE/HOL LS11 36 A3
WOR/ARM LS12 27 E5
Stocks Ri SCFT LS14 31 F1
Stocks Rd SCFT LS14 31 F1
Stocks St CHAL LS7 28 C2
Stonebridge Ap
WOR/ARM LS12 * 34 A2
Stonebridge Av WOR/ARM LS12 34 B2
Stonebridge Gv WOR/ARM LS12 34 A2
Stonebridge La WOR/ARM LS12 34 B2
Stone Brig Gn RTHW LS26 50 B2
Stone Brig La RTHW LS26 50 C2
Stonechat Ri MOR LS27 47 E2
Stonecliffe Crs WOR/ARM LS12 34 A2
Stonecliffe Dr WOR/ARM LS12 33 H2
Stonecliffe Garth
WOR/ARM LS12 34 A2
Stonecliffe Gv WOR/ARM LS12 33 H2
Stonecliffe Mt WOR/ARM LS12 34 A2
Stonecliffe Ter WOR/ARM LS12 33 H2
Stonecliffe Wy WOR/ARM LS12 33 H3
Stonedene HDGY LS6 19 H2
Stonegate CHAL LS7 28 C2
Stonegate Ap CHAL LS7 19 H4
Stonegate Cha CHAL LS7 19 H3
Stonegate Cl AL/HA/HU LS17 13 H4
Stonegate Crs CHAL LS7 20 A3
Stonegate Farm Cl CHAL LS7 19 H3
Stonegate Gdns CHAL LS7 19 H3
Stonegate Gn CHAL LS7 19 H4
Stonegate La CHAL LS7 19 H3
Stonegate Ms CHAL LS7 19 H4
Stonegate Pl CHAL LS7 * 19 H4
Stonegate Rd AL/HA/HU LS17 13 H5
Stonegate Wk CHAL LS7 20 A4
Stonehurst MSTN/BAR LS15 31 H1
Stonelea Ct CHAL LS7 20 A3
HDGY LS6 19 F5
Stoneleigh Av AL/HA/HU LS17 14 B3
Stoneleigh Cl AL/HA/HU LS17 14 B3
Stoneleigh La AL/HA/HU LS17 14 B4
Stone Mill Ap HDGY LS6 19 G3
Stone Mill Ct HDGY LS6 19 G3
Stone Mill Wy HDGY LS6 19 G3
Stone Vls HDGY LS6 19 F4
Stoneycroft HORS LS18 17 F2
Stoney Ri HORS LS18 17 F2
Stoney Rock Ct OSM LS9 29 F4
Stoney Rock Gv OSM LS9 29 F4
Stoney Rock La OSM LS9 29 F4
Stoneythorpe HORS LS18 17 F2
Stony Royd PDSY/CALV LS28 24 A2
Storey Pl SCFT LS14 30 C4
Stott Rd HDGY LS6 * 27 G2
Stott St WOR/ARM LS12 35 F1
Stowe Gv OSM LS9 30 A5
Stradbroke Wy WOR/ARM LS12 35 E2
Stratford Av BEE/HOL LS11 36 A5
Stratford St BEE/HOL LS11 36 C5
Stratford Ter BEE/HOL LS11 36 B5
Strathmore Av OSM LS9 29 G3
Strathmore Dr OSM LS9 29 G2
Strathmore St OSM LS9 29 G3
Strathmore Vw OSM LS9 29 G3
Strawberry La WOR/ARM LS12 35 E1
Strawberry Rd WOR/ARM LS12 35 E1
Streamside HDGY LS6 19 G4
Street La AL/HA/HU LS17 13 H5
Stretton Av HDGY LS6 19 G1
Strickland Av AL/HA/HU LS17 15 H3
Strickland Cl AL/HA/HU LS17 15 H3
Strickland Crs AL/HA/HU LS17 15 H3
Studfold Vw SCFT LS14 31 E2
Studio Rd BVRD LS3 [illegible]
Styebank La RTHW LS26 44 D5
Suffolk Ct YEA LS19 5 H5
Sugar Hill Cl RTHW LS26 51 G3
Sugar Well Ap CHAL LS7 * 20 A5
Sugar Well Ct CHAL LS7 * 28 B1
Sugar Well Mt CHAL LS7 20 A5
Sugar Well Rd CHAL LS7 20 A5
Summerfield Av BRAM LS13 25 E2
Summerfield Dr BRAM LS13 25 E2
Summerfield Gdns BRAM LS13 25 E2
Summerfield Gn BRAM LS13 25 E2
Summerfield Pl BRAM LS13 25 E2
Summerfield Rd BRAM LS13 24 D2
Summerhill Gdns RHAY LS8 14 D4
Summerhill Pl RHAY LS8 14 D4
Summerville Rd
PDSY/CALV LS28 24 A3
Sunbeam Av BEE/HOL LS11 36 B5
Sunbeam Gv BEE/HOL LS11 36 B5
Sunbeam Pl BEE/HOL LS11 36 B5
Sunbeam Ter BEE/HOL LS11 36 B5
EARD/LOFT WF3 * 47 G5
Sun Fld PDSY/CALV LS28 24 B4
Sunfield Cl PDSY/CALV LS28 24 B3
Sunfield Dr PDSY/CALV LS28 24 B3
Sunfield Gdns PDSY/CALV LS28 24 B3
Sunfield Pl PDSY/CALV LS28 24 C4
Sunningdale Av AL/HA/HU LS17 13 E3
Sunningdale Dr AL/HA/HU LS17 13 E3
Sunningdale Gn AL/HA/HU LS17 13 E3
Sunny Bank CHAL LS7 21 F5
MOR LS27 41 E3
Sunnybank Av HORS LS18 17 F3
Sunnybank Ct YEA LS19 6 B5
Sunnybank Crs YEA LS19 6 B5
Sunny Bank Gv RHAY LS8 21 E5
Sunnybank Rd HORS LS18 17 F3
Sunny Bank Vw RHAY LS8 * 21 F5
Sunnydene SCFT LS14 30 D4
Sunnyside Rd BRAM LS13 25 F4
Sunnyview Av BEE/HOL LS11 35 H5
Sunnyview Gdns BEE/HOL LS11 35 H5
Sunnyview Ter BEE/HOL LS11 35 H5
Sunset Av HDGY LS6 19 G2
Sunset Dr HDGY LS6 19 G3
Sunset Hilltop HDGY LS6 19 G2
Sunset Mt HDGY LS6 19 G3
Sunset Ri HDGY LS6 19 G2
Sunset Rd HDGY LS6 19 G2
Sunset Vw HDGY LS6 19 G2
Sun St PDSY/CALV LS28 24 C4
YEA LS19 6 A5
Surrey Gv PDSY/CALV LS28 24 C5
Surrey Rd PDSY/CALV LS28 24 C5
Sussex Av HORS LS18 10 C4
MID LS10 37 F5
Sussex Gdns MID LS10 37 F5
Sussex Gn MID LS10 37 F5
Sussex Pl MID LS10 37 F5
Sussex St OSM LS9 37 E1
Sutherland Av RHAY LS8 21 G1
Sutherland Crs RHAY LS8 14 C5
Sutherland Mt OSM LS9 29 G3
Sutherland Rd OSM LS9 29 G3
Sutherland St WOR/ARM LS12 * 35 G2
Sutherland Ter OSM LS9 29 G3
Sutton Ap SCFT LS14 30 C4
Sutton Crs SCFT LS14 30 C4
Sutton Gv MOR LS27 * 46 C3
Sutton St WOR/ARM LS12 2 B7
Swaine Hill Crs YEA LS19 5 G5
Swaine Hill St YEA LS19 5 G5
Swaine Hill Ter YEA LS19 5 G5
Swallow Av WOR/ARM LS12 34 C2
Swallow Cl AL/HA/HU LS17 14 B3
Swallow Crs WOR/ARM LS12 34 C2
Swallow Dr AL/HA/HU LS17 14 B3
Swallow Mt WOR/ARM LS12 34 C2
Swallow V MOR LS27 47 F2
Swarcliffe Ap SCFT LS14 31 G1
Swarcliffe Av SCFT LS14 31 G1
Swarcliffe Bank SCFT LS14 23 G5
Swarcliffe Dr SCFT LS14 31 G1
Swarcliffe Dr East
MSTN/BAR LS15 31 H1
Swarcliffe Gn SCFT LS14 31 H1
Swarcliffe Rd SCFT LS14 23 G5
Swardale Gn SCFT LS14 31 G1
Swardale Rd SCFT LS14 31 G1
Sweet St BEE/HOL LS11 36 B2
Sweet St West BEE/HOL LS11 36 A2
Swincar Av YEA LS19 5 H5
Swinegate LDS LS1 3 G6
Swinnow Av BRAM LS13 25 E4
Swinnow Cl BRAM LS13 25 E4
Swinnow Crs PDSY/CALV LS28 25 E3
Swinnow Dr BRAM LS13 25 E4
Swinnow Gdns BRAM LS13 25 E4
Swinnow Garth
PDSY/CALV LS28 25 E5
Swinnow Gn PDSY/CALV LS28 24 D5
Swinnow Gv BRAM LS13 25 E4
Swinnow La BRAM LS13 25 E3
Swinnow Rd PDSY/CALV LS28 25 E5
Swinnow Vw BRAM LS13 25 E4
Swinnow Wk BRAM LS13 25 E4
Swithens Ct RTHW LS26 50 D2
Swithens Dr RTHW LS26 50 C2
Swithens Gv RTHW LS26 50 C2
Swithen's La RTHW LS26 50 D4
Swithen's St RTHW LS26 50 D2
Sycamore Av MSTN/BAR LS15 31 E5
RHAY LS8 21 F5
Sycamore Cha PDSY/CALV LS28 32 D1
Sycamore Cl CHAL LS7 19 H3
HDGY LS6 28 A1
Sycamore Cft BEE/HOL LS11 36 B5
Sycamore Fold BEE/HOL LS11 36 B5
Sycamore Rw BRAM LS13 25 E1
The Sycamores GSLY LS20 5 E2
Sycamore Wk PDSY/CALV LS28 24 B3
Sydenham St BEE/HOL LS11 35 H2
Sydney St PDSY/CALV LS28 24 B3
RTHW LS26 45 H5

T

Talbot Av AL/HA/HU LS17 14 A5
BULY LS4 27 E2
Talbot Ct RHAY LS8 21 F1
Talbot Crs RHAY LS8 14 B5
Talbot Fold RHAY LS8 21 F1
Talbot Gdns RHAY LS8 14 B5
Talbot Gv RHAY LS8 14 B5
Talbot Mt BULY LS4 27 E2
Talbot Ri RHAY LS8 14 B5
Talbot Rd RHAY LS8 14 B5
Talbot Ter BULY LS4 27 E2
RTHW LS26 50 C2
Talbot Vw BULY LS4 27 E2
Tall Trees AL/HA/HU LS17 13 G4
Tanglewood BEE/HOL LS11 42 A4
Tanhouse Hl HORS LS18 18 A2
Tannery Ct PDSY/CALV LS28 * 32 D1
Tannery Sq HDGY LS6 19 G3
Tarnside Dr SCFT LS14 30 D2
Tarn View Rd YEA LS19 6 A5
Tatham Wy RHAY LS8 22 A4
Tavistock Cl WOR/ARM LS12 35 F2
Tavistock Ms WOR/ARM LS12 35 F2
Tavistock Pk WOR/ARM LS12 35 F2
Tavistock Wy WOR/ARM LS12 35 F2
Tawny Beck WOR/ARM LS12 33 G1
Tawny Cl MOR LS27 47 F2
Taylors Cl SCFT LS14 31 F1
Tealby Cl BHP/TINH LS16 11 E5
Teal Dr MOR LS27 47 F2
Teale Dr CHAL LS7 21 E5
Teal Ms MID LS10 48 D1
Telephone Pl CHAL LS7 3 K1
Telford Cl MID LS10 43 E1
Telford Pl MID LS10 43 E1
Telford Ter MID LS10 37 E5
Temperance St
PDSY/CALV LS28 * 24 C4
Tempest Pl BEE/HOL LS11 * 36 A5
Tempest Rd BEE/HOL LS11 36 A5
Templar La LDSU LS2 3 J4
MSTN/BAR LS15 31 H1
Templar Pl LDSU LS2 3 J4
Templar St LDSU LS2 3 J3
Temple Av MSTN/BAR LS15 39 E2
RTHW LS26 44 D4
Temple Cl MSTN/BAR LS15 39 E2
Temple Ct MSTN/BAR LS15 38 D1
RTHW LS26 44 D4
Temple Crs BEE/HOL LS11 36 A5
Temple Ga MSTN/BAR LS15 39 F1
Templegate Av MSTN/BAR LS15 39 E2
Templegate Cl MSTN/BAR LS15 39 F1
Templegate Crs
MSTN/BAR LS15 39 F2
Temple Gate Dr MSTN/BAR LS15 39 E1
Templegate Gn MSTN/BAR LS15 39 F1
Templegate Ri MSTN/BAR LS15 39 E2
Templegate Rd MSTN/BAR LS15 39 F2
Templegate Vw
MSTN/BAR LS15 39 E2
Templegate Wk
MSTN/BAR LS15 39 F1
Templegate Wy
MSTN/BAR LS15 39 F2
Temple Gn RTHW LS26 45 E4
Temple Gv MSTN/BAR LS15 39 E1
Temple La MSTN/BAR LS15 39 F1
Temple Lea MSTN/BAR LS15 39 E1
Temple Moor MSTN/BAR LS15 * 31 F5
Templenewsam Rd
MSTN/BAR LS15 38 D1
Templenewsam Vw
MSTN/BAR LS15 38 D2
Temple Park Cl
MSTN/BAR LS15 39 E1
Temple Park Gdns
MSTN/BAR LS15 39 E1
Temple Park Gn
MSTN/BAR LS15 39 E1
Temple Ri MSTN/BAR LS15 39 E2
Templestowe Crs
MSTN/BAR LS15 31 G4
Templestowe Dr
MSTN/BAR LS15 31 G5
Templestowe Gdns
MSTN/BAR LS15 31 F5
Templestowe Hl
MSTN/BAR LS15 31 F4
Temple Vw EARD/LOFT WF3 50 A5
Temple View Gv OSM LS9 37 G1
Temple View Pl OSM LS9 37 F1
Temple View Rd OSM LS9 37 F1
Temple View Ter OSM LS9 37 F1
Temple Vue HDGY LS6 19 F4
Temple Wk MSTN/BAR LS15 31 F5
Tennyson Cl PDSY/CALV LS28 32 D2
Tennyson St GSLY LS20 5 F4
MOR LS27 46 D2
PDSY/CALV LS28 24 B3
PDSY/CALV LS28 32 D2
Tennyson Ter MOR LS27 * 46 D2
Terminus Pde MSTN/BAR LS15 * 31 G3
The Terrace PDSY/CALV LS28 32 C4
Texas St MOR LS27 46 D4
Thackray St MOR LS27 46 C3
Theaker La WOR/ARM LS12 26 D5
Thealby Cl OSM LS9 * 29 E5
Thealby Lawn OSM LS9 29 E4
Thealby Pl OSM LS9 29 E5
Theodore St BEE/HOL LS11 42 A2
Third Av RTHW LS26 44 D4
WOR/ARM LS12 35 F2
Thirlmere Cl BEE/HOL LS11 41 G3
Thirlmere Gdns BEE/HOL LS11 41 G3
Thirsk Gv MID LS10 48 D3
Thirsk Rw LDS LS1 2 E5
Thomas St HDGY LS6 28 A2
Thoresby Pl LDS LS1 [illegible]
Thornbury Av BHP/TINH LS16 19 E3
Thorn Cl RHAY LS8 29 H2
Thorn Crs RHAY LS8 29 H2
Thorn Dr RHAY LS8 29 H2
Thorne Gv RTHW LS26 44 D5
Thornfield Av PDSY/CALV LS20 24 A2
Thornfield Ct MSTN/BAR LS15 31 F3
Thornfield Dr MSTN/BAR LS15 31 F3
Thornfield Ms MSTN/BAR LS15 31 F3
Thornfield Rd BHP/TINH LS16 18 D2
Thornfield Wy MSTN/BAR LS15 31 F3
Thorn Gv RHAY LS8 29 H2
Thornhill Ct WOR/ARM LS12 34 D2
Thornhill Cft WOR/ARM LS12 34 D2
Thornhill Pl WOR/ARM LS12 34 D2
Thornhill Rd WOR/ARM LS12 34 D2
Thornhill St WOR/ARM LS12 34 D2
Thorn La RHAY LS8 21 F4
Thornlea Cl YEA LS19 8 B2
Thornleigh Gdns OSM LS9 * 37 F2
Thornleigh Gv OSM LS9 37 F2
Thornleigh Mt OSM LS9 37 F2
Thornleigh St OSM LS9 37 F2
Thornleigh Vw OSM LS9 37 F2
Thorn Mt RHAY LS8 30 A1
Thorn Ter RHAY LS8 29 H1
Thornton Av WOR/ARM LS12 34 C1
Thornton Gdns WOR/ARM LS12 34 C1
Thornton Gv WOR/ARM LS12 34 C1
Thorntons Ar LDS LS1 3 G4
Thorntons Dl HORS LS18 17 F4
Thorn Vw RHAY LS8 29 H2
Thornville MOR LS27 40 D4
Thornville Av HDGY LS6 27 G3
Thornville Ct HDGY LS6 * 27 G3
Thornville Crs HDGY LS6 27 G2
Thornville Gv HDGY LS6 27 G2
Thornville Mt HDGY LS6 27 G2
Thornville Pl HDGY LS6 27 G3
Thornville Rd HDGY LS6 * 27 G3
Thornville St HDGY LS6 27 G3
Thornville Ter HDGY LS6 27 G2
Thornville Vw HDGY LS6 27 G3
Thorn Wk RHAY LS8 30 A2
Thorpe Cl GSLY LS20 4 B4
Thorpe Ct MID LS10 48 C3
Thorpe Crs MID LS10 48 C3
Thorpe Dr GSLY LS20 4 B3
Thorpe Gdns MID LS10 48 C2
Thorpe Garth MID LS10 48 B3
Thorpe Gv MID LS10 48 C2
Thorpe La EARD/LOFT WF3 47 G5
GSLY LS20 4 A4
Thorpe Lower La
EARD/LOFT WF3 49 G3
Thorpe Mt MID LS10 48 B3
Thorpe Rd MID LS10 48 C2
PDSY/CALV LS28 24 B5
Thorpe Sq MID LS10 48 D3
Thorpe St MID LS10 48 C2
MSTN/BAR LS15 31 E5
Thorpe Vw EARD/LOFT WF3 49 E4
MID LS10 48 C3
Throstle Av MID LS10 48 B3
Throstle Dr MID LS10 48 A3
Throstle Hl MID LS10 48 B3
Throstle La MID LS10 48 C3
Throstle Mt MID LS10 48 B3
Throstle Nest Vw HORS LS18 17 G3
Throstle Pde MID LS10
Throstle Pl MID LS10
Throstle Rd MID LS10
MID LS10
Throstle Rw MID LS10
Throstle Sq MID LS10
Throstle St MID LS10
Throstle Ter MID LS10
Throstle Vw MID LS10
Throstle Wk MID LS10
Thwaite Ga MID LS10
Thwaite La MID LS10
Tilbury Av BEE/HOL LS11 *
Tilbury Gv BEE/HOL LS11 *
Tilbury Mt BEE/HOL LS11 *
Tilbury Pde BEE/HOL LS11 *
Tilbury Rd BEE/HOL LS11
Tilbury Rw BEE/HOL LS11
Tilbury Ter BEE/HOL LS11
Tilbury Vw BEE/HOL LS11 *
Tile La BHP/TINH LS16
Tingley Av EARD/LOFT WF3
Tingley Common
EARD/LOFT WF3
MOR LS27
Tingley Crs EARD/LOFT WF3
Tinshill Av BHP/TINH LS16
Tinshill Cl BHP/TINH LS16
Tinshill Crs BHP/TINH LS16
Tinshill Dr BHP/TINH LS16
Tinshill Garth BHP/TINH LS16
Tinshill Gv BHP/TINH LS16
Tinshill La BHP/TINH LS16
Tinshill Mt BHP/TINH LS16
Tinshill Rd BHP/TINH LS16
Tinshill Vw BHP/TINH LS16
Tofts House Cl PDSY/CALV LS
Tofts Rd PDSY/CALV LS28
Toft St WOR/ARM LS12
Tonbridge St LDS LS1
Tong Ap WOR/ARM LS12
Tong Dr WOR/ARM LS12
Tong Ga WOR/ARM LS12
Tong Gn WOR/ARM LS12
Tong Rd WOR/ARM LS12
Tongue La HDGY LS6
Tong Wy WOR/ARM LS12
Topcliffe Av MOR LS27
Topcliffe Cl EARD/LOFT WF3
Topcliffe Garth MOR LS27
Topcliffe Gv MOR LS27
Topcliffe La EARD/LOFT WF3
Topcliffe Md MOR LS27
Topfield Fold MOR LS27
Tordoff Ter KSTL LS5 *
Toronto Pl CHAL LS7
Torre Cl OSM LS9
Torre Crs OSM LS9
Torre Dr OSM LS9
Torre Gv OSM LS9
Torre Hl OSM LS9
Torre La OSM LS9
Torre Mt OSM LS9
Torre Pl OSM LS9
Torre Rd OSM LS9
Torre Sq OSM LS9
Torre Vw OSM LS9
Torre Wk OSM LS9
Tower Gv WOR/ARM LS12
Tower House St LDSU LS2
Tower La WOR/ARM LS12
Tower Pl WOR/ARM LS12
Towers Sq HDGY LS6
The Towers WOR/ARM LS12
Towers Wy HDGY LS6
Town Cl HORS LS18
Townend Pl PDSY/CALV LS28
Townend Rd WOR/ARM LS12
Town Ga GSLY LS20
Town Gate Cl GSLY LS20
Town Hall Sq YEA LS19
Town St BEE/HOL LS11
BRAM LS13
CHAL LS7
EARD/LOFT WF3
GSLY LS20
HORS LS18
MID LS10
PDSY/CALV LS28
WOR/ARM LS12
YEA LS19
YEA LS19
Town Street Ms CHAL LS7
Town Street Wk CHAL LS7
Trafalgar Gdns MOR LS27
Trafalgar St LDSU LS2
Trafford Av OSM LS9
Trafford Gv OSM LS9
Trafford Ter OSM LS9
Tranbeck Rd GSLY LS20
Tranfield Av GSLY LS20
Tranfield Cl GSLY LS20
Tranfield Gdns GSLY LS20
Tranmere Ct GSLY LS20
Tranmere Dr GSLY LS20
Tranquility MSTN/BAR LS15
Tranquility Ct MSTN/BAR LS1
Trans Pennine Trail MID LS10
Tranter Pl MSTN/BAR LS15
Tree Tops Ct RHAY LS8
Trelawn Av HDGY LS6
Trelawn Pl HDGY LS6
Trelawn St HDGY LS6
Trelawn Ter HDGY LS6
Tremont Gdns MID LS10
Trenic Crs HDGY LS6
Trenic Dr HDGY LS6
Trentham Av BEE/HOL LS11
Trentham Gv BEE/HOL LS11
Trentham Pl BEE/HOL LS11
Trentham Rw BEE/HOL LS11
Trentham St BEE/HOL LS11
Trent Rd OSM LS9
Trent St BEE/HOL LS11
Trescoe Av WOR/ARM LS12

q LDS LS1 * ...3 C5
DS LS1 ...3 C4
BEE/HOL LS11 ...36 A2
PI PDSY/CALV LS28 ...32 D3
ns PDSY/CALV LS28 ...33 F1
r PDSY/CALV LS28 ...33 F2
LS27 * ...46 C1
RS LS18 ...10 C5
...46 C2
OR/ARM LS12 ...27 E5
PSY/CALV LS28 ...44 C1
BEE/HOL LS11 ...41 G1
ns RHAY LS8 ...21 H3
BEE/HOL LS11 ...24 C3
OSM LS9 ...3 K6
AV AL/HA/HU LS17 ...13 F5
CI AL/HA/HU LS17 ...13 F5
Fold AL/HA/HU LS17 ...13 F5
PI AL/HA/HU LS17 ...13 F5
GV AL/HA/HU LS17 ...13 F5
RI AL/HA/HU LS17 ...13 F5
Vw AL/HA/HU LS17 * ...13 F5
PDSY/CALV LS28 ...24 B2
OSM LS9 ...48 D1
ys HDGY LS6 ...27 E1
M LS9 ...37 H1
ct CHAL LS7 ...32 A2
k CHAL LS7 ...20 A4
t AL/HA/HU LS17 * ...13 E4
1 AL/HA/HU LS17 ...13 E4
t AL/HA/HU LS17 ...13 E4
t AL/HA/HU LS17 ...13 E4
t AL/HA/HU LS17 ...13 E5

U

Crs MSTN/BAR LS15 ...38 C2
126 ...45 C3
/HOL LS11 ...36 A2
DSU LS3 ...3 H4
2 ...41 E5
CHAL LS7 ...20 C4
GY LS6 ...19 H5
RD/LOFT WF3 ...50 B3
Rd LDSU LS28 ...28 A3
RHAY LS8 ...21 G5
s RHAY LS8 ...29 C1
r RHAY LS8 ...29 C1
rn St BRAM LS13 ...15 E5
odview PI
LS11 * ...42 B1
rtley Ct
M LS12 ...34 C1
rtley Dr
rtley Rd
M LS12 ...34 D1

V

HAY LS8 ...14 C4
HDGY LS6 ...19 H5
L/HA/HU LS17 ...13 C2
MSTN/BAR LS15 ...31 F4
s CHAL LS7 ...20 C2
PDSY/CALV LS28 ...32 C2
PDSY/CALV LS28 ...25 E5
BRAM LS13 ...15 E5
BRAM LS13 ...17 G5
27 ...46 D1
ALV LS28 ...32 D2
PDSY/CALV LS28 ...32 D2
AL/HA/HU LS17 ...13 E4
r PI CHAL LS7 ...21 E4
PDSY/CALV LS28 ...24 B1
SCFT LS14 ...30 C5
St BRAM LS13 ...25 E3
PDSY/CALV LS28 ...24 A1
d LDS LS1 ...2 E1
r LDSU LS3 ...3 F3
LS5 ...18 A4
LS5 ...18 A4
ns KSTL LS5 ...18 B5
ate Crs KSTL LS5 ...18 B5
ate Dr KSTL LS5 ...18 A4
ate Mt KSTL LS5 ...18 A4
r KSTL LS5 ...18 C1
y KSTL LS5 ...26 C1
KSTL LS5 ...18 A4
1 KSTL LS5 ...18 A4
y KSTL LS5 ...18 C1
d WOR/ARM LS12 ...27 F4
Dr PDSY/CALV LS28 ...32 B1
St KSTL LS5 ...26 D1
e KSTL LS5 ...26 D1

Vicarage Vw KSTL LS5 ...26 D1
Vicar La LDS LS1 ...3 H4
Vicars Rd RHAY LS8 ...29 F1
Vicars Ter RHAY LS8 * ...29 F1
Vickers Av KSTL LS5 ...26 B2
Vickersdale PDSY/CALV LS28 ...24 C5
Vickers St MOR LS27 ...46 B4
Victor Dr GSLY LS20 ...5 E4
Victoria Av HORS LS18 ...17 E3
   MOR LS27 ...46 C1
   OSM LS9 ...37 G1
   RTHW LS26 ...50 C2
Victoria CI HORS LS18 ...17 E3
   YEA LS19 ...6 B5
Victoria Court Ms HDGY LS6 * ...17 E3
Victoria Crs HORS LS18 ...17 E3
   PDSY/CALV LS28 ...32 A1
Victoria Dr HORS LS18 ...17 E3
   MOR LS27 ...40 D5
Victoria Gdns HORS LS18 ...17 F3
   PDSY/CALV LS28 ...32 A1
Victoria Grange Dr RHAY LS8 ...21 G2
Victoria Ms HORS LS18 ...17 E4
   OSM LS9 ...37 G1
Victoria Mt HORS LS18 ...17 E3
Victoria Park Av BRAM LS13 ...26 A2
Victoria Park Gv BRAM LS13 ...26 B2
Victoria PI BEE/HOL LS11 ...36 B3
   YEA LS19 ...5 G5
Victoria RI HORS LS18 ...17 E3
Victoria Rd BEE/HOL LS11 ...36 B3
   GSLY LS20 ...4 D4
   HDGY LS6 ...27 G2
   KSTL LS5 ...26 C1
   MOR LS27 ...46 C1
   PDSY/CALV LS28 * ...24 B3
   PDSY/CALV LS28 ...32 A1
   RTHW LS26 ...44 B5
   SCFT LS14 ...23 F3
Victoria Sq LDS LS1 ...3 H4
Victoria St BVRD LS3 ...2 B4
   MID LS10 ...36 D3
   MOR LS27 ...41 E4
   MOR LS27 ...46 B1
Victoria Ter BVRD LS3 ...2 B2
   HDGY LS6 ...19 H5
   KSTL LS5 ...26 C1
   PDSY/CALV LS28 ...24 D3
Victoria Wk HORS LS18 ...17 E3
The View AL/HA/HU LS17 ...12 D1
   RHAY LS8 ...21 F2
Village Av BULY LS4 ...27 F3
Village PI BULY LS4 ...27 F3
The Village St BULY LS4 ...27 F3
Village Ter BULY LS4 ...27 F2
Vinery Av OSM LS9 ...29 G5
Vinery Gv OSM LS9 ...29 G5
Vinery Mt OSM LS9 ...37 G1
Vinery PI OSM LS9 ...37 F1
Vinery Rd BULY LS4 ...27 F3
Vinery St OSM LS9 ...37 G1
Vinery Ter OSM LS9 ...37 G1
Vinery Vw OSM LS9 ...37 G1
Vollan's Ct SCFT LS14 ...23 E5

W

Wade La LDSU LS2 ...3 G2
Wade St PDSY/CALV LS28 ...24 B2
Wadlands CI PDSY/CALV LS28 ...24 A1
Wadlands Dr PDSY/CALV LS28 ...24 A1
Wadlands Gv PDSY/CALV LS28 ...24 A1
Wadlands Ri PDSY/CALV LS28 ...24 A1
Waincliffe Crs BEE/HOL LS11 ...41 H2
Waincliffe Dr BEE/HOL LS11 ...41 H3
Waincliffe Garth BEE/HOL LS11 ...41 H3
Waincliffe PI BEE/HOL LS11 ...41 H3
Waincliffe Ter BEE/HOL LS11 ...41 H3
Wakefield Av SCFT LS14 ...30 D4
Wakefield Rd MID LS10 ...49 H1
   RTHW LS26 ...51 D3
Walesby Ct BHP/TINH LS16 ...11 E5
Walford Av OSM LS9 ...29 G5
Walford Gv OSM LS9 ...29 G5
Walford Mt OSM LS9 ...29 G5
Walford Rd OSM LS9 ...29 G5
Walford Ter OSM LS9 ...29 G5
Walker PI MOR LS27 * ...40 D4
Walker Rd HORS LS18 ...17 F1
Walkers Gn WOR/ARM LS12 ...35 E4
Walker's La WOR/ARM LS12 ...35 E4
Walkers Ms HDGY LS6 ...19 H5
Walkers Rw YEA LS19 ...8 C1
The Walk RHAY LS8 ...21 G5
Walmer Gv PDSY/CALV LS28 ...32 D5
Walmsley Rd HDGY LS6 ...27 G2
Walnut CI SCFT LS14 ...23 G2
Walter Crs OSM LS9 ...37 F1
Walter St BULY LS4 ...27 F4
Walton St BEE/HOL LS11 ...36 A2
   MID LS10 ...37 E4
Wand La MID LS10 ...42 D2
Ward St MID LS10 ...36 D3
Warm La YEA LS19 ...8 C1
Warrel's Av BRAM LS13 ...25 G3
Warrel's Ct BRAM LS13 ...25 G3
Warrel's Mt BRAM LS13 ...25 G3
Warrel's PI BRAM LS13 ...25 G3
Warrel's Rd BRAM LS13 ...25 G2
Warrel's St BRAM LS13 * ...25 G3
Warrel's Ter BRAM LS13 ...25 G3
Warren House La YEA LS19 ...6 B5
Washington PI BRAM LS13 ...25 E5
Washington St BRAM LS13 ...25 E5
   BVRD LS5 ...27 G5
Washington Ter BRAM LS13 ...25 E5

Water La BEE/HOL LS11 ...2 D7
   HORS LS18 ...16 C1
   PDSY/CALV LS28 ...24 B2
   WOR/ARM LS12 ...33 H1
Waterloo Crs BRAM LS13 ...25 H2
Waterloo La BRAM LS13 ...25 H2
Waterloo St MID LS10 ...3 H6
Waterloo Wy BRAM LS13 ...25 H2
Waterside Rd MID LS10 ...43 H1
Watson Rd SCFT LS14 ...30 D4
Watson St MOR LS27 ...46 B3
Waveney Rd WOR/ARM LS12 ...35 E2
Waverley Garth BEE/HOL LS11 ...36 B4
Wayland Ap BHP/TINH LS16 ...12 B3
Wayland Dr BHP/TINH LS16 ...12 B3
Weaver Gdns WOR/ARM LS12 ...34 A1
Weavers CI PDSY/CALV LS28 ...32 D2
Weavers Gra GSLY LS20 ...5 E3
Weavers Rw PDSY/CALV LS28 ...32 D2
Weaver St BULY LS4 ...27 F4
Webster Rw WOR/ARM LS12 ...34 D1
Wedgewood Dr RHAY LS8 ...21 G2
Wedgewood Gv RHAY LS8 ...21 G2
Weetwood Av BHP/TINH LS16 ...19 F3
Weetwood Ct BHP/TINH LS16 ...19 E2
Weetwood Crs BHP/TINH LS16 ...19 F2
Weetwood Grange Gv
   BHP/TINH LS16 ...18 D2
Weetwood House Ct
   BHP/TINH LS16 ...18 D2
Weetwood La BHP/TINH LS16 ...19 E1
Weetwood Mill La
   BHP/TINH LS16 ...19 F2
Weetwood Park Dr
   BHP/TINH LS16 ...18 D2
Welbeck Rd BHP/TINH LS16 ...19 E3
Welburn Av BHP/TINH LS16 ...18 D3
Welburn Dr BHP/TINH LS16 ...18 D3
Welburn Gv BHP/TINH LS16 ...18 D3
Well CI YEA LS19 ...9 E4
Well Close Rt CHAL LS7 ...28 C3
Well Garth MSTN/BAR LS15 ...31 G3
Well Garth Bank BRAM LS13 ...25 F1
Well Garth Mt MSTN/BAR LS15 ...31 G3
Well Garth Wk BRAM LS13 ...25 F1
Well Hill YEA LS19 ...5 H5
Well Holme Md WOR/ARM LS12 ...34 A5
Well House Av RHAY LS8 ...21 G5
Well House Crs RHAY LS8 ...21 G5
Well House Dr RHAY LS8 ...21 G5
Well House Gdns RHAY LS8 ...21 G5
Well House Rd RHAY LS8 ...21 G5
Wellington Ap WOR/ARM LS12 ...2 A6
Wellington Bridge St BVRD LS3 ...2 B4
Wellington Gdns BRAM LS13 ...25 H1
Wellington Garth BRAM LS13 ...25 H1
Wellington Gv BRAM LS13 ...25 H1
   PDSY/CALV LS28 ...32 A1
Wellington Mt BRAM LS13 ...25 H1
Wellington PI LDS LS1 ...2 C5
Wellington Rd WOR/ARM LS12 ...2 B5
   BRAM LS13 ...2 B4
Wellington St BVRD LS3 ...2 B4
   MOR LS27 ...46 C2
Wellington Ter BRAM LS13 ...25 H1
Well La CHAL LS7 ...4 E2
   GSLY LS20 ...5 E3
   YEA LS19 ...8 D1
   YEA LS19 ...9 E4
Wells Cft HDGY LS6 ...19 G3
Wells Rd GSLY LS20 ...4 C5
Wellstone Av BRAM LS13 ...25 F5
Wellstone Dr BRAM LS13 ...25 F5
Wellstone Gdns BRAM LS13 ...25 F5
Wellstone Garth BRAM LS13 ...25 F4
Wellstone Gn BRAM LS13 ...25 F4
Wellstone Ri BRAM LS13 ...25 F5
Wellstone Rd BRAM LS13 ...25 F5
Wellstone Wy BRAM LS13 ...25 F5
Well Ter GSLY LS20 ...5 E3
Welton Gv HDGY LS6 ...27 G2
Welton Mt HDGY LS6 ...27 G2
Welton PI HDGY LS6 ...27 G2
Welton Rd HDGY LS6 ...27 G2
Wensley Av CHAL LS7 ...20 C3
Wensley Crs CHAL LS7 ...20 C3
Wensleydale Av WOR/ARM LS12 ...26 B3
Wensleydale Crs
   WOR/ARM LS12 ...26 B3
Wensleydale Dr WOR/ARM LS12 ...26 B3
Wensleydale Ms
   WOR/ARM LS12 ...26 B3
Wensleydale Ri
   WOR/ARM LS12 * ...26 B3
Wensley Dr CHAL LS7 ...20 C3
Wensley Gn CHAL LS7 ...20 B3
Wensley Lawn MID LS10 ...48 C2
Wensley Rd CHAL LS7 ...20 B2
Wensley Vw CHAL LS7 ...20 C3
Wentworth Av AL/HA/HU LS17 ...13 C5
Wentworth Wy AL/HA/HU LS17 ...13 C5
Wepener Mt OSM LS9 ...29 H4
Wepener PI OSM LS9 ...29 H4
Wesley Ap BEE/HOL LS11 ...41 H1
Wesley Av WOR/ARM LS12 ...35 E1
Wesley Ct BEE/HOL LS11 ...41 H1
   HDGY LS6 ...28 A2
Wesley Cft BEE/HOL LS11 ...35 H5
Wesley Garth BEE/HOL LS11 ...41 H1
Wesley PI OSM LS9 ...37 E1
   WOR/ARM LS12 ...35 E1
Wesley Rw PDSY/CALV LS28 ...24 C5
Wesley Sq PDSY/CALV LS28 * ...24 C5
Wesley St BEE/HOL LS11 ...36 A2
   BRAM LS13 ...16 D5
   MOR LS27 ...46 B2
   PDSY/CALV LS28 ...24 B2
Wesley Ter BRAM LS13 ...16 D5
   BRAM LS13 ...25 H2

PDSY/CALV LS28 ...24 C5
Wesley Vw BRAM LS13 * ...16 D5
   PDSY/CALV LS28 ...32 C1
West Av RHAY LS8 ...22 A2
Westbourne Av BEE/HOL LS11 ...36 B5
Westbourne Dr GSLY LS20 ...4 C5
Westbourne Mt BEE/HOL LS11 ...36 B5
Westbourne PI BEE/HOL LS11 ...36 B5
   PDSY/CALV LS28 ...24 A3
Westbourne St BEE/HOL LS11 ...36 B5
Westbrook CI HORS LS18 ...10 B5
Westbrook La HORS LS18 ...10 B5
Westbury CI MID LS10 ...43 F1
Westbury Gv MID LS10 ...43 G1
Westbury PI North MID LS10 ...43 F1
Westbury PI South RTHW LS26 ...43 F2
Westbury St MID LS10 ...43 F1
Westbury Ter RTHW LS26 ...43 G1
Westcombe Av RHAY LS8 ...14 C5
West Ct RHAY LS8 ...22 A3
Westdale Dr PDSY/CALV LS28 ...24 B5
Westdale Gdns PDSY/CALV LS28 ...24 B5
Westdale Gv PDSY/CALV LS28 ...24 B5
Westdale Ri PDSY/CALV LS28 ...24 B5
Westdale Rd PDSY/CALV LS28 ...24 B5
West Dene AL/HA/HU LS17 ...14 B2
West End WOR/ARM LS12 ...33 H5
West End CI HORS LS18 ...16 D1
West End Dr HORS LS18 ...17 E1
West End Gv HORS LS18 ...16 D1
West End La HORS LS18 ...9 F5
West End PI BEE/HOL LS11 ...36 A3
West End Ter HORS LS18 ...16 D1
   SCFT LS14 ...8 B1
Westerly Cft WOR/ARM LS12 ...27 E5
Westerly Ri WOR/ARM LS12 ...27 E5
Western Gv WOR/ARM LS12 ...34 D3
Western Mt WOR/ARM LS12 ...34 D3
Western PI WOR/ARM LS12 ...34 D3
Western St WOR/ARM LS12 ...34 D3
West Farm Av MID LS10 ...48 B1
Westfield PDSY/CALV LS28 ...24 B4
Westfield Av HORS LS18 ...17 E1
   YEA LS19 ...8 B1
Westfield CI RTHW LS26 ...50 A2
Westfield Ct RTHW LS26 ...50 A2
   WOR/ARM LS12 ...34 D3
Westfield Crs BVRD LS3 ...2 A1
Westfield Dr YEA LS19 ...8 A1
Westfield Mt YEA LS19 ...8 A1
Westfield Rd BVRD LS3 ...2 A1
   MOR LS27 ...46 C2
   RTHW LS26 ...50 A2
Westfield Ter BVRD LS3 ...2 A1
Westgate GSLY LS20 ...4 C4
   LDS LS1 ...2 C4
West Grange CI MID LS10 ...42 D2
West Grange Dr MID LS10 ...42 D2
West Grange Fold MID LS10 ...42 D2
West Grange Gdns MID LS10 ...42 D2
West Grange Garth MID LS10 ...42 D2
West Grange Rd MID LS10 ...42 D2
West Grange Wk MID LS10 ...42 D2
West Grove St
   PDSY/CALV LS28 ...32 C1
West Hill Av CHAL LS7 ...20 C3
Westland Rd BEE/HOL LS11 ...42 B3
Westland Sq BEE/HOL LS11 ...42 B3
West Lea CI AL/HA/HU LS17 ...20 B1
West Lea Crs YEA LS19 ...5 F5
West Lea Dr AL/HA/HU LS17 ...20 D1
West Lea Gdns AL/HA/HU LS17 ...20 B1
West Lea Garth AL/HA/HU LS17 ...20 B1
West Lea Gv YEA LS19 ...5 F5
Westlock Av OSM LS9 ...29 G4
West Lodge Gdns CHAL LS7 ...20 C4
Westminster CI BRAM LS13 ...24 D1
Westminster Crs
   MSTN/BAR LS15 ...38 C2
Westminster Cft BRAM LS13 * ...25 C2
Westminster Dr BRAM LS13 ...24 D1
Westmoor PI BRAM LS13 ...25 F2
Westmoor Ri BRAM LS13 ...25 F2
Westmoor St BRAM LS13 ...25 F2
Westmoreland Mt BRAM LS13 * ...25 H1
West Mount St BEE/HOL LS11 * ...36 A5
Westover Gdns
   PDSY/CALV LS28 ...32 A1
Westover Gn BRAM LS13 * ...25 G2
Westover Gv BRAM LS13 * ...25 G2
Westover Mt BRAM LS13 * ...25 G2
Westover Rd BRAM LS13 ...25 G2
Westover Ter BRAM LS13 ...25 G2
Westover Vw BRAM LS13 ...25 G2
West Pde BHP/TINH LS16 ...18 C2
   GSLY LS20 ...4 C4
West Pk BHP/TINH LS16 ...18 C2
   RTHW LS26 ...50 D1
West Park Av RHAY LS8 ...14 B4
West Park CI RHAY LS8 ...14 C4
West Park Crs RHAY LS8 ...14 C4
West Park Dr BHP/TINH LS16 ...14 A4
West Park Dr East RHAY LS8 ...14 C4
West Park Dr West RHAY LS8 ...14 C4
West Park Gv RHAY LS8 ...14 C4
West Park Rd PDSY/CALV LS28 ...32 B1
West Pasture CI HORS LS18 ...10 A5
Westroyd PDSY/CALV LS28 ...32 A2
Westroyd Av PDSY/CALV LS28 ...32 A2
Westroyd Crs PDSY/CALV LS28 ...32 A2
Westroyd Gdns
   PDSY/CALV LS28 ...32 A2
West St BVRD LS3 ...2 B4
   MOR LS27 ...46 B3
   PDSY/CALV LS28 ...24 C5
West V WOR/ARM LS12 ...34 A5
Westvale Ms BRAM LS13 ...25 G3
West Vw BEE/HOL LS11 ...36 A4
   RTHW LS26 ...51 G1
   YEA LS19 ...5 F5

West View Ct YEA LS19 ...5 F5
West Villa Rd GSLY LS20 ...5 E5
Westway GSLY LS20 ...4 B4
   PDSY/CALV LS28 ...24 A2
Westways Dr RHAY LS8 ...22 A5
Westwinn Garth SCFT LS14 ...23 G1
Westwinn Vw SCFT LS14 ...23 G1
Westwood CI WOR/ARM LS12 ...40 D5
West Wood Ct MID LS10 ...48 A1
Westwood Ri WOR/ARM LS12 ...40 D5
West Wood Rd MOR LS27 ...47 H2
Westwood Side MOR LS27 ...40 D4
Wetherby Gv BULY LS4 ...27 E5
Wetherby PI BULY LS4 ...27 F5
Wetherby Rd RHAY LS8 ...21 H3
   SCFT LS14 ...22 D1
Wetherby Ter BULY LS4 ...27 E5
Whack House CI YEA LS19 ...8 C1
Wharfe CI HORS LS18 ...16 C1
Wharfedale Av CHAL LS7 ...28 B1
Wharfedale Ct SCFT LS14 ...22 D5
Wharfedale Gv HDGY LS6 ...28 B1
Wharfedale Mt HDGY LS6 ...28 B1
Wharfedale RI HDGY LS6 ...28 B1
Wharfedale St HDGY LS6 ...28 B1
Wharfedale Vw HDGY LS6 ...28 B1
Wharf St LDSU LS2 ...3 J5
Wheatfield Ct PDSY/CALV LS28 ...32 B2
Wheatlands PDSY/CALV LS28 ...24 A2
Wheaton Av MSTN/BAR LS15 ...31 E5
Wheelwright Av
   WOR/ARM LS12 ...34 C3
Wheelwright CI WOR/ARM LS12 ...34 C3
Whimbrel Ms MOR LS27 ...47 E3
Whinbrook Crs AL/HA/HU LS17 ...20 C1
Whinbrook Gdns
   AL/HA/HU LS17 ...20 C1
Whinbrook Gv AL/HA/HU LS17 ...20 C1
Whincover CI WOR/ARM LS12 ...34 B3
Whincover Cross
   WOR/ARM LS12 ...34 B3
Whincover Dr WOR/ARM LS12 ...34 B3
Whincover Gdns
   WOR/ARM LS12 ...34 B3
Whincover Gv WOR/ARM LS12 ...34 B3
Whincover HI WOR/ARM LS12 ...34 B3
Whincover Mt WOR/ARM LS12 ...34 B3
Whincover Rd WOR/ARM LS12 ...34 B3
Whincover Vw WOR/ARM LS12 ...34 B3
Whinfield BHP/TINH LS16 ...11 H3
Whingate Av WOR/ARM LS12 ...26 C5
Whingate CI WOR/ARM LS12 ...34 C1
Whingate Gn WOR/ARM LS12 ...34 C1
Whingate Gv WOR/ARM LS12 ...34 C1
Whingate Rd WOR/ARM LS12 ...34 C1
Whinmoor Ct SCFT LS14 ...23 E1
Whinmoor Crs SCFT LS14 ...23 E1
Whinmoor Gdns SCFT LS14 ...23 D1
Whinn Moor La AL/HA/HU LS17 ...15 G4
Whitaker St PDSY/CALV LS28 ...24 B3
Whitebeam La MID LS10 ...42 D3
Whitebridge Av
   MSTN/BAR LS15 ...30 C4
Whitebridge Sp SCFT LS14 ...30 C4
Whitebridge Vw OSM LS9 ...30 C4
Whitechapel CI RHAY LS8 ...21 H4
Whitechapel Wy RHAY LS8 ...21 H4
Whitecote Gdns BRAM LS13 ...25 F1
Whitecote HI BRAM LS13 ...25 F1
Whitecote La BRAM LS13 ...25 F1
Whitecote Ri BRAM LS13 ...25 F1
White Gv RHAY LS8 ...21 G2
Whitehall Est RTHW LS26 ...50 D1
Whitehall Est WOR/ARM LS12 * ...34 B4
Whitehall Quay LDS LS1 ...2 E5
Whitehall Rd WOR/ARM LS12 ...2 C5
   WOR/ARM LS12 ...34 C4
Whitehouse La YEA LS19 ...6 D4
White Laith Av SCFT LS14 ...23 F2
White Laith Ap SCFT LS14 ...23 F2
White Laith CI SCFT LS14 ...23 F2
White Laith Cft SCFT LS14 ...23 F2
White Laith Gdns SCFT LS14 * ...23 F2
White Laith Garth SCFT LS14 ...23 F2
White Laith Gn SCFT LS14 ...23 F2
White Laith Rd SCFT LS14 ...23 F2
White Laith Wk SCFT LS14 ...23 F2
White Lands YEA LS19 ...8 C3
Whiteleas St CHAL LS7 ...3 J1
Whitestone Crs YEA LS19 ...5 H5
White St RTHW LS26 ...45 C5
Whitfield Av MID LS10 ...37 E4
Whitfield Gdns MID LS10 * ...37 E4
Whitfield PI MID LS10 ...37 E4
Whitfield Sq MID LS10 ...37 E4
Whitfield St RHAY LS8 ...29 F2
Whitfield Wy MID LS10 ...37 E4
Whitkirk La MSTN/BAR LS15 ...31 G4
Whitley Gdns RHAY LS8 ...29 E2
The Wickets HDGY LS6 ...19 H3
Wickham St BEE/HOL LS11 ...36 A5
Wide La MOR LS27 ...47 E2
Wigeon Ap MOR LS27 ...47 E2
Wigton Cha AL/HA/HU LS17 ...14 A1
Wigton Gn AL/HA/HU LS17 ...14 A1
Wigton Gn AL/HA/HU LS17 ...14 B2
Wigton La AL/HA/HU LS17 ...14 B2
Wigton Park CI AL/HA/HU LS17 ...14 B1
Wike Ridge Av AL/HA/HU LS17 ...14 C1
Wike Ridge CI AL/HA/HU LS17 ...14 D1
Wike Ridge Fold AL/HA/HU LS17 ...14 C1
Wike Ridge Gv AL/HA/HU LS17 ...14 D2
Wike Ridge La AL/HA/HU LS17 ...14 D1
Wike Ridge Ms AL/HA/HU LS17 ...14 C2
Wike Ridge Mt AL/HA/HU LS17 ...14 C2
Wike Ridge Vw AL/HA/HU LS17 ...14 C2
Wilfred Av MSTN/BAR LS15 ...31 F5
Wilfred St MSTN/BAR LS15 ...31 F5

Wilfrid Ter *WOR/ARM* LS12 ....**34** C4
Willans Av *RTHW* LS26 ....**44** C4
William Av *MSTN/BAR* LS15 * **30** C5
William Hey Ct *OSM* LS9 * **29** H5
William Ri *MSTN/BAR* LS15.........**30** D5
William St *HDGY* LS6 ....**27** C2
  MOR LS27 ....**41** E5
  PDSY/CALV LS28 ....**24** B4
William Vw *MSTN/BAR* LS15 ....**30** C5
Willis St *OSM* LS9 ....**37** E1
Willoughby Ter *BEE/HOL* LS11 ...**35** H5
Willow Ap *BULY* LS4 ....**27** C4
Willow Av *BULY* LS4 ....**27** C4
Willow Cl *BULY* LS4 ....**27** C4
Willow Crs *MSTN/BAR* LS15 ....**38** D1
Willow Gdns *GSLY* LS20...............**5** E3
Willow Rd *BULY* LS4 ....**27** C4
  PDSY/CALV LS28 ....**24** A3
The Willows *AL/HA/HU* LS17 ....**13** C5
Willow Terrace Rd *LDSU* LS2 ....**2** D1
Willow Well Rd *MSTN/BAR* LS15 ..**30** D5
Wills Gill *GSLY* LS20 ....**5** F3
Wilmington Gv *CHAL* LS7 * **28** C2
Wilmington St *CHAL* LS7 * **28** D3
Wilmington Ter *CHAL* LS7 ....**28** D3
Wilsons Yd *PDSY/CALV* LS28 ....**24** B4
Wilton Gv *HDGY* LS6 ....**19** G4
Winchester St *WOR/ARM* LS12 ....**35** F1
Windermere Dr *AL/HA/HU* LS17 ..**12** D1
Winders Dl *MOR* LS27 ....**40** B5
Winding Wy *AL/HA/HU* LS17 ....**13** F2
Windmill Ap *MID* LS10 ....**43** E3
Windmill Cha *RTHW* LS26 ....**50** C2
Windmill Cl *MID* LS10 ....**43** E4
Windmill Ct *SCFT* LS14 ....**23** F4
Windmill Field Rd *RTHW* LS26 ......**50** C2
Windmill Gdns *MSTN/BAR* LS15 ..**39** H1
Windmill Gn *RTHW* LS26 ....**50** C2
Windmill Hl *PDSY/CALV* LS28 ......**32** A2
Windmill La *RTHW* LS26 ....**50** C2
  YEA LS19 ....**9** E1
Windmill Rd *MID* LS10.................**43** E3
Windsor Av *MSTN/BAR* LS15 ....**31** F5
Windsor Crs *RTHW* LS26 ....**44** C5
Windsor Mt *MSTN/BAR* LS15 ....**31** F5
Wine St *LDS* LS1 ....**3** F4
Winfield Gv *LDSU* LS2 ....**28** B3
Winfield Pl *LDSU* LS2 ....**28** B3
Winfield Ter *LDSU* LS2 * **28** B3
Winnipeg Pl *CHAL* LS7 ....**20** C4
Winrose Ap *MID* LS10...................**43** E4
Winrose Av *MID* LS10 ....**42** D3
Winrose Crs *MID* LS10 ....**42** D3
Winrose Dr *MID* LS10 ....**42** D3
Winrose Garth *MID* LS10 ....**42** D3
Winrose Gv *MID* LS10 ....**43** E3
Winrose Hl *MID* LS10 ....**43** F2
Winstanley Ter *HDGY* LS6.............**27** G2
Winston Gdns *HDGY* LS6 ....**19** E5
Winston Mt *HDGY* LS6 ....**19** E5
Winterbourne Av *MOR* LS27 ....**40** D5
Winthorpe Av *EARD/LOFT* WF3 ....**48** D4
Winthorpe Crs *EARD/LOFT* WF3 ...**48** D4
Wintoun St *CHAL* LS7 ....**3** J1

Wolley Av *WOR/ARM* LS12 ....**33** H5
Wolley Ct *WOR/ARM* LS12 ....**33** H5
Wolley Dr *WOR/ARM* LS12 ....**33** H5
Wolley Gdns *WOR/ARM* LS12 ....**33** H5
Wolseley Rd *BULY* LS4 ....**27** F4
Womersley Pl *PDSY/CALV* LS28 ....**32** B2
Woodbine Ter *BRAM* LS13 * **25** G2
  HDGY LS6 ....**19** G4
Woodbourne Av
  AL/HA/HU LS17 ....**20** C1
Woodbridge Cl *HDGY* LS6 ....**18** D5
Woodbridge Crs *HDGY* LS6 ....**18** C4
Woodbridge Fold *KSTL* LS5 ....**18** C5
Woodbridge Gdns *HDGY* LS6 ....**18** C5
Woodbridge Garth *HDGY* LS6 ....**18** C5
Woodbridge Gn *HDGY* LS6 ....**18** C5
Woodbridge Lawn *HDGY* LS6 ....**18** C5
Woodbridge Pl *HDGY* LS6 ....**18** C5
Woodbridge Rd *HDGY* LS6 ....**18** C5
Woodbridge V *HDGY* LS6 ....**18** D5
Wood Cl *BHP/TINH* LS16 ....**12** B4
  CHAL LS7 ....**20** C3
  RTHW LS26 ....**44** B5
Wood Crs *RTHW* LS26 ....**44** B5
Woodcross *MOR* LS27 ....**40** C5
Woodcross End *MOR* LS27 ....**40** C4
Woodcross Fold *MOR* LS27 ....**40** C5
Woodcross Gdns *MOR* LS27 ....**40** C5
Woodcross Garth *MOR* LS27 ....**40** C4
Wood Dr *RTHW* LS26 ....**44** A5
Woodeson Ct *BRAM* LS13.............**16** D5
Wood Gv *WOR/ARM* LS12 ....**33** H1
Woodhall Av *KSTL* LS5 ....**18** A4
Woodhall Ct *MSTN/BAR* LS15.......**39** H2
Woodhall Dr *KSTL* LS5 ....**18** A4
Wood Hl *RTHW* LS26 ....**44** B5
Wood Hill Ct *BHP/TINH* LS16 ....**10** D3
Wood Hill Crs *BHP/TINH* LS16 ......**10** C4
Wood Hill Gdns *BHP/TINH* LS16 ...**10** D3
Wood Hill Ri *BHP/TINH* LS16 ....**10** D3
Wood Hill Rd *BHP/TINH* LS16 ....**10** D3
Woodhouse Cliff *HDGY* LS6 ....**27** H1
Woodhouse Hill Av *MID* LS10 * **43** F4
Woodhouse Hill Gv *MID* LS10 * **43** E1
Woodhouse Hill Pl *MID* LS10 ....**43** E1
Woodhouse Hill Rd *MID* LS10 ....**43** E1
Woodhouse Hill Ter *MID* LS10 * **43** E1
Woodhouse La *HDGY* LS6 ....**28** A2
  LDSU LS2 ....**3** G2
Woodhouse Sq *BVRD* LS3 ....**2** E4
Woodhouse St *HDGY* LS6 ....**28** A2
Woodland Cl *MSTN/BAR* LS15 ......**31** G5
Woodland Ct *RHAY* LS8.................**21** F5
Woodland Crs *RTHW* LS26 ....**44** B4
Woodland Dr *CHAL* LS7 ....**20** C5
Woodland Gv *CHAL* LS7 ....**29** E1
Woodland La *METH/HALD LS15 .....**45** F4
Woodland La *CHAL* LS7 ....**20** D3
Woodland Mt *CHAL* LS7 * **29** E1
Woodland Pk *RTHW* LS26 ....**51** G1
Woodland Park Rd *HDGY* LS6 ....**19** G5
Woodland Ri *MSTN/BAR* LS15 ......**31** F5
Woodlands Av *PDSY/CALV* LS28 ...**24** A4

Woodlands Ct *BHP/TINH* LS16......**18** D1
Woodlands Dr *IDLE* BD10 ....**8** C5
  MOR LS27 ....**40** B5
Woodlands Gv *PDSY/CALV* LS28 ..**24** A4
Woodlands Park Rd
  PDSY/CALV LS28 ....**32** B3
Woodlands Sq *WOR/ARM* LS12 ....**26** B5
Woodlands Rd *PDSY/CALV* LS28 ..**24** A4
Woodlands Ter *PDSY/CALV* LS28 ..**24** A4
The Woodlands *RTHW* LS26 * **51** G1
Woodlands Vw *AL/HA/HU* LS17 ....**14** C4
Woodland Ter *CHAL* LS7................**20** A5
Wood La *BRAM* LS13 ....**25** H5
  BRAM LS13 ....**25** H5
  CHAL LS7 ....**20** C3
  HDGY LS6 ....**19** G5
  HORS LS18 ....**17** H2
  RTHW LS26 ....**44** C5
  WOR/ARM LS12 ....**34** A1
Wood Lane Ct *HDGY* LS6 ....**19** G5
Woodlea Ap *HDGY* LS6 ....**19** H1
  YEA LS19 ....**8** B1
Woodlea Cha *HDGY* LS6 ....**19** H2
Woodlea Cl *YEA* LS19 ....**8** B2
Woodlea Ct *HDGY* LS6 ....**19** H1
Woodlea Dr *HDGY* LS6 ....**19** H1
  YEA LS19 ....**8** B2
Woodlea Fold *HDGY* LS6 ....**19** H2
Woodlea Gdns *HDGY* LS6 ....**19** H1
Woodlea Garth *HDGY* LS6.............**19** H1
Woodlea Ga *HDGY* LS6 ....**19** H1
Woodlea Gn *HDGY* LS6 ....**19** H2
Woodlea Gv *BEE/HOL* LS11 * **35** H5
  HDGY LS6 ....**19** H2
Woodlea Holt *HDGY* LS6 ....**19** H1
Woodlea La *HDGY* LS6..................**19** H1
Woodlea Lawn *HDGY* LS6 ....**19** H1
Woodlea Mt *BEE/HOL* LS11 ....**35** H5
  YEA LS19 ....**8** B1
Woodlea Pk *HDGY* LS6 ....**19** H2
Woodlea Pl *BEE/HOL* LS11 ....**35** H5
Woodlea Rd *YEA* LS19 ....**8** B1
Woodlea Sq *HDGY* LS6 * **19** H1
Woodlea St *BEE/HOL* LS11 ....**35** H5
Woodlea Vw *HDGY* LS6 ....**19** H2
Woodleigh Hall Vw *YEA* LS19 * **16** C1
Woodliffe Ct *CHAL* LS7 ....**20** C5
Woodliffe Dr *CHAL* LS7 ....**20** C5
Woodman St *MSTN/BAR* LS15 ......**31** E5
Wood Mt *RTHW* LS26 ....**44** A5
Woodnook Cl *BHP/TINH* LS16.......**10** D5
Woodnook Dr *BHP/TINH* LS16 ......**10** D5
Woodnook Garth
  BHP/TINH LS16 ....**10** D5
Woodnook Rd *BHP/TINH* LS16 .....**10** D4
Wood Nook Ter
  PDSY/CALV LS28 ....**24** A4
Wood Pl *BEE/HOL* LS11 ....**36** A5
Woodside Av *BULY* LS4 ....**27** E3
  CHAL LS7 ....**19** H4
Woodside Cl *MOR* LS27 ....**40** C5
Woodside Ct *HORS* LS18 ....**18** A2

Woodside Dr *MOR* LS27 ....**40** C4
Woodside Gdns *MOR* LS27 ....**40** C4
Woodside Hill Cl *HORS* LS18.........**17** H2
Woodside La *MOR* LS27 ....**40** C4
Woodside Ms *CHAL* LS7................**19** H3
Woodside Park Av *HORS* LS18 ......**17** H2
Woodside Park Dr *HORS* LS18 ......**17** H2
Woodside Pl *BULY* LS4 ....**27** E3
Woodside Rd *BULY* LS4 ....**27** E3
Woodside Ter *BULY* LS4 ....**27** E3
Woodside Vw *BULY* LS4 ....**27** E3
Woodsley Gn *HDGY* LS6 ....**27** H5
Woodsley Rd *BVRD* LS3 ....**27** G4
Woodsley Ter *LDSU* LS2 ....**2** C1
Wood's Rw *PDSY/CALV* LS28 ....**24** C4
Woodstock Cl *BHP/TINH* LS16 ......**12** B4
Wood St *MOR* LS27 ....**46** B1
Woodthorne Cft
  AL/HA/HU LS17 ....**14** B3
Wood Vw *MOR* LS27 ....**41** E3
Woodview Cl *HORS* LS18 ....**10** C5
Woodview Gv *BEE/HOL* LS11 ....**42** B1
Woodview Mt *BEE/HOL* LS11 ....**42** B1
Woodview Rd *BEE/HOL* LS11 ....**42** B1
Woodview St *BEE/HOL* LS11 ....**42** B1
Woodview Ter *BEE/HOL* LS11 ....**42** B1
Woodville Av *HORS* LS18 ....**17** H1
Woodville Ct *RHAY* LS8 ....**21** H1
Woodville Crs *HORS* LS18 ....**17** H1
Woodville Gv *HORS* LS18 ....**17** H2
  MID LS10 * **43** E2
Woodville Pl *HORS* LS18 ....**18** A1
Woodville Sq *MID* LS10 ....**43** E2
Woodville St *HORS* LS18 ....**18** A1
Woodville Ter *HORS* LS18 ....**17** H1
Wood Vine Rd *PDSY/CALV* LS28 ...**24** A4
Woodway *HORS* LS18 ....**17** G5
Woodway Dr *HORS* LS18 ....**17** G5
Wooler Av *BEE/HOL* LS11 ....**42** A1
Wooler Dr *BEE/HOL* LS11 ....**42** A1
Wooler Gv *BEE/HOL* LS11 ....**42** A1
Wooler Pl *BEE/HOL* LS11 ....**42** A1
Wooler Rd *BEE/HOL* LS11 * **41** H1
Wooler St *BEE/HOL* LS11 ....**41** H1
Worcester Av *MID* LS10 ....**49** F2
Worcester Cl *EARD/LOFT* WF3 ......**48** C5
Worcester Dr *MID* LS10 ....**49** F2
Wordsworth Ct *RTHW* LS26 ....**51** G5
Wordsworth Dr *RTHW* LS26 ....**51** G5
Wormald Rw *LDS* LS1 ....**3** G5
Worrall St *MOR* LS27 ....**46** B3
Wortley Hts *WOR/ARM* LS12 ....**35** F2
Wortley La *WOR/ARM* LS12 ....**35** H2
Wortley Moor La
  WOR/ARM LS12 ....**34** D2
Wortley Moor Rd
  WOR/ARM LS12 ....**34** C1
Wortley Pk *WOR/ARM* LS12 ....**35** G2
Wortley Rd *WOR/ARM* LS12 ....**34** D1
Wrangthorn Av *HDGY* LS6 ....**27** H2
Wrangthorn Pl *HDGY* LS6 ....**27** H2
Wrangthorn Ter *HDGY* LS6 ....**27** H2
Wrenbury Av *BHP/TINH* LS16 ....**10** D2
Wrenbury Crs *BHP/TINH* LS16 ......**10** D2
Wrenbury Gv *BHP/TINH* LS16 ....**11** E2

Wren Dr *MOR* LS27 ....**40** C4
Wycliffe Cl *BRAM* LS13.................
Wycliffe Dr *AL/HA/HU* LS17 ....
Wykebeck Av *OSM* LS9 ....
Wykebeck Crs *OSM* LS9 ....
Wykebeck Gv *OSM* LS9 ....
Wykebeck Mt *OSM* LS9 ....
Wykebeck Pl *OSM* LS9 ....
Wykebeck Rd *OSM* LS9 ....
Wykebeck Sq *OSM* LS9 ....
Wykebeck St *OSM* LS9 ....
Wykebeck Ter *OSM* LS9 ....
Wykebeck Valley Rd *OSM* LS9 ......
Wynciffe Gdns *AL/HA/HU* LS17 ...
Wynford Av *BHP/TINH* LS16 ....
Wynford Gv *BHP/TINH* LS16 ....
Wynford Mt *BHP/TINH* LS16 ....
Wynford Ri *BHP/TINH* LS16 ....
Wynford Ter *BHP/TINH* LS16 ....
Wynyard Dr *MOR* LS27 ....
Wyther Dr *KSTL* LS5 ....
Wyther La *KSTL* LS5 ....
Wyther Park Av *WOR/ARM* LS12 ..
Wyther Park Cl *WOR/ARM* LS12 ...
Wyther Park Crs *WOR/ARM* LS12 .
Wyther Park Gv *WOR/ARM* LS12 ..
Wyther Park Hl *WOR/ARM* LS12 ..
Wyther Park Mt *WOR/ARM* LS12 ..
Wyther Park Pl *WOR/ARM* LS12 ...
Wyther Park Rd *WOR/ARM* LS12 ..
Wyther Park Sq *WOR/ARM* LS12 ..
Wyther Park St *WOR/ARM* LS12 ...
Wyther Park Ter *WOR/ARM* LS12 ..
Wyther Park Vw *WOR/ARM* LS12 ..

Yarn St *MID* LS10 ....
Yeadon Moor Rd *HORS* LS18 ....
  YEA LS19 ....
Yewdall Rd *BRAM* LS13................
York Pl *LDS* LS1 ....
York Rd *OSM* LS9 ....
  SCFT LS14 ....
  SCFT LS14 ....
York St *LDSU* LS2 ....

Zermatt Gv *CHAL* LS7 ....
Zermatt Mt *CHAL* LS7 * ....
Zermatt St *CHAL* LS7 ....
Zermatt Ter *CHAL* LS7 ....
Zetland Pl *RHAY* LS8 ....
Zoar St *MOR* LS27 ....

Index - featured places

Abbey Grange CE High School
  BHP/TINH LS16 ....**18** B2
Abbey House Museum
  KSTL LS5 ....**18** B5
Acorn Business Park
  SCFT LS14 ....**30** C4
Adel Primary School
  BHP/TINH LS16 ....**12** C4
Adel St John the Baptist
  CE Primary School
  BHP/TINH LS16 ....**12** A3
Agnes Stewart CE High School
  OSM LS9 ....**29** E5
Aireborough Leisure Centre
  GSLY LS20 ....**5** E3
Aireside Business Centre
  LDS LS1 ....**2** E5
Aireside Retail Park
  LDS LS1 ....**2** D5
Aireview Primary School
  BRAM LS13 ....**24** C1
The Alcuin School
  CHAL LS7 ....**20** D3
Allerton Grange School
  AL/HA/HU LS17 ....**21** F1
Allerton High School
  AL/HA/HU LS17 ....**13** F3
Alwoodley Golf Club
  AL/HA/HU LS17 ....**14** A1
Alwoodley Primary School
  AL/HA/HU LS17 ....**13** E4
AMF Bowling
  LDSU LS2 ....**3** G2
Apex Business Park
  BEE/HOL LS11 ....**36** C3
Aragon Hotel
  CHAL LS7 ....**20** A3
Archbishop Cranmer
  CE Primary School
  AL/HA/HU LS17 ....**13** F4
Arlington Business Centre
  MOR LS27 ....**41** F3
Armley Clinic
  WOR/ARM LS12 ....**27** E5
Armley Gaol
  WOR/ARM LS12 ....**35** G1
Armley Link Trading Estate
  WOR/ARM LS12 ....**27** F5
Armley Primary School
  WOR/ARM LS12 ....**27** E5
Armley Sports & Leisure Centre
  WOR/ARM LS12 ....**34** D1
Arndale Centre
  HDGY LS6 ....**19** F5

Ashfield Medical Centre
  MSTN/BAR LS15 ....**31** G3
Ashley Business Centre
  LDSU LS2 ....**3** J3
Ashley Industrial Estate
  CHAL LS7 ....**28** C2
Ashton Road Industrial Estate
  RHAY LS8 ....**29** G2
Ashton View Medical Centre
  RHAY LS8 ....**29** F3
Asquith Primary School
  MOR LS27 ....**40** B5
Astra Business Park
  BEE/HOL LS11 ....**42** C3
Balm Road Industrial Estate
  MID LS10 ....**36** D5
Bankside Primary School
  RHAY LS8 ....**29** E2
Barras Garth Industrial Estate
  WOR/ARM LS12 ....**34** D2
BBC North
  OSM LS9 ....**3** K4
BBC North Studios
  LDSU LS2 ....**3** F1
Beckett Park Athletics Centre
  HDGY LS6 ....**18** D5
Beckett Park Campus
  HDGY LS6 ....**18** D5
Beckett Park Primary School
  HDGY LS6 ....**18** D5
Beechwood Primary School
  SCFT LS14 ....**23** E5
Beecroft Primary School
  HDGY LS6 ....**26** D2
Beeston Hill St Lukes
  CE Primary School
  BEE/HOL LS11 ....**36** B4
Beeston Primary School
  BEE/HOL LS11 ....**41** G1
Beeston Royds
  Industrial Estate
  BEE/HOL LS11 ....**35** E5
Belle Isle Medical Centre
  RTHW LS26 ....**43** F3
Bentley Primary School
  HDGY LS6 ....**19** H4
Benton Park School
  YEA LS19 ....**8** D2
Bero Bu School
  LDSU LS2 ....**3** F3
Bewley's Hotel
  BEE/HOL LS11 ....**36** B2
Blenheim Primary School
  LDSU LS2 ....**28** B3

Bracken Edge Primary School
  CHAL LS7 ....**21** E5
Bradford Golf Club
  GSLY LS20 ....**4** A5
Braim Wood Boys
  High School
  RHAY LS8 ....**22** B3
Bramley Business Centre
  BRAM LS13 ....**25** F3
Bramley Grange College
  BRAM LS13 ....**23** G1
Bramley Health Centre
  BRAM LS13 ....**25** G2
Bramley RUFC
  BRAM LS13 ....**25** G2
Bramley St Peters
  CE Primary School
  BRAM LS13 ....**25** G3
Brandon Golf Club
  AL/HA/HU LS17 ....**15** F2
Bridge Court Business Park
  BEE/HOL LS11 ....**36** A3
Broadgate Primary School
  HORS LS18 ....**17** G1
Brodetsky Primary School
  AL/HA/HU LS17 ....**13** C3
Bronte House School
  IDLE BD10 ....**8** B5
Brownhill Primary School
  OSM LS9 ....**29** G4
Brudenell Primary School
  HDGY LS6 ....**27** G2
Bruntcliffe High School
  MOR LS27 ....**46** A2
Burley FC
  KSTL LS5 ....**18** B4
Burley Hill Trading Estate
  BULY LS4 ....**27** E2
Burley Park Medical Centre
  BULY LS4 ....**27** F3
Burley St Matthias
  CE Primary School
  BULY LS4 ....**27** F3
Burmantofts Health Centre
  OSM LS9 ....**29** E4
Cape Industrial Estate
  PDSY/CALV LS28 ....**24** C2
Cardigan Trading Estate
  BULY LS4 ....**27** F4
Cardinal Heenan
  RC High School
  HDGY LS6 ....**19** H1
Carlton CC
  EARD/LOFT WF3 ....**50** B4

Carlton Mills
  Trading Estate
  WOR/ARM LS12 ....**27** F5
Carlton Northfield AFC
  EARD/LOFT WF3 ....**50** B4
Carlton Primary School
  EARD/LOFT WF3 ....**50** B3
Carr Manor High School
  AL/HA/HU LS17 ....**20** A2
Carr Manor Primary School
  AL/HA/HU LS17 ....**20** A2
Castleton Primary School
  WOR/ARM LS12 ....**35** F1
Central Library, Museum &
  Art Gallery
  LDS LS1 ....**3** F3
Chapel Allerton Hospital
  CHAL LS7 ....**21** E5
Chapel Allerton
  Medical Centre
  CHAL LS7 ....**20** D4
Chapel Allerton
  Primary School
  CHAL LS7 ....**20** C4
Chapeltown Business Centre
  CHAL LS7 ....**28** D1
Chapeltown Health Centre
  CHAL LS7 ....**29** E2
Chel Business Centre
  CHAL LS7 ....**28** D3
Chesney Park Industrial Estate
  MID LS10 ....**36** D4
Christ Church Upper Armley
  CE Primary School
  WOR/ARM LS12 ....**26** D5
Christ the King RC
  Primary School
  BRAM LS13 ....**26** A4
Churwell Primary School
  MOR LS27 ....**40** D4
City Art Gallery
  LDS LS1 ....
City of Leeds School
  HDGY LS6 ....**28** A1
City Park Industrial Estate
  BEE/HOL LS11 ....**35** E5
City Tennis Club
  BEE/HOL LS11 ....**42** A1
City Varieties Music Hall
  LDS LS1 ....**3** G4
Clapgate Primary School
  MID LS10 ....**49** F1
Cobden Primary School
  WOR/ARM LS12 ....**34** B4

Cockburn High School
  BEE/HOL LS11 ....**36** B5
College of Technology
  LDSU LS2 ....
College of Technology
  LDSU LS2 ....
Conway Medical Centre
  RHAY LS8 ....
Cookridge Hall Golf &
  Country Club
  BHP/TINH LS16 ....
Cookridge Hospital
  BHP/TINH LS16 ....
Cookridge Primary School
  BHP/TINH LS16 ....
Copley Hill Trading Estate
  WOR/ARM LS12 ....
Corpus Christi Catholic College
  OSM LS9 ....
Corpus Christi Primary School
  OSM LS9 ....
Cottage Road Picture House
  HDGY LS6 ....
Cottingley Community
  Health Centre
  BEE/HOL LS11 ....
Cottingley Hall Crematorium
  BEE/HOL LS11 ....
Cottingley Primary School
  BEE/HOL LS11 ....
Craven Road Medical Centre
  HDGY LS6 ....
Crawshaw School
  PDSY/CALV LS28 ....
Cross Flatts Park
  Primary School
  BEE/HOL LS11 ....
The Crossgates Centre
  MSTN/BAR LS15 ....
Cross Gates Primary School
  SCFT LS14 ....
Cross Green Light
  Industrial Estate
  OSM LS9 ....
Cross Hall Junior School
  MOR LS27 ....
Crown Point Retail Park
  MID LS10 ....
Dental Institute
  LDSU LS2 ....
De Vere Oulton Hall Hotel
  RTHW LS26 ....
De Vere Village Hotel
  BHP/TINH LS16 ....

St Marys Catholic
Comprehensive School
ILK LS29 ....4 C1
St Marys Hospital
WOR/ARM LS12 ....26 B5
St Marys RC Primary School
HORS LS18 ....17 G1
RTHW LS26 ....50 D2
St Matthews
CE Primary School
CHAL LS7 ....20 C3
St Michaels Catholic College
LDSU LS2 ....2 B1
St Michaels CE Primary School
HDGY LS6 ....19 G5
St Nicholas RC Primary School
OSM LS9 ....30 B2
St Oswalds CE Junior School
GSLY LS20 ....5 E4
St Patricks RC Primary School
OSM LS9 ....29 G5
St Pauls RC Primary School
OSM LS9 ....13 E3
St Peter & St Paul
RC Primary School
YEA LS19 ....8 B1
St Peters CE Primary School
OSM LS9 ....3 K3
St Philips RC Primary School
MID LS10 ....48 B1
St Stephens CE Primary School
KSTL LS5 ....26 C1
St Theresas C Primary School
MSTN/BAR LS15 ....31 G2
St Urbans RC Primary School
HDGY LS6 ....20 A1
Sand Moor Golf Club
AL/HA/HU LS17 ....13 G1
School of Art Architecture &
Design (Leeds Metropolitan
University)
LDSU LS2 ....3 G2
School of Education &
Prof Studies
HDGY LS6 ....18 C4
School of Teacher
Education Studies
HDGY LS6 ....18 C4
Scotch Park Trading Estate
WOR/ARM LS12 ....27 F5
Seacroft Clinic
SCFT LS14 ....23 F5
Seacroft Industrial Estate
SCFT LS14 ....23 F3
Seven Hills Primary School
MOR LS27 ....46 D2

Shadwell CP School
AL/HA/HU LS17 ....15 H3
Shadwell Medical Centre
AL/HA/HU LS17 ....14 A4
Shakespeare Primary School
OSM LS9 ....29 F4
Sharma Park
Industrial Estate
RHAY LS8 ....29 E3
Sharp Lane Primary School
MID LS10 ....49 E1
Sherwood Industrial Estate
EARD/LOFT WF3 ....49 H3
South Leeds Art College
MID LS10 ....43 E3
South Leeds Business Park
MID LS10 ....36 D3
South Leeds Golf Club
BEE/HOL LS11 ....42 A4
South Leeds High School
BEE/HOL LS11 ....35 H4
South Leeds Sports Centre
BEE/HOL LS11 ....36 B4
South Leeds Stadium
BEE/HOL LS11 ....42 C3
Southroyd Primary School
PDSY/CALV LS28 ....32 C2
South Side Aviation Centre
YEA LS19 ....6 C5
Southview Business Park
GSLY LS20 ....5 E5
Southview
Business Park Centre
GSLY LS20 ....5 E2
Springbank Junior School
PDSY/CALV LS28 ....24 B2
Spring Bank Primary School
HDGY LS6 ....27 F1
Stanningley Industrial Centre
PDSY/CALV LS28 ....24 B4
Stanningley Primary School
PDSY/CALV LS28 ....24 D3
Stanningley RLFC
PDSY/CALV LS28 ....25 E3
Summerfield Primary School
BRAM LS13 ....24 D2
Sunfield Medical Centre
PDSY/CALV LS28 ....24 B4
Swinnow Primary School
PDSY/CALV LS28 ....25 E5
Swinnow Shopping Centre
BRAM LS13 ....25 E5
Tainton Park Trading Estate
WOR/ARM LS12 ....35 G2
Takalani Dance Theatre
RHAY LS8 ....30 A1

Talbot Primary School
RHAY LS8 ....21 F1
The Tandy Trading Estate
BULY LS4 ....27 E4
Temple Moor High School
MSTN/BAR LS15 ....39 F1
Temple Newsam Country Park
MSTN/BAR LS15 ....39 F2
Temple Newsam Golf Club
MSTN/BAR LS15 ....38 D2
Temple Newsam Halton
Primary School
MSTN/BAR LS15 ....31 E5
Temple Newsam House
MSTN/BAR LS15 ....39 F3
Tetley's Brewery
MID LS10 ....3 H7
Thackray Museum
RHAY LS8 ....29 F3
Thomas Danby College
CHAL LS7 ....28 D3
Thorpe Primary School
HORS LS18 ....49 E4
Thwaite Mills Watermill
OSM LS9 ....37 H5
Tranmere Park
Primary School
GSLY LS20 ....4 B4
Travelodge
LDS LS1 ....3 G6
YEA LS19 ....6 D4
Trinity & All Saints College
HORS LS18 ....10 A4
Tropical World
RHAY LS8 ....21 H1
Tulip Street Retail Park
MID LS10 ....36 D5
University of Leeds
BHP/TINH LS16 ....19 E1
HDGY LS6 ....27 H1
LDSU LS2 ....2 D1
University Sports Centre
LDSU LS2 ....2 D1
Victoria Industrial Park
SCFT LS14 ....23 F2
Victoria Junior School
RTHW LS26 ....44 B5
Victoria Park School
BRAM LS13 ....26 A2
Victoria Primary School
OSM LS9 ....29 H5
VUE Cinema
BULY LS4 ....27 E4
Wakefield Tutorial
Preparatory School
MOR LS27 ....46 C2

Waterloo Primary School
PDSY/CALV LS28 ....32 A1
Waterside Industrial Park
OSM LS9 ....37 H5
Weetwood Primary School
BHP/TINH LS16 ....19 F3
Wellington Road
Industrial Estate
WOR/ARM LS12 ....2 B4
Westbrook Lane Primary School
HORS LS18 ....10 A4
West End Primary School
HORS LS18 ....9 H5
Westfield Industrial Estate
YEA LS19 ....8 C1
Westfield Junior School
YEA LS19 ....8 B1
Westfield Medical Centre
CHAL LS7 ....20 D5
West Leeds High School
WOR/ARM LS12 ....34 B1
West Oaks School Oakwood
RHAY LS8 ....30 B1
Westroyd Infant School
PDSY/CALV LS28 ....24 B3
West Side Retail Park
GSLY LS20 ....5 F5
West Specialist Inclusive
Learning Centre
BRAM LS13 ....26 A2
Westwood Primary School
MID LS10 ....48 A2
West Yorkshire Playhouse
OSM LS9 ....3 K4
Whingate Business Park
WOR/ARM LS12 ....34 D1
Whingate Primary School
WOR/ARM LS12 ....34 C1
Whitecote Primary School
BRAM LS13 ....25 H1
Whitehall Industrial Estate
WOR/ARM LS12 ....34 B4
Whitehall Trading Estate
WOR/ARM LS12 ....34 A4
White Laith Primary School
SCFT LS14 ....23 G3
White Rose Shopping Centre
MOR LS27 ....41 G4
Whitkirk Medical Centre
MSTN/BAR LS15 ....31 H5
Whitkirk Primary School
MSTN/BAR LS15 ....39 F1
Wigton Moor Primary School
AL/HA/HU LS17 ....14 B2
Windmill Primary School
MID LS10 ....45 E5

Wira Business Park
BHP/TINH LS16 ....
Woodhouse CC
CHAL LS7 ....
Woodhouse Health Centre
HDGY LS6 ....
Woodkirk High School
EARD/LOFT WF3 ....
Woodlands Primary School
OSM LS9 ....
Woodlesford Primary Scho
RTHW LS26 ....
Woodside Trading Estate
HORS LS18 ....
Woodsley Health Centre
HDGY LS6 ....
Wortley High School
WOR/ARM LS12 ....
Wortley Moor Lane
Trading Estate
WOR/ARM LS12 ....
Wykebeck Infant School
OSM LS9 ....
Wykebeck Primary School
OSM LS9 ....
Wyther Lane Industrial Esta
KSTL LS5 ....
Yarnbury RUFC
HORS LS18 ....
Yeadon Airport
Industrial Estate
YEA LS19 ....
Yeadon Cemetery
YEA LS19 ....
Yeadon CC
YEA LS19 ....
Yeadon Health Centre
YEA LS19 ....
Yeadon Westfield Infant Se
YEA LS19 ....
Yorkshire Amateurs FC
CHAL LS7 ....
Yorkshire Bank Sports Grou
AL/HA/HU LS17 ....
Yorkshire CCC (Headingley
Cricket Ground)
HDGY LS6 ....
Yorkshire College of
Music & Drama
HDGY LS6 ....
Yorkshire Post Offices
LDS LS1 ....
Yorkshire Post Sports Club
BHP/TINH LS16 ....
Yorkshire Television Studio
BVRD LS3 ....

Acknowledgements

The Post Office is a registered trademark of Post Office Ltd. in the UK and other countries.

Schools address data provided by Education Direct.

Petrol station information supplied by Johnsons

One-way street data provided by © Tele Atlas N.V. Tele Atlas

Garden centre information provided by

Garden Centre Association 🌼 Britains best garden centres

Wyevale Garden Centres 🌳

The statement on the front cover of this atlas is sourced, selected and quoted
from a reader comment and feedback form received in 2004

Notes

Notes

AA Street by Street QUESTIONNAIRE

Dear Atlas User
Your comments, opinions and recommendations are very important to us.
So please help us to improve our street atlases by taking a few minutes
to complete this simple questionnaire.

You do not need a stamp (unless posted outside the UK). If you do not want to remove
this page from your street atlas, then photocopy it or write your answers on a plain sheet
of paper.

Send to: The Editor, AA Street by Street, FREEPOST SCE 4598,
Basingstoke RG21 4GY

ABOUT THE ATLAS...

Which city/town/county did you buy?

Are there any features of the atlas or mapping that you find particularly useful?

Is there anything we could have done better?

Why did you choose an AA Street by Street atlas?

Did it meet your expectations?

Exceeded ☐   **Met all** ☐   **Met most** ☐   **Fell below** ☐

Please give your reasons

Where did you buy it?

For what purpose? (please tick all applicable)

To use in your own local area ☐   To use on business or at work ☐

Visiting a strange place ☐   In the car ☐   On foot ☐

Other (please state)

LOCAL KNOWLEDGE...

Local knowledge is invaluable. Whilst every attempt has been made to make the information contained in this atlas as accurate as possible, should you notice any inaccuracies, please detail them below (if necessary, use a blank piece of paper) or e-mail us at *streetbystreet@theAA.com*

ABOUT YOU...

Name (Mr/Mrs/Ms)
Address

Postcode

Daytime tel no   Mobile tel no
E-mail address

Please only give us your e-mail address and mobile phone number if you wish to hear from us about other products and services from the AA and partners by e-mail or text or mms.

Which age group are you in?

Under 25 ☐   25-34 ☐   35-44 ☐   45-54 ☐   55-64 ☐   65+ ☐

Are you an AA member?   YES ☐   NO ☐

Do you have Internet access?   YES ☐   NO ☐

Thank you for taking the time to complete this questionnaire. Please send it to us as soon as possible, and remember, you do not need a stamp (unless posted outside the UK).   ML14y